Web-Based Instruction

A Guide for Libraries

Susan Sharpless Smith

AMERICAN LIBRARY ASSOCIATION
Chicago and London
2001

Susan Sharpless Smith, technology team leader for the Z. Smith Reynolds Library at Wake Forest University in Winston–Salem, N.C., leads the planning, development, implementation, maintenance, and evaluation of the library's technology activities. Prior to assuming this position, she was the library's electronic resources librarian, and in this capacity her responsibilities included managing and authoring the reference department's Web site and participating in the provision of library instruction. Her interest in Web-based library instruction emerged when studying for her MA in Educational Technology Leadership at George Washington University, where her focus of study was on the development of educational Web sites. She teaches classes for faculty, students, and staff on a wide range of topics relating to technology, including Web authoring and design. Smith participates regularly in regional and national conferences, speaking on a variety of technology issues. She currently chairs the North Carolina Library Association's Technology and Trends Round Table.

The paper used in this publication meets the minimum requirements of American National Standard for Information Sciences—Permanence of Paper for Printed Library Materials, ANSI Z39.48-1992. ∞

Library of Congress Cataloging-in-Publication Data
Smith, Susan Sharpless.
    Web-based instruction : a guide for libraries / Susan Sharpless Smith.
      p.   cm.
    Includes bibliographical references and index.
    ISBN 0-8389-0805-5
    1. Library orientation—Computer-assisted instruction.   2. Web sites—
Design.   3. Library information networks.   I. Title.
Z711.2.S59 2001
005.7'2—dc21   2001022050

Printed in the United States of America.

05 04 03 02 01   5 4 3 2 1

Contents

Figures   vii

Acknowledgments   xi

Acronyms   xiii

Introduction   *1*

The Problem with Traditional Bibliographic Instruction   *1*
Why Use Web-Based Instruction?   *2*
When Is Web-Based Instruction Inappropriate?   *3*
The Effectiveness of Web-Based Instruction   *3*
What Can you Expect from This Book?   *4*

1 Library Instruction on the Web   *5*

Characteristics of Good Library Instruction   *5*
Types and Examples of Web-Based Library Instruction   *6*

2 Design and Development Cycle   *15*

Preproduction   *15*
Production   *22*
Publication   *22*
Postproduction   *23*
Testing and Evaluation   *24*
Project Management   *24*

3 Selecting Project Development Tools   *28*

User Constraints   *28*
Development Hardware   *32*
Authoring Software Programs   *40*

4 Designing the User Interface   *53*

User-Centered Design   *54*
Instructional Design and Content   *54*
Basic Guidelines and Principles for User-Interface Design   *59*
Navigation   *61*
Screen Layout and Presentation Aids   *72*
Visual Design Considerations   *75*
User Accessibility   *92*
Page Optimization   *95*

5 Multimedia: Using Graphics, Sound, Animation, and Video   *97*

Multimedia and Instruction   *97*
Types of Multimedia   *105*

6 Interactivity   *136*

Categories of Interaction   *136*
Interactivity Methods   *140*
Interactivity Languages and Technologies   *156*
Interactivity Development Tools for Nonprogrammers   *166*

7 Evaluation and Testing   *170*

Why, What, and How Much Evaluation?   *170*
Categories of Evaluation   *171*
Evaluation Methods   *172*
Content Mastery   *177*

Resources   *179*

Accessibility   *179*
Animation   *179*
Applications for Building Interactivity   *180*
Audio   *180*
Browser Compatibility   *181*

Cascading Style Sheets   *181*
Clip Art   *181*
Colors   *181*
Communication Tools   *181*
Course Shells   *181*
Design and Development Cycle   *182*
Evaluation and Testing   *182*
Glossaries   *183*
Graphics   *183*
Image Optimization   *183*
Library Instruction on the Web   *183*
Markup Languages   *184*
Multimedia   *184*
Navigation   *184*
Page Optimization   *184*
Research Literature   *184*
Rollovers   *185*
Script Languages and Web Interaction Technologies   *185*
Script Libraries   *186*
Selecting Development Tools   *186*
SMIL   *187*
Streaming Media   *187*
Typography   *187*
User Interface Design   *187*
Video   *187*
Virtual Experiences   *188*
Web Development Sites   *188*
Web Editors   *188*

Index   **189**

Figures

1.1 General Research and Reference Skills Tutorial *7*
1.2 Online Catalog Research Skills Tutorial *8*
1.3 Database- and Software-Specific Search Skills Tutorial *9*
1.4 Subject- and Course-Specific Research Skills Tutorial *10*
1.5 Assignment-Specific Research Skills Tutorial *11*
1.6 Internet Skills Tutorial *12*
1.7 General Library Orientation Tutorial *13*
1.8 Information Literacy Course *14*
2.1 The Design and Development Cycle for Web-Based Instruction *16*
2.2 Potential Comparison Criteria for Evaluation of Web-Based Instruction *19*
2.3 Script Outline for Research *20*
2.4 Sample Flowchart *21*
2.5 Gantt Chart for a Web Project Using Microsoft Project Software *25*
3.1 Browser Chart from Webmonkey *30*
3.2 Netscape Netcenter's Web Site Garage Browser-Compatibility Check *31*
3.3 Netscape Netcenter's Web Site Garage Page-Load Time Check *32*
3.4 Web Page Viewed in Code-Based Editor HomeSite *41*
3.5 Web Page Viewed in WYSIWYG Editor Macromedia Dreamweaver *42*
3.6 Web Page Viewed in Code-Based Editor First Page with Layout View *43*
3.7 CorelDRAW Illustration Software for Vector Graphics *45*
3.8 Macromedia Director Interactive Multimedia Authoring Software with Time Line *49*
3.9 Blackboard's Free Service to Create an Online Course *51*
4.1 Pop-up Window to Present Additional Information *57*
4.2 CNET's Window Builder Tool to Make Pop-up Windows *58*
4.3 Page Optimized for Scannability *59*
4.4 Tutorial with Location Marker *62*

4.5   Multiple Navigation System Example   63
4.6   Text for a Navigation System   65
4.7   Flowchart Example   66
4.8   Menu Tree Example   66
4.9   Drop-Down Menu Example   67
4.10 Linear Navigation Design Example   70
4.11 Frame Displays   71
4.12 Tables Used as Layout Tools   73
4.13 Effective Use of White Space Example   76
4.14 Color Meanings and Perceptions   77
4.15 Color Wheel and Color Schemes   79
4.16 High and Low Color Contrasts and Legibility   80
4.17 Effective Use of Color Example   81
4.18 Browser-Safe Color Palette   82
4.19 Free Color Utilities Example   83
4.20 Advantages and Disadvantages of Highlighting Techniques   84
4.21 Textured Background Image   86
4.22 Comparison of Typefaces at Same Point Size   86
4.23 Comparison of Windows and Macintosh Displays   90
4.24 Comparison of Resolution and Text Size   91
4.25 Bobby Accessibility-Check Tool   94
5.1   Images Used for Navigation   99
5.2   Graphics Used to Set a Mood   99
5.3   Logo Used for Identification   100
5.4   Photo and Map in Virtual Tour   101
5.5   Screen Capture Used in Searching Tutorial   102
5.6   Lotus ScreenCam Demonstration Used in Searching Tutorial   102
5.7   Screen-Capture Demonstration Used in Author-Search Tutorial   103
5.8   Animation Used for Visualization of Boolean Logic Concepts   104
5.9   Zoom-in View of Raster Image Pixels   106
5.10 Vector Images   107
5.11 Comparison of Raster and Vector Images   108
5.12 Advantages, Disadvantages, and Uses of GIF and JPEG Formats   109
5.13 Useful Web Icons for Tutorials   112
5.14 Creating an Image Map with Dreamweaver   113
5.15 CNET Builder's Mouseover Machine   114
5.16 Netscape Netcenter's Web Site Garage GIF Lube Image Optimizing
      Utility   116
5.17 Image before and after Slicing   117
5.18 Two Control Options for Sound Files on Web Pages   120
5.19 Creation of an Animated GIF   123
5.20 Macromedia Flash Application Interface   124
5.21 Flash Animation Used in Texas Information Literacy Tutorial   125
5.22 Director Shockwave Used in Organize and Synthesize Information
      Tutorial   126
5.23 Macromedia Dreamweaver Used to Create Layer-Based
      Animation   127

5.24   Axes of Three-Dimensional Graphics   *128*
5.25   VRML Used to Tour a Library   *129*
5.26   Video File, Load-Time, and Run-Time Indicators   130
5.27   QuickTime Virtual Reality Tour   *131*
6.1   Social Interaction through a Discussion Forum   137
6.2   Information Transfer through Use of a Feedback Form   *138*
6.3   Remote Access to a Database   *139*
6.4   Knowledge Building through Formulating Search Strategies   *140*
6.5   Virtual Experiences Designed for Live Interaction and
         Collaboration   *141*
6.6   Hyperlinks to Create Interactivity in a Library Catalog Tutorial   *142*
6.7   Image Map with Hyperlinks to Provide an Interactive Activity   *143*
6.8   E-Mail Links to an Instructor   *144*
6.9   Discussion Forum as a Communication Method   *145*
6.10   Chat Program for Real-Time Distance Learning Communication   *146*
6.11   Online Survey Using Forms   *147*
6.12   Exercise Using Forms in Library Catalog Tutorial   *148*
6.13   Activity Using Forms for Developing Research Strategies   *148*
6.14   Self-Assessment Using Forms   *149*
6.15   Testing Using Forms   *150*
6.16   Evaluation Using Forms   *151*
6.17   Skills Practice through Simulation of Database Searches   *152*
6.18   Skills Practice through Simulation Created in Macromedia
         Authorware   *153*
6.19   Skills Practice through Live Access   *154*
6.20   Interactive Movement to Organize Notes   *155*
6.21   Rollovers Used in a URL Exercise   *155*
6.22   Web Programming Languages Comparison Chart   *158*
6.23   Java Applets Used in a Library Information Access Tutorial   *159*
6.24   JavaScript Source Script Library   *167*
6.25   Hot Potatoes Quiz Creation Tool   *168*

Acknowledgments

I want to thank the people who helped make this book a reality. Writing a book is certainly not a solitary process; it is one that relies on the support and encouragement of colleagues and family.

It would have never occurred to me to attempt this project if not for ALA Editions acquisitions editor Tarshel Beards. She saw the nucleus of a potential book topic in a presentation I gave at a LITA National Forum and encouraged me to develop it. She guided me throughout the entire authoring process. Editorial manager Joan Grygel's skillful efforts made this book more readable, understandable, and useful for readers.

There are many people at Z. Smith Reynolds Library to thank also. Rhoda Channing, our director, has always encouraged her staff to extend our reach professionally. She provides a positive example by the way in which she conducts her professional life and has always given total support to her staff's professional development endeavors, including this project. My fellow technology team members provided moral support and handholding through the long months of writing and served as sounding boards on many technology questions. My colleagues in our reference department were instrumental in teaching me how to deliver traditional library instruction and how to translate this effectively into our library's Web-based library instruction tutorials.

I would like to thank all of the libraries and other organizations that have allowed me to use their sites as examples throughout the book.

Finally, without the support from my husband, Ron, this book would not exist. He took over the management of all aspects of the domestic front for many months so that I could concentrate on this project. He has always been my main source of inspiration because of his unfailing belief in my abilities to accomplish anything.

Acronyms

AIFF	Audio Interchange File Format
ASP	Active Server Page
AU	Audio File Format
AVI	Audio Video Interleave
BMP	bitmap
CDR	CorelDRAW
CD-ROM	compact disc–read only memory
CD-RW	compact disc–rewritable
CGI	Common Gateway Interface
CODEC	*Co*mpressor/*dec*ompressor
CPU	Central Processing Unit
CSS	cascading style sheets
dHTML	dynamic HTML
DOM	document object model
dpi	dots per inch
DV	digital video
FTP	File Transfer Protocol
GB	gigabyte
GHz	gigahertz
GIF	Graphics Interchange Format
HTML	HyperText Markup Language
IE	Internet Explorer
IIS	Internet Information Server
IT	information technology
JPEG, JPG	Joint Photographic Experts Group
JSP	JavaServer Page
LCD	liquid crystal display
MB	megabyte
MHz	megahertz
MIDI	Musical Instrument Digital Interface
MNG	Multiple-image Network Graphics

MOO	Multiuser domain, Object Oriented
MPEG	Moving Pictures Expert Group
MP3	MPEG-1 Audio Layer-3
OCR	optical character recognition
PC	personal computer (IBM compatible)
PCI	Peripheral Component Interconnect
PDF	Portable Document Format
Perl	Practical Extraction and Reporting Language
PFR	Portable Font Resource
PHP	[Personal Home Page] PHP Hypertext Processor
PNG	Portable Network Graphics
ppi	pixels per inch
RAM	random access memory
SCSI	Small Computer System Interface
SGML	Standard Generalized Markup Language
SMIL	Synchronized Multimedia Integration Language
SVG	Scalable Vector Graphics
SVGA	Super Video Graphics Array
Tcl	Tool Command Language
TIFF	Tag Image File Format
Tk	tool kit
3-D	three dimensional
UID	User Interface Design
URL	Uniform Resource Locator
USB	Universal Serial Bus
VGA	Video Graphics Array
VRML	Virtual Reality Modeling Language
WAV	Waveform Audio File Format
W3C	World Wide Web Consortium
WYSIWYG	what you see is what you get
WWW	World Wide Web
XHTML	Extensible Hypertext Markup Language
XML	Extensible Markup Language

Introduction

The Web has become an everyday part of most libraries' delivery of services. Over the past few years we have come to rely on the Web to perform all types of job functions. It's not surprising that the Web has become a potential tool to extend our library-instruction capabilities.

THE PROBLEM WITH TRADITIONAL BIBLIOGRAPHIC INSTRUCTION

There are common themes that appear in discussions about traditional bibliographic instruction, also called "library instruction." This instruction is designed to teach library users how to use the library and its resources effectively. Increasingly, library instruction goals are expanding to encompass a more-comprehensive concept—information literacy, in which library users gain "the ability to locate, evaluate, and use information to become independent life-long learners" (Commission 1996). Instruction has traditionally been delivered face-to-face in a lecture style by a librarian with subject knowledge of the course, but research has shown that using some sort of practice to reinforce the instruction is more effective than offering just a straight lecture. The information environment has become more complex with the growth of online resources. In addition to teaching students about traditional print library resources, now it is imperative to include electronic databases and journals as well as World Wide Web resources. This requires greater attention to instruction on search and evaluation methods.

There are more newly important issues to consider also. Many libraries are finding that their constituencies have undergone a change. For example, students for whom English is a second language may find it difficult to retain all that is taught in a face-to-face class. Furthermore, some libraries are now supporting distance education programs and must find a way to reach out to those students.

These situations present challenges to providing effective library instruction. It means (and this comes as no surprise) that instruction librarians have to do more with limited staff, resources, and time. Planning subject-specific, interactive classes is very time consuming and labor intensive. Hiring more instruction librarians is usually not an option. Classroom space is finite, and access to a classroom that is configured for interactive hands-on learning is even more difficult to find.

WHY USE WEB-BASED INSTRUCTION?

In light of all these difficulties that stand in the way of providing effective library instruction, there is a growing recognition of the need to develop alternative solutions. Because we have turned to the World Wide Web for so many of our day-to-day activities, it is an obvious place to turn to for a possible answer to the library instruction problem. Some characteristics of the Web are very attractive: It is a way that library skills can be taught to large numbers of students. It is interactive and can be programmed to give immediate feedback to students as they proceed through the lessons. There is no limitation of time or space; students can access the instruction twenty-four hours a day from wherever they can connect to the Internet. Finally, one of the most appealing attractions is that instruction on the Web presents the same information to all students, removing the unavoidable variations in human delivery.

Personal Sources of Interest in Web-Based Instruction Potential

My interest in exploring what Web-based library instruction could do for my library originated from a few different directions. First, Wake Forest University, where I work, has no requirement that students take a basic library skills class as part of the required curriculum, as is the case in many other higher education institutions. Here, it is up to the professor whether to expose his or her students to instruction about how to conduct research. As you might imagine, some professors bring their classes to the library faithfully every semester, but the majority of them don't. It's not necessarily that they think it's unimportant, but they don't want to forfeit a class period out of their schedule. However, that doesn't stop them from assigning research projects!

Second, our library has only two classrooms that can be used for instruction, and originally only one of those was wired so that students could have hands-on practice during the class. Having just two classrooms causes scheduling problems. Because much of the library instruction is needed during particular periods of the class term, there is a lot of competition for the available space.

Third, this university is a ThinkPad campus, which means that every undergraduate student has his or her own laptop computer. Network connections are available in every dorm room, in the dining halls, in most classrooms, and throughout the library. This year, Internet access has been extended to all corners of the campus with the addition of a wireless network. Therefore, students at Wake Forest are comfortable with using the Web as a learning tool; in fact, it is emphasized in many of their classes.

Taking all of these facts into consideration, we decided that we could use the Web to reach out to those students who do not have the opportunity to come to the library for instruction and as a supplement to traditional face-to-face instruction, which will remain the backbone of our program.

WHEN IS WEB-BASED INSTRUCTION INAPPROPRIATE?

Web-based library instruction may not be the answer for everyone. It's important to understand your institution's mission and decide whether Web-based instruction supports that mission. For example, if your institution places a high value on classroom instruction, not only in the library but also throughout the campus, then Web-based instruction may be determined to be inappropriate for that environment. There is also the risk of losing the personal contact that face-to-face instruction provides. Many students are hesitant to ask for help with their research problems, but when they have become acquainted with a librarian through instruction, they feel more comfortable in seeking assistance. Finally, such basic roadblocks as inadequate infrastructure may be a legitimate reason to reconsider the desire to turn to Web-based instruction. If your institution is limited in its hardware, software, and networking capabilities, you may be doing your students a disservice if you attempt to channel instruction through an online environment.

THE EFFECTIVENESS OF WEB-BASED INSTRUCTION

Before embarking on a major undertaking to produce an interactive Web-based tutorial, you may well ask about the effectiveness of such instruction. Developing an effective Web-based tutorial is a time-consuming task, and it would be foolish to devote limited resources to a project that will not be a worthwhile tool. However, a review of the literature on the effectiveness of computer-based instruction in general, and its value in delivering library instruction specifically, is reassuring. In almost every study reviewed, neither instruction delivery method (face-to-face or computer-based) was found to be significantly different from the other. A list of the research that was reviewed can be found in the research literature resources at the end of this book.

You may want to carry out your own local research to see if Web-based instruction is right for you. A study conducted at Wake Forest University involved six sections of a survey course, Business 100. Half of the sections received face-to-face instruction while the other half were administered the same content in a Web-based tutorial. Effectiveness was compared by analyzing the differences in pretest and posttest scores. The findings were consistent with what others have determined. That is, in this study, neither face-to-face instruction nor Web-based instruction was found to be more effective: students increased their pretest to posttest scores in both methods of delivery. These results helped confirm that our method of incorporating Web-based instruction is the right course for this university where we have chosen to supplement traditional instruction with Web-based instruction.

WHAT CAN YOU EXPECT FROM THIS BOOK?

Web-Based Instruction: A Guide for Libraries will help you decide if you would like to implement Web-based instruction, and if so, it will lead you through the process. It is aimed toward the library instruction practitioner who has some basic knowledge of and experience with Web-authoring procedures but who has no previous experience in creating interactive educational Web sites. If you are completely unfamiliar with Web authoring and its terminology, you will want to read one of the many books available on HTML (HyperText Markup Language), the language of the Web, first. Although Web-based instruction is concentrated in academic environments, public libraries are also finding it to be a valuable way to instruct their patrons about the Internet and about research in an online setting.

This book is organized in the order that planning and executing a Web project takes place; therefore, you may encounter an early mention of some technical terms that are fully explained in later chapters, where the sequence of dealing with those topics would normally take place during a project. Chapter 1 presents best practices for library instruction and explores the different types of Web-based instruction now being created by institutions. Chapter 2, Design and Development Cycle, is geared to help you organize a project from start to finish. Chapter 3 presents considerations for selecting development tools for a Web project and identifies and assesses potential hardware and software authoring tools. The importance of user interface design guidelines and principles is explained in chapter 4. Use of multimedia and the importance of interactivity are looked at in detail in chapters 5 and 6, where tools that will help accomplish their use are also discussed. Chapter 7 focuses on an overview of evaluation and testing methods that can help you determine the best assessment method for your project. Each chapter includes practical information to ensure that a library Web project is a manageable, enriching experience.

NOTE

Commission on Colleges, Southern Association of Colleges and Schools. Dec. 1996. Criteria for Accreditation, Section 5.1.2 [Library and Other Information Resources] Services. Accessed 5 March 2001 at http://www.sacs.org/pub/coc/cri70. htm#SECTIONV.

1

Library Instruction
on the Web

CHARACTERISTICS OF GOOD
LIBRARY INSTRUCTION

As you start to think about how to develop a Web-based library instruction project, a primary goal will be to incorporate the characteristics of good library instruction. What constitutes the best practices for library instruction? Much research has been done over the years to identify these characteristics. This list gathered by Nancy Dewald (1999) provides a compilation of best practices:

1. *Library instruction is best received when it is course-related, and more specifically, assignment-related.* Anyone who has worked with students has found that the retention of materials is much higher when it relates to a specific subject being taught to them or when there is an assignment attached. In these situations, students are more highly motivated to learn. When instruction is delivered for some unknown future use, students tend to dismiss what is being covered.

2. *Incorporating active learning into instruction is more effective than instruction by lecture style alone.* Providing exercises or other activities helps reinforce the lessons being taught and determine whether the students are grasping the material. With straight lecture, a one-way dissemination of information, it is difficult to assess the students' mental engagement.

3. *Collaborative learning can be beneficial.* Having students interact together in small groups to help each other learn is a powerful way to encourage critical thinking and problem-solving skills. Although this technique may not lend itself to a one-shot instruction class, it can be used in a longer information literacy course.

4. *Information provided in more than one medium is helpful.* Students have different learning styles. Some learn primarily through visual means; others prefer auditory means. Combining a lecture delivery with a visual demonstration can reinforce the message through two mediums.

5. *Establishing clear objectives is important.* Students are much more likely to grasp what is being taught if they know the direction the instruction is heading.

6. *Teaching concepts is preferable to simply teaching mechanics.* When students understand the concepts being taught, they can transfer that knowledge to other learning situations. For example, information literacy concepts include Boolean logic, keyword versus controlled-vocabulary searching, evaluating resources, and methods for focusing a search.

7. *Good library instruction does not end with the class session but includes the option of asking the librarian for help in the future.* Often, library instruction is just the beginning of the research process. Students usually have a need for follow-up help and should be assured that it is available and is an anticipated part of the process.

Is it possible to incorporate these criteria into Web-based instruction? Does it make a difference if the instruction is totally online rather than a supplement to face-to-face instruction? As you start to consider how to transfer these characteristics over to a new medium, you will find, as Dewald did in her analysis of twenty online tutorials, that there are comparable techniques in Web tutorials that demonstrate the use of best practices. In this and subsequent chapters, these techniques will be identified and examples from different tutorials will illustrate the incorporation of good instruction criteria including active learning, collaborative learning, and the use of multiple mediums. A main goal of this book is to teach you how to integrate active learning and collaboration into your Web-based instruction through using interactive technologies and to use graphics, sound, and/or animation to deliver information through more than one medium.

Dewald's list of good library instruction characteristics also covers items that are not necessarily solved by simply using a certain Web technique. Delivering course-related content, establishing objectives, teaching concepts, and providing ongoing assistance are pedagogical issues that you and your team must build into the instructional design of your tutorial. No matter what format your instruction takes, these are issues that every good instructor addresses when developing a class or course.

TYPES AND EXAMPLES OF WEB-BASED LIBRARY INSTRUCTION

What kind of library instruction can be delivered via the Web? An examination of existing tutorials shows that you are limited only by your imagination. Still, there are several major categories of tutorials. The following sections deal with each of these and provide examples.

General Research or Reference Skills

One common type of Web-based library tutorial deals with how to do research in general. Although at first it might appear that this type of instruction will not meet the criteria of a course-based focus, it can be integrated into many different disciplines as a supplement since the research process follows a similar path in many subject areas. Furthermore, as mentioned previously, Web-based tutorials can also be the primary method of instruction for distance education students who will not have an opportunity to receive face-to-face course instruction.

The tutorial shown in figure 1.1 from the University of Cincinnati Libraries is a typical example of general research instruction. It contains modules on planning research, using the online catalog, finding books, finding articles, locating periodical titles, finding items on reserve, and using the World Wide Web for research. Other popular topics that are covered in general research tutorials are evaluating information, citing resources, and differentiating between various resource types.

FIGURE 1.1
General Research and Reference Skills Tutorial

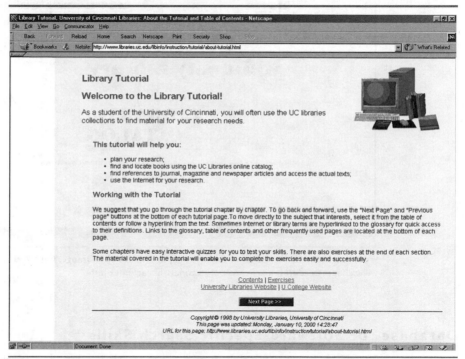

From University of Cincinnati Libraries. Available: http://www.libraries.uc.edu/libinfo/instruction/tutorial/about-tutorial.html.

Online Catalog Skills

A library's online catalog is its main tool for finding materials in its collection. A tutorial that instructs library users on how to search that specific system can be helpful to all concerned. Most online systems today are sophisticated enough to permit very complex search strategies. If the tutorial is developed to teach the concept of searching in one system, the strategies learned can be transferred to other online systems. Concepts that can be conveyed in an online catalog tutorial include keyword versus subject searching, the meaning of call numbers and how they are structured, when to try different access points to find materials (author, title, subject, keyword), and how to search different fields simultaneously using Boolean logic. Students can be taught about different types of information available in the library and how to interpret and refine the results they retrieve from the catalog. Figure 1.2 illustrates an interactive tutorial from Thurmond Clarke Memorial Library at Chapman University that teaches freshmen how to use the library's online catalog.

FIGURE 1.2
Online Catalog Research Skills Tutorial

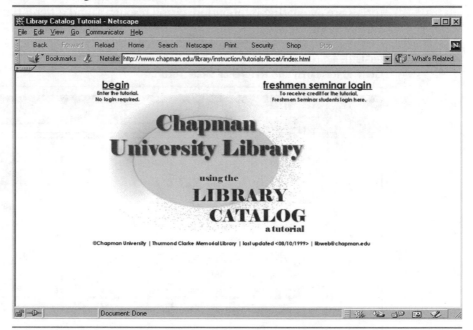

From Thurmond Clarke Memorial Library, Chapman University, Orange, Calif. Available: http://www.chapman.edu/library/instruction/tutorials/libcat/index.html.

Database- or Software-Specific Search Skills

This category of tutorials covers those that are developed to teach users to use specific databases or to master particular search-software interfaces. Because there are so many different interfaces to databases, it is necessary to help users learn how to navigate them. Some search software, such as Ovid or SilverPlatter's WebSPIRS, provides one interface to search multiple databases. Tutorials designed to teach how to search specific interfaces can be integrated into subject-specific and course-related instruction by focusing on an appropriate database for that field. Mastery of the search software can be translated into knowledge of how to use the program in another discipline.

Shippensburg University of Pennsylvania's Ezra Lehman Library has created two similar tutorials that teach students how to search PsyINFO (see figure 1.3) and Sociological Abstracts via SilverPlatter's WebSPIRS interface. In this tutorial the student is taught how to do a basic search, narrow a search, use advanced search strategies, output results, and use special features available in WebSPIRS.

FIGURE 1.3
Database- and Software-Specific Search Skills Tutorial

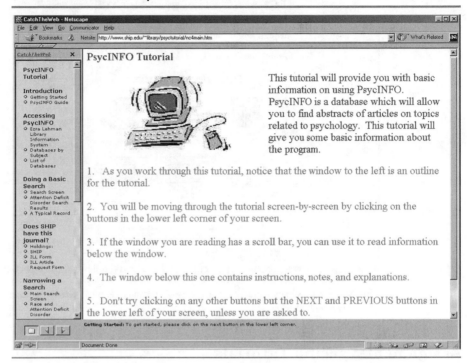

From Ezra Lehman Library, Shippensburg University of Pennsylvania. Available: http://www.ship.edu/~library/psyctutorial/nc4main.htm.

Discipline- or Course-Specific Research Skills

Tutorials in this category zero in on teaching a student to conduct research in a certain discipline. A humanities student approaches a research project in a much different manner than a physics student does. Usually a discipline-specific tutorial supports a particular course, often a survey course with multiple sections. This type of tutorial will be very focused and provides the student with in-depth instruction on how to do research in a particular field. It will include information about appropriate sources and research processes unique to that discipline.

Australia's Monash University Library has developed several research tutorials that are course-specific. Figure 1.4 is an example of a tutorial developed for the course Origins of Western Civilisation 1: The Bronze Age. Exercises within the tutorial use subject headings suitable for the topic and show appropriate databases for archeology research.

FIGURE 1.4
Subject- and Course-Specific Research Skills Tutorial

From Monash University Library, Victoria, Australia. Available: http://www.lib.monash.edu.au/vl/ary11/ary1con.htm.

Assignment-Specific Tutorials

A tutorial can also be developed to guide a student through a specific assignment for a course. This is a perfect opportunity for a librarian to collaborate with a professor to create an interactive Web research project.

In an art history course at Wake Forest University, the professor had a set assignment that she used to teach students how to conduct research. The art history librarian and this author started with the written assignment and developed a tutorial that would make the assignment an interactive lesson that was much more engaging to the student than a text handout. (See figure 1.5.)

Internet Skills

In many libraries, teaching Internet skills has become a standard part of the instruction mission. This type of instruction can range from teaching the mechanics of navigating the Internet to using the Web for research. Different libraries have included a vast assortment of instruction topics about the Internet in their lessons. The following list of potential Internet topics will give you an idea of the possibilities:

FIGURE 1.5
Assignment-Specific Research Skills Tutorial

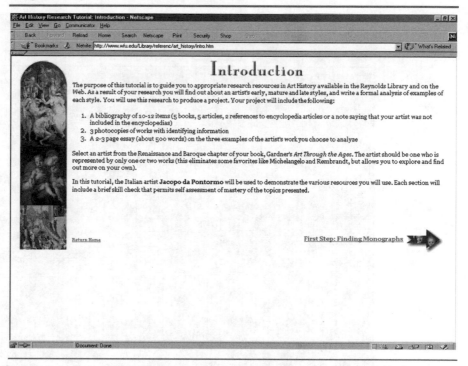

From Z. Smith Reynolds Library, Wake Forest University, Winston–Salem, N.C. Available: http://www.wfu.edu/Library/referenc/art_history.

> introduction to the Internet
>
> Web browser navigation
>
> history of the Internet
>
> communication on the Internet
>
> Web search tools
>
> Web search strategies
>
> evaluation of Web resources
>
> supplying information on the Web

An interesting example of an Internet tutorial comes from Spencer S. Eccles Health Sciences Library, University of Utah, shown in figure 1.6. Internet Navigator is a multi-institutional Internet course that is available to all ten Utah institutions of higher learning. It contains four modules: introduction to the Internet, communication, Internet information navigation, and providing information on the World Wide Web.

FIGURE 1.6
Internet Skills Tutorial

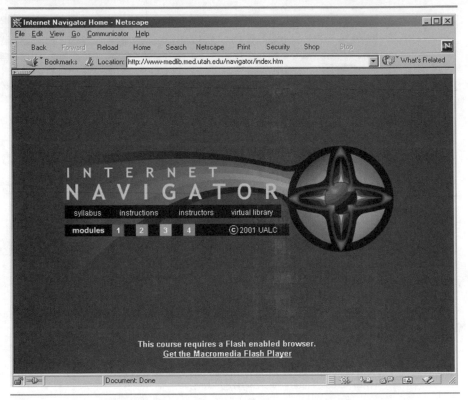

From Spencer S. Eccles Health Sciences Library, University of Utah, Salt Lake City. Available: http://www-medlib.med.utah.edu/navigator/index.html.

General Library Orientation

Most academic libraries hold library orientation tours each semester when new students arrive on campus. An academic library can be an intimidating structure to new freshmen. Helping students learn where departments, services, and materials are located in the library is the first step to transforming them into independent information seekers. A virtual library tour can serve the same purpose. It provides the students with a map that they can use to become acquainted with the library building and its services.

Duke University Libraries created virtual tours for four of its libraries. Each tour includes floor plans, images, and a description of the services available. They offer two versions—one in which the student can browse the library by floor or decide where to go and a guided tour for freshmen that provides a short introduction to the departments that they need to know about. (See figure 1.7.)

FIGURE 1.7
General Library Orientation Tutorial

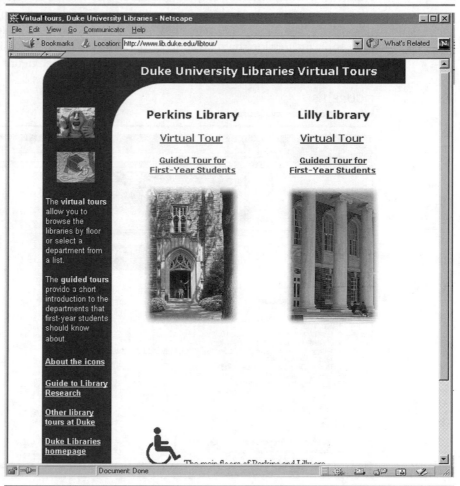

From Duke University Libraries, Durham, N.C. Available: http://www.lib.duke.edu/libtour.

Information Literacy Courses

As the world of information becomes more complex, information literacy has become an increasingly important part of the education process. Many higher education institutions include an information literacy class as a required part of the curriculum, often during a student's first year. It may be offered as a separate class for credit or may be incorporated into a survey course such as freshman English. These courses allow concepts to be covered in an in-depth manner because the time constraints of a "one-shot" class are removed. In this type of forum, there are many opportunities for incorporating active learning, collaborative learning, multiple mediums to present information, and the other characteristics of good library instruction.

Fort Lewis College; Durango, Colorado, requires that students pass a one-credit information literacy class to graduate. The lessons developed by the library instruction coordinator serve as a course pack that contains all the readings for the class. The course has been designed so that students can self-pace their progression, but classes meet on a weekly basis and assignments and tests are given throughout the semester-long schedule. (See figure 1.8.)

FIGURE 1.8
Information Literacy Course

From John F. Reed Library, Fort Lewis College, Durango, Colo. Available: http://library.fortlewis.edu/
~instruct/lib150/contents.html.

NOTE

Dewald, N. H. Jan. 1999. "Transporting Good Library Instruction Practices into the Web Environment: An Analysis of Online Tutorials." *Journal of Academic Librarianship* 25, no. 1: 26–32.

2

Design and
Development Cycle

As with any undertaking, it is important to set up a systematic process to follow that will guide you as the project proceeds. In the software industry, this is known as the design and development cycle. It incorporates the planning, development, production, and evaluation of a product from start to finish, and it's a cycle because it is a circular process rather than a linear one. It is much like the design and development of software. By the time one version is released, the next one is already being worked upon. This chapter discusses the various components that make up a typical design and development cycle. You will find that the components don't always surface in the same place in the cycle, and they often overlap. In fact, the process can be very fluid.

No matter what size project you are embarking upon, it is important to understand the different aspects of this cycle and to incorporate them into your process. Establishing a system will permit the project to be developed within a specified time frame and evaluated according to objective criteria. It will allow you to execute the project efficiently, saving you time overall. The four main stages that you will deal with are preproduction, production, publication, and postproduction. In addition, two facets appear in all stages of the cycle: project management and evaluation. Figure 2.1 provides a graphical representation of the design and development cycle for Web-based instruction.

PREPRODUCTION

No matter how simple the project appears at first consideration, if you jump right in and start creating Web pages immediately, it is going to end up taking much longer than if you take the time up front to carefully plan each aspect of the project. This planning step is called the preproduction phase and can normally encompass about two-thirds of the entire cycle.

FIGURE 2.1
The Design and Development Cycle for Web-Based Instruction

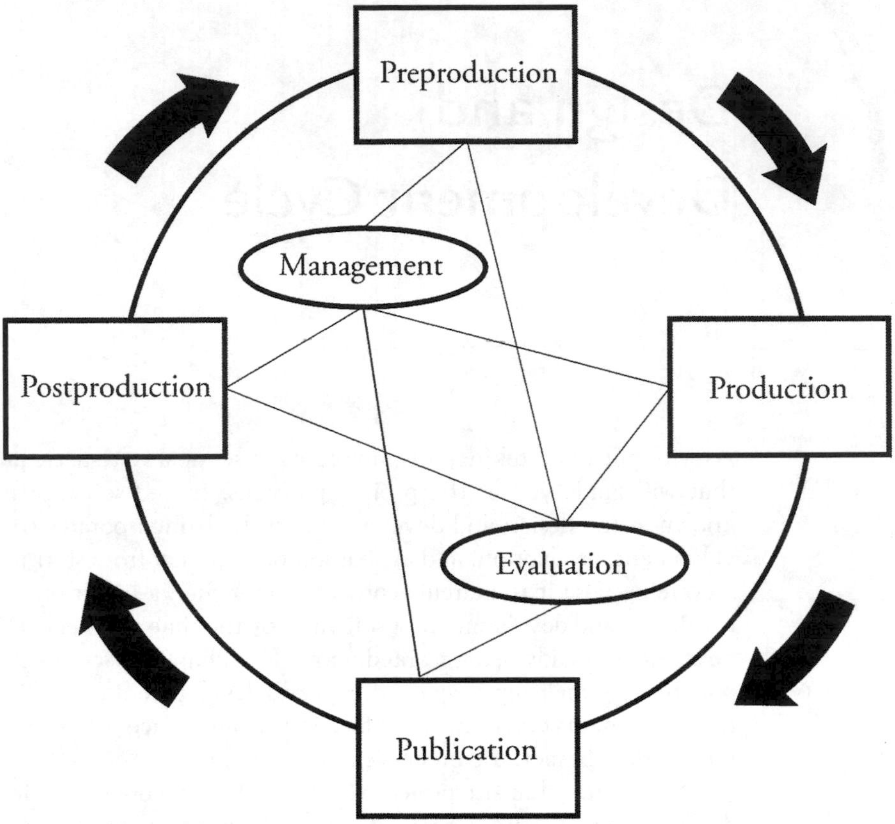

Needs Analyses

Preproduction starts with an idea. Maybe you and your colleagues have decided that an online tutorial is a good objective, or perhaps a faculty member who would like a tutorial for a specific class has approached you. Whatever the origin of the idea, it has been formed in response to some perceived need. You must develop a good understanding of what that need is. So, the first step in the cycle is to perform needs analyses of the client, audience, information, and resources.

Client Needs Analysis

Start by interviewing your client (who may be a fellow librarian, an entire academic department, or a faculty member). You want to determine what the client hopes to accomplish with an online tutorial. Does the client have some specific goal in mind? What is it? For instance, will the tutorial replace face-to-face library instruction, or will it be a supplement to it? Is a Web-based tutorial really the best approach to provide the outcome the client is seeking? What resources does the client have for this project? Is there a departmental budget that will pay for the project, or does the client expect it to come from your library budget?

Audience Needs Analysis

Who is the audience you will be addressing in the tutorial? You will want to "get into their heads" before you design your tutorial. What are the characteristics of this audience—gender, age, ethnicity, socioeconomic level, educational background, learning style, and the degree of familiarity with the proposed subject matter? It is also essential to know the audience's level of computer competence. If you are dealing with an audience with mixed characteristics, you should recognize and factor that into your design.

Information Needs Analysis

Determining information needs involves researching, selecting, and arranging the content that will be included in the tutorial. You will want to consult with the client or a content specialist to determine what is to be included and how to organize it for optimum retention. Often the client is not the person who understands the best way to present the content. For example, a faculty member who is the client probably knows the discipline but not necessarily how it relates to doing library research. Content to be included may also depend on the audience mix. For instance, if the targeted audience is made up of distance education students, the tutorial may want to emphasize online resources over print resources that require a trip to the library to use.

Resource Needs Analysis

What resources are available to support your project? Hardware and software resources need to be considered. Do you have what you need to produce the tutorial, or will you require additional applications or peripherals such as a scanner? What about the students' existing hardware and software? (Chapter 3 focuses in detail on hardware and software considerations.)

How much time is available to complete the project? What human resources are needed? Is there sufficient money in the budget to cover expenses? What delivery system is going to be used, and will your existing infrastructure support it? In the case of Web-based delivery, will it be delivered over a fiber-optic network or an analog phone line? The answer will shape what you decide to develop.

When you have worked through these analyses and have clearly outlined the results, you have the information you'll need to start on the next step in preproduction: design and prototyping.

Design and Prototyping

During the design and prototyping stage of the preproduction phase of the cycle, important preliminary work takes place. This is the time you will develop design ideas and instruction content and organize these into a detailed plan that sets the stage for production of your tutorial. In this section you will be introduced to brainstorming for design ideas, developing scripts, and creating visual tools that will become the blueprint for your tutorial.

Design Brainstorming

The beginning of the design stage is a good time to brainstorm. Assemble your project team (discussed later in this chapter under project management). Have each person contribute his or her ideas on what would be included in the perfect tutorial. Consider both content and functionality. With content, consider the message to be communicated. Start identifying what content can be included that will help develop the research skills the students will need to have. When discussing functionality, consider the level of interactivity that you will use to convey the content. When brainstorming, the sky's the limit, and no idea is too far-fetched. This is particularly true when discussing functionality. Maybe you think that some interactivities that you might desire are beyond the technical capabilities of your team, but this isn't the time to reject anything out of hand. It's a time to see the range of ideas and expectations that each team member is bringing to the project and to establish the beginning of teamwork by learning about each other. You'll find that part of the fun of doing a project like this is that you will have the opportunity to further your knowledge and expertise as you meet the challenge of learning new technologies.

One tool that can help your team reach an agreement about what a good tutorial might consist of is to "shop the competition." That is, visit sites and take a look at what other libraries or educational organizations have done on similar projects. Use the various sites to trigger conversation about what each team member likes or dislikes about a particular site. It will be helpful to compile a list of criteria or questions to consider that you have identified as being important to your project so that you have a basis for comparison. (See figure 2.2.)

A good portal to library tutorial sites can be found on LIRT's (Library Instruction Round Table) site at http://diogenes.baylor.edu/Library/LIRT/lirtproj. html. This exercise will serve to start the design process. You will discover your team's design and organization awareness. Which team member has a good eye for design? Who on the team understands content organization? As you proceed, the skeleton of your site's architecture will start to emerge, and each team member's role will become defined.

Once you have determined the basics of what you desire, the more-detailed tasks of developing a script, planning the tutorial's progression through a flowchart or storyboard, and creating the interface design can begin.

Script

The script will become the nuts and bolts of the message you want to convey. It is a good idea to start with an outline that defines the main points to be made in the tutorial. Often the outline becomes apparent once the site architecture is

FIGURE 2.2
Potential Comparison Criteria for Evaluation of Web-Based Instruction

EVALUATION CATEGORY	QUESTIONS TO ASK
Instructional design	Are the objectives clear?
	Is there provision for interactive practice?
	Is there a feedback mechanism in place?
	Are illustrations and examples incorporated into the instruction?
Subject content	Does it contain the right amount and quality of information?
	Is the language jargon-free?
	Is the content presented in concise chunks to facilitate easy recall?
Audience considerations	Is the material delivered in an appropriate manner for the targeted audience?
	Will the material engage the students' attention?
	Is the material covered pertinent to students' needs?
	Does the site permit student control of movement through the tutorial?
Use of media	Do the graphics, sound, and other multimedia help further the instruction?
	Do multimedia components download quickly?
	Do they require use of a plug-in; if so, are instructions provided?
Visual design	Is the screen design layout clearly organized and easy to understand?
	Is the layout consistent between screens?
	Is the interface aesthetically pleasing?
	Is the site easily identifiable as a cohesive unit?
	Does the color scheme used contribute to the tone of the site?
Ease of use	Is it intuitive to use?
	Is it easy to navigate?
	Do pages load quickly?
Evaluation	Are there evaluation mechanisms built into the tutorial?
Accessibility	Is the tutorial accessible to disabled users?

determined. Site architecture is the design of the site, not in terms of artistic design elements, such as color or graphics, but in terms of the organization, navigation, and functional systems of the site. Figure 2.3 shows an example of a typical outline for a library instruction Web project. The script will include all aspects of the content: the wording for the text you want to include, media that illustrate the content (i.e., images, sound files, movie clips), activities to reinforce a concept, and skill checks to provide an assessment of retention of what has been taught.

FIGURE 2.3
Script Outline for Research

I.   Introduction
II. Selecting Your Topic
    A.   What to write about?
    B.   Background reading
    C.   State the research topic
III. Finding Library Materials
    A.   Online catalog—a definition
    B.   Searching the catalog
    C.   Interpreting catalog search results
IV. Finding Journal Articles
    A.   Periodical databases and indexes
        1.   General versus subject specific
        2.   Electronic databases versus print indexes
        3.   Citation indexes versus full text
    B.   Selecting a database
    C.   Database searching
        1.   Building a search strategy
        2.   Basic search
        3.   Advanced search
    D.   Interpreting results
    E.   Locating the article
V.   Getting Materials from Other Libraries
VI. Using the Internet
    A.   Search indexes
    B.   Search engines
    C.   Meta search engines
VII. Citing Research
VIII. Getting Help
IX. Glossary

From Z. Smith Reynolds Library, Wake Forest University, Winston–Salem, N.C. Available: http://www.wfu.edu/Library/referenc/research.

Flowchart/Storyboard

Both a flowchart and a storyboard are tools to illustrate the step-by-step progression through the tutorial. A flowchart is a visual representation of the sequence of the content of the tutorial. It will show what comes first, second, third, etc., as well as what pages link to each other, what actions your audience will take, and what will occur when each action is taken. It is a road map of your project. Figure 2.4 illustrates a simple flowchart created from the first several screens of the interactive tutorial Falcon: An Interactive Web Tutorial, from Bowling Green State University Libraries.

FIGURE 2.4
Sample Flowchart

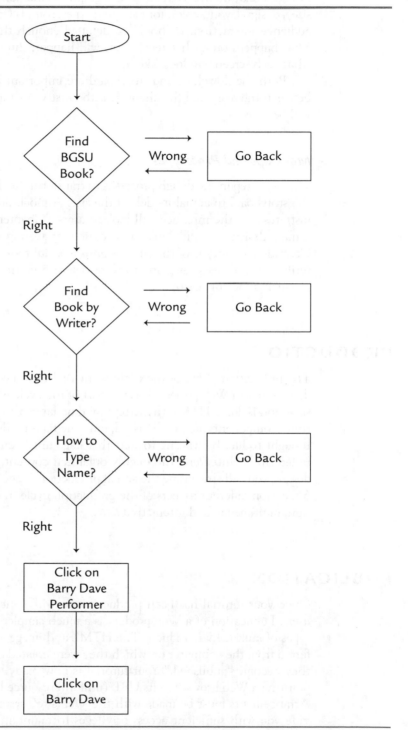

Modeled from Falcon: An Interactive Web Tutorial, Bowling Green State University, Bowling Green, Ohio. Available: http://www.bgsu.edu/colleges/library/infosrv/tutorial/tutor1.html.

The storyboard goes a step farther. It contains a sketch for each screen that includes text, information about the graphics (including placement, color, and size), design layout, color, font size and types, sounds (including narration), and audience interaction. It should be detailed enough that team members know what happens on each screen, what will happen throughout the tutorial, and what each screen will look like.

Both the flowchart and storyboard are important tools of communication between the team and the client. It is the first visualization of what the project will become.

Mock-ups and Prototypes

The next step in the design process is to transform the design ideas contained in the storyboard to actual models of the site. A mock-up of the screen design illustrates how the interface will look to users. (Chapter 4 discusses the user interface design; we will look more closely at testing usability in chapter 7.) Creating a prototype of the site design is a useful tool in the early stages to determine if the design is going to work before investing a great deal of time in producing the entire site.

PRODUCTION

The production phase of the cycle is the one most people think of when they decide to do a Web project. It is the part of the cycle where the actual site construction is done. HTML (hypertext markup language) code is written, interactivity components are programmed, multimedia is produced, and your tutorial is brought to life. By waiting to start this stage until you have put in place a detailed site architecture, thoroughly organized content, and a set page and site design, you will streamline the actual production of the site. Chapters 4 through 6 focus on different aspects of the production cycle in detail: user interface design, multimedia, and interactivity.

PUBLICATION

Once your tutorial has been produced, you will want to make it available to users. Publication of a Web product is a much simpler process than with other types of multimedia products. The HTML and image and sound files are transferred from the computer on which they were created onto a Web server where they become "published." Your tutorial is now ready to be accessed simply by pointing a Web browser to its URL (uniform resource locator, or Web address). Arrangements must be made with the Web site's system administrator to provide you with sufficient access privileges to maintain and update the files as needed.

POSTPRODUCTION

The postproduction phase of the cycle is as important as the planning phase. It includes such tasks as developing a marketing strategy, site indexing, site maintenance, and planning for the next version of the tutorial.

Marketing Strategy

If your tutorial is designed to be used by only a specific group of students, then it may not be necessary to do more than provide a professor with the URL of the site. However, if you are targeting a broader audience, it may be advisable to develop specific methods to get the word out about your tutorial so users can find and use it. Marketing strategies can range from simple to elaborate, but often such methods as notifying appropriate mailing lists, posting an announcement on your organization's home page, or sending out a broadcast e-mail announcement are effective. Your team can explore the best means for your particular situation.

Site Indexing

Site indexing is the process of indexing your tutorial on external Web search engines (as opposed to the indexing done on a search engine installed on your organization's Web server). To improve the potential for users to find your tutorial via the major search engines like HotBot or AltaVista, you will want to use available tools to describe your site accurately. The main way to accomplish this is to use <meta> tags to specify accurate descriptions in the <head> of your document. Also, use descriptive terms in the <title> tag because many search engines index from this tag. The process may also be speeded up by taking a proactive approach by submitting your site manually to various search engines rather than waiting for their automated indexing programs (called "robots") to visit your site and find you.

Site Maintenance

Once your tutorial is published, it is important to take steps to ensure that it stays functional and current. For example, the Web is notorious for being ever-changing, and you will want to make sure that you regularly check for broken links and update them.

Planning for the Next Version

Publishing a Web tutorial isn't a finite project. As you proceed through the postpublication evaluation process you will start to gather information that will form the nucleus for revisions and improvements.

TESTING AND EVALUATION

Testing and evaluation are very important components of the design and development cycle, but they can't be neatly assigned into just one phase of the cycle. Testing and evaluation are the primary vehicles you have to receive essential information to help ensure that your tutorial is effective. Because they are essential elements of a successful Web instruction project, this subject is covered in depth in chapter 7.

PROJECT MANAGEMENT

No matter whether your project is large or small, it will require management from start to finish. A large project may call for a dedicated project manager; a small project may have one of the team members also wearing a management hat. There are many facets of a project to manage: the time line, the budget, the staff/team, resources, reports, client relations, and quality control.

Time Line

Usually time is one of the constraints on a project. For example, a university's general research and reference tutorial needs to be ready at the start of the fall term, or a professor needs a course-related tutorial two weeks before the research assignment is due. Any project is more effective if there is a detailed time line to follow. A time line will include the project schedule that details tasks and activities, projected completion dates, and persons assigned to each task. Project management software is available to track time lines (for example, Microsoft Project), but it can be done without investing in expensive software. To create a time line, make a list of all activities involved in each phase of the project, put them in sequential order, estimate the time it will take to complete each task, and assign responsibility. You may want to set up different views of the time line—weekly, monthly, and overall view. A good model that will work is a Gantt chart, also known as a bar chart. Figure 2.5 illustrates a simple Gantt chart of a Web project.

Budget

Managing the project budget can be a major task in a large-scale project. If you are starting with nothing, you may have to create a budget prior to your project's being approved. Using the results from the initial resource needs analysis, you may have to consider expenditures for hardware and software to produce the tutorial. If you don't have trained staff, application training may have to be factored into the budget. Human resources, even if you aren't paying an extra salary to someone on staff, are a major budget item since staff hours spent on the project will most likely be one of the largest costs for which you must account.

FIGURE 2.5
Gantt Chart for a Web Project Using Microsoft Project Software

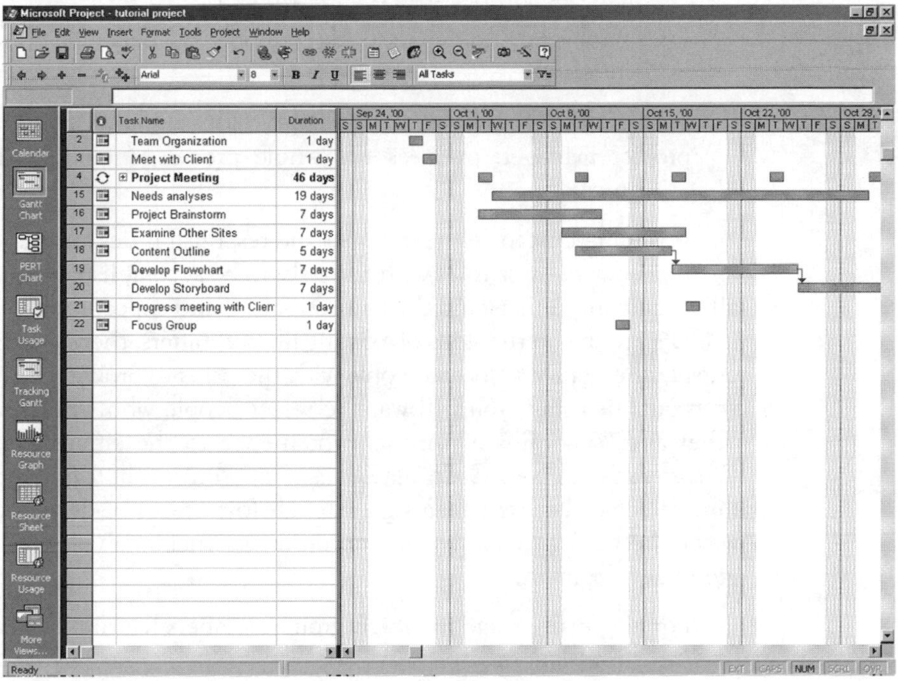

Screen shot reprinted by permission from Microsoft Corporation.

Staffing and Teamwork

Forming the right team for your project and managing the resulting team dynamics may well be one of the most challenging aspects of the project. As you are forming your team, keep in mind the roles that may need to be filled:

Web author: creates the HTML pages for the tutorial

scripting programmer: adds interactivity into the tutorial through scripting or other technologies

instructional designer: determines the best way to present the content in an online environment to optimize retention

content specialist: determines the content to include; this may be the library's bibliographic instructor or the subject specialist for the content being presented

writer: writes the script and content

editor: edits the script and content

graphic/animation designer or videographer: understands user interface design and creates graphics and other multimedia systems designer: designs how the tutorial will work from a technical standpoint; works with instructional designer on flowcharts and storyboard; manages authors; selects authoring tools

information technology specialist: provides the expertise on server and network issues

evaluation specialist: creates evaluation plan and tools

project manager: oversees the whole process, including the evaluation process

It is important to define the roles and responsibilities for each team member and to associate these roles with the tasks to be accomplished. This ensures that all participants understand the team structure and expectations.

Depending on the skills of existing library staffers, there may be a need to go outside the library to locate people with the skills to produce the tutorial. Even with qualified staff, you will want to select people who will complement each other and "subordinate personal prominence to the efficiency of the whole" (*Webster's Ninth New Collegiate Dictionary* definition of *teamwork*). It is important to remember that teams go through four stages of development on their way to becoming a cohesive unit according to Tuckman's (1965) model of small group development:

Forming is the stage in which group members learn about each other and the task at hand.

Storming develops as group members reach a level of comfort with each other and may start vying for status within the group and argue.

Norming is the stage in which the group structure is developed. Rules are established for achieving goals, roles are defined, and the group is ready to get down to the business at hand.

Performing is the stage in which the team begins to function as a system and focuses attention on the work or content. Emphasis here is on productivity and achievement. Collaboration and cooperation are incorporated to work toward the shared goal.

Coaching staff to put the good of the team before individual considerations is a skill that requires patience, maturity, and a good sense of humor.

Resource Allocation

Most organizations don't have unlimited resources. Even if you've determined that you have the necessary resources to complete your project, you may well be sharing those resources with others in your organization. For example, your content specialist may be the library's bibliographic instructor; the site designer may be the systems administrator; etc. Most likely, your team members won't be able to devote 100 percent of their time to this project. Scheduling the time that team members can commit to a particular project is important to meeting the project time lines. You also may be sharing hardware and software resources with others (including the public) in your organization, and the project manager will have to become involved in allocating those resources so they are available when needed by team members.

Reports

Depending on the scope of the project, it may be necessary to submit progress reports to your client at crucial points throughout the design and development cycle. In addition, regular reports can serve as an effective record-keeping method that will be a valuable tool for project evaluation. Reports can also be a good way to communicate the overall project progress to team members.

Client Relations

If you are working with a client, you will want the client to stay informed and satisfied with the progress of the project. Therefore, you must make time to communicate regularly. Maintaining a good relationship with the client can make a world of difference if the project gets off-schedule for whatever reason. The client is much more likely to be understanding of extenuating circumstances if he or she has been kept in the loop in a positive manner.

Quality Control

Overseeing the emergence of an exemplary tutorial calls for quality checks at each step of the production cycle. You may incorporate both formal and informal methods for evaluating if your tutorial is meeting expectations of the criteria established in the preproduction stage. These methods will be discussed in detail in chapter 7.

It should be evident by now that even though the design and development cycle provides a structure to follow, it is a nonlinear process with more than one way to implement each phase. There is plenty of room for variations depending on the team you have assembled, the characteristics of your client, and the leadership style of the project manager. Keep in mind the main factors that will influence how you proceed: money (budget), time (scheduling), staffing (expertise), and facilities (hardware/software). Finally, remember that no matter how important it is to be systematic, it is just as imperative to provide space for creativity.

NOTE

Tuckman, B. 1965. "Developmental Sequence in Small Groups." *Psychological Bulletin* 63 (June): 384–99.

3

Selecting Project Development Tools

As discussed in the previous chapter, analyzing hardware and software resource needs is an important part of the preproduction stage of your Web project. There are three major areas of consideration:

- constraints that may exist depending upon the hardware and software available to users
- development hardware
- authoring software

USER CONSTRAINTS

One of the main benefits of a Web-based delivery system is that it can be used across platforms. A platform is the underlying hardware or software for a system, commonly called the operating system. Customarily, software application programs were developed to run on a particular platform. A developer that wanted an application to run on multiple platforms would be forced to write two separate programs. But with HTML, the language of the Web, it doesn't matter if your users are on PC-compatible computers or use Macintoshes. However, you do have to worry about what hardware and software your audience uses to access your tutorial.

So, what do you need to be concerned about? Your main concerns fall into three categories: hardware issues, browser issues, and access methods.

Hardware Issues

It is doubtful that you are in the envious situation where all of your users have late-model, identical computers. Therefore, you must take into account the range of hardware being used to access your tutorial.

Monitor Screen Size and Display Capabilities

Display capabilities can vary greatly. If your users have older monitors, they may only be capable of displaying a resolution of 640 × 480 pixels (the number of individual points of color; in this case, 640 horizontally and 480 vertically). When you start to lay out the design for your user interface, you will select a window size that will display. If you design your site to display at 800 × 600 and your user's screen can only display 640 × 480, that user will not be able to view the entire screen and may have to scroll both horizontally and vertically to read what is on it. This is very wearisome for the person who is trying to focus on the content. The site's display resolution should be no larger than the lowest resolution screen that a user may have.

Although color monitors are common today, there are still monochrome or gray-scale display screens in use (particularly with notebook and smaller computers). If you know that some of your audience members may be accessing your tutorial with noncolor screens, this should influence how you plan your color design.

Processor Speed

The clock speed of a processor, or central processing unit (CPU), determines how fast it interprets and executes program instructions (commands). This is measured in megahertz (MHz). A 500 MHz computer will execute 5 million cycles per second. Since every instruction requires a specific number of cycles, the clock speed helps determine how fast those instructions will be executed. Today you will see computers that have 1 GHz (gigahertz, 1 billion hertz), but there are still plenty of 133 MHz computers in use. If your audience members have lower speed CPUs in their computers and you create a tutorial that requires a great number of commands to be issued simultaneously, the audience will have a hard time using the tutorial because the tutorial will respond slowly.

Random Access Memory

RAM is the second part of the equation for speed, along with the processor. It is the place in the computer where data is stored during the short term for easy access. When RAM fills up, the computer must pull the data from the hard drive, which slows down the process considerably. Computers with more RAM installed will be able to run programs faster than those with minimal RAM. Keep in mind that your tutorial isn't the only thing that is running on a computer at a given time. The operating system, Web browser, and other applications are using available RAM also.

Sound

Although it seems self-evident, if you are planning to incorporate audio into your tutorial, make sure that your audience has access to a computer with sound capabilities. In many public areas, including computer labs, the sound has been disabled so that others will not be disturbed. If part of the tutorial will convey important information in audio format, you will need to decide how to deliver it in public environments (perhaps providing access to headphones).

Browser Issues

Several different Web browsers are available, and the two most popular are Internet Explorer and Netscape. Furthermore, many different versions of these browsers are in use. Because users don't necessarily abandon their current browser and update to the newest version and because latest versions incorporate new technologies that have been developed since the previous update, you may find you have browser-compatibility issues. If you decide to incorporate a certain type of scripting to provide interaction or use some of the more recent HTML elements, in older browsers your page may not function as you had planned. Some features that are not supported in all browsers include cascading style sheets, layers, frames, and JavaScript. These features are defined and discussed in later chapters. At this point, it is important only to know what browsers support the features you plan to use. As shown in figure 3.1, Webmon-

FIGURE 3.1
Browser Chart from Webmonkey

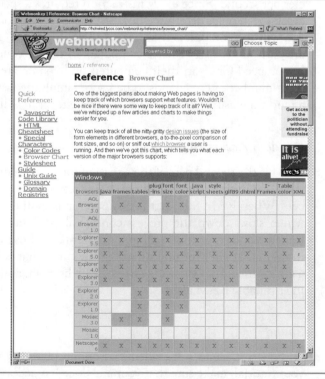

key provides a browser chart that specifies which features are supported by various browser types and versions. In addition, there are utilities available on the Web that you can use to test the compatibility of browsers with your pages. For example, Netscape Netcenter's Web Garage (see figure 3.2) checks how well your pages display in different browsers.

FIGURE 3.2
Netscape Netcenter's Web Site Garage Browser-Compatibility Check

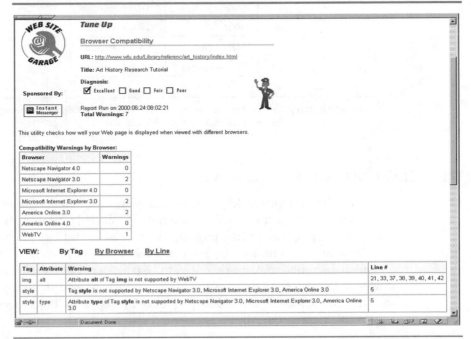

Netscape Netcenter's Web Site Garage screenshot © 2000 Netscape Communications Corp. Used with permission. Available: http://websitegarage.netscape.com.

Access Method

How are your users going to access the tutorial? Are they all on the local network using a T-1 high-speed, digital connection? Do any of them connect to your site via a modem? If there are modem users, you will want to be able to gauge how fast your pages will load under different connect rates. The Netscape Netcenter Web Site Garage chart in figure 3.3 shows a page that takes only one second to load on a T-1 connection will take 35 seconds to load on a 14.4K modem connection. Slow load times can result in frustration to your users.

Determining the constraints that your users have with their software and hardware will help you make decisions about what type of authoring systems are required for graphics, video, and audio. That, in turn, will help with decision making on selecting development hardware.

FIGURE 3.3
Netscape Netcenter's Web Site Garage Page-Load Time Check

This diagnostic checks how fast your page loads up under 6 common modem speeds.

Connect Rate	Connect Time
14.4K	35.47 seconds
28.8K	19.19 seconds
33.6K	16.34 seconds
56K	12.63 seconds
ISDN 128K	4.11 seconds
T1 1.44 Mbps	1.00 seconds

Netscape Netcenter's Web Site Garage screenshot © 2000 Netscape Communications Corp. Used with permission. Available: http://websitegarage.netscape.com.

DEVELOPMENT HARDWARE

Having the appropriate development hardware to create a multimedia project will make the project move along much more smoothly. Nothing is harder than trying to create multimedia programs with substandard equipment. However, budgets can vary enormously, and concessions may have to be made. This is a general discussion of items that need to be considered when selecting the hardware to be used. For help in researching specific hardware and selection criteria, refer to the resources section at the end of this book for links to sites that can help you focus specifically on hardware research.

Computer Selection

Before you can design and produce your Web-based tutorial, you will need to select the computer workstations to be used. You may decide to have one central computer where the entire production will take place, or you may choose to do different portions of the production on different computers. Deciding which workstations to use must be done in conjunction with the choice of authoring software (discussed later in this chapter). Software is developed according to what platform it will run on, so if you decide on an application that is available only for Windows, then you must use a computer that runs Windows. Similarly, each different software application has minimum system requirements for it to perform properly. You must be aware of those requirements so you use a computer that meets those specifications. Requirements include such stipulations as processor speed, operating system, amount of RAM, quantity of available hard disk space, color display capability of the video card, and availability of a CD-ROM drive, sound card, and a network interface card (NIC) or modem. Normally, the software manufacturer will give minimum requirements as well as recommended specifications. Don't be surprised if you discover that running a certain application on a computer that has just the minimum specifications results in less than satisfactory performance. As mentioned previously, any application you run is competing for your system's resources with other programs and utilities running on the computer. It is always a good idea to try to configure a computer to exceed the bare minimum requirements listed.

Peripheral Selection

A peripheral is any external device that attaches to a computer. Although you might not know them by this term, as a computer user you are familiar with many computer peripherals. Typically their purpose is to input or output data; some do both. Common input peripherals are the keyboard and the mouse. One of the most common output devices is the printer. Peripherals that serve both functions include hard disks, floppy disks, and modems. Several devices that you will want to consider for a Web project include monitors, video adapters, sound cards, scanners, cameras, camcorders, video cards, and removable file storage systems.

Monitor

The monitor is the most common output device, and it is not one you can choose to do without. However, as briefly described previously, there are considerations that should be made in selecting the appropriate monitor for a multimedia project.

Screen Size   The first factor used to describe a monitor is its size. In general, the larger the screen size, the more pixels it can display horizontally and vertically. The size is measured in the same manner as a television screen—diagonally from one corner to its opposite. The size specified for a particular monitor may be misleading since there is always an area around the edge of the screen that can't be used. Look for the "viewable area" size to determine how much screen is actually available. For a long time, the most common size used has been the 15-inch screen. Now, however, 17-inch screens are becoming more popular because it is much easier to work with multiple windows when you have more "real estate." A 21-inch monitor is deluxe to have for a multimedia project, but it is very expensive.

Resolution   The higher the resolution of the monitor, the sharper the image will be. It is useful to have a monitor that can display multiple resolutions so you can test your page design in the different resolutions your audience will use. Displays that specify a maximum resolution number (for instance, 1280×1023 pixels) will probably support lesser resolutions (1024×768, 800×600, and 640×480).

Color Capability   Over the years, monitors have come in different display modes that determined the number of colors capable of being displayed as well as the maximum resolution. Today, the most common display mode is SVGA (super video graphics array). An SVGA monitor can display more than 16 million colors. VGA (video graphics array) mode displays 256 colors. One important point to remember when you are relying on the colors displayed on a monitor is that different monitors display the same colors differently. It's not a good idea to get your mind set on a particular hue because it will not look the same on another display. In addition, there are only 216 colors that display consistently in Web browsers. In chapter 4 we will discuss how to select Web-safe colors to ensure the color you intend is the one your audience sees.

Video Adapter

The performance of your monitor is partially dependent on the video adapter (also called a graphics card). This card is usually installed in an expansion slot on the system board; sometimes it is integrated into the system board rather than being a separate component. The adapter contains a video controller so that data can be sent to and be refreshed or repainted on the display, and it provides digital-to-analog conversion (converting strings of binary zeros and ones to output that is meaningful to humans, in this case a picture). Video adapters contain their own memory so that the computer's RAM isn't used for storing displays. Increased video RAM is required for higher resolutions to be displayed. When working on a multimedia project, the computer should have the highest quality video adapter possible that is within the budget.

Sound Card

To include audio in the project, a sound card is required. A sound card serves as both an input device (from a microphone or a CD-ROM) and output device (via speakers or headphones). It will be used in both capacities to capture audio and play it back. The sound card records normal analog (electronic transmission via signals of varying frequency) signals and converts them to digital ones (electronic technology that stores and processes data as zeros and ones) and copies it onto the hard drive or another storage device. To hear what's been recorded, the sound card works in reverse, converting the digital information back to analog and feeding to a speaker that generates the sound.

Most late-model computers include a sound card as part of the basic configuration. A basic sound card should have a line in and a line out, but it may go beyond that and have additional I/O (input/output) connectors for things such as CD audio and video. Your sound card should support the two digital audio standards: MIDI (Musical Instrument Digital Interface), a standard for representing music electronically, and Sound Blaster, which is the de facto standard for PC sound. If possible, choose a PCI (Peripheral Component Interconnect) sound card over an ISA (Industry Standard Architecture) because the PCI card is faster. PCI connections allow data to flow at 32 bits at a time versus the 16 bits that ISA supports.

In addition, don't forget to acquire a microphone and speakers so that you can input and play back the audio you create. Headphones can also be a useful tool for working on an audio digitization project.

Scanners

Scanners come in a variety of types and price ranges. A flatbed scanner is the most popular format and will serve well for most Web projects. It can be used to scan photos, pictures, and pages from books. It consists of a flat surface where the document or image is placed. When a light passes over the document, the scanner converts the light to a computer-readable format. A color scanner has three light sources, one each for red, blue, and green. The term you see most often in discussions of scanners is *resolution*. You will see scanner specifications that talk about 600 × 600 dpi (dots per inch) or 1200 × 1200 dpi. It's not necessary to use a scanner that has the highest resolution possible. Web images only display at a maximum of 72 or 96 dpi, depending on the operating system, so to ensure small file size for faster downloading, you will want to scan your graphics at 72 dpi, not any higher. Other features to consider when choosing a scanner include mode of connectivity to the computer, maximum scan size, and scan speed. Most scanners come bundled with imaging and OCR (optical character recognition) software, so that may become a factor in choosing a particular brand or model.

Cameras

You may choose to work with either a conventional camera or a digital camera. With a conventional camera, you can develop your film into prints or slides and then digitize them using a flatbed scanner.

Digital cameras have become increasingly popular as their image quality has improved and the prices have dropped. Good quality digital cameras are now affordable and may soon be a standard peripheral for most systems. A major benefit for a Web project is that a digital camera removes the step of having to scan an image into digital format. With a digital camera, the image is captured in a digital format that is immediately ready for transfer into the computer, which can then be manipulated with graphics editing software. In a digital camera, the imaging is performed by a charge coupled device (CCD) or CMOS (complementary metal-oxide semiconductor) sensors. The CCD or CMOS replaces both the shutter and the film found in traditional cameras. For an in-depth discussion of digital camera technologies, refer to the PC Technology Guide at http://www.pctechguide.com/19digcam.htm.

There are four fundamental issues to consider when selecting a digital camera: computing platform, image quality, memory storage, and connectivity. Each is discussed in the following sections. In addition, there are several other qualities to check for: camera features such as lens type, battery life, flash capability, and file formats. Whether they are crucial depends on the parameters of your project.

Computing Platform   The platform used was more of an issue a few years ago than it is now because most digital cameras today will interface with both Windows and Macintosh. Make sure you get a camera that is packaged with the software that works with your platform. It can be discouraging to end up with a camera that you can't interface with your computer.

Image Quality   The quality of the image depends on many things, but the most important determinant is the resolution of the CCD. It wasn't too long ago that the typical resolution for a digital camera was 640 × 480 pixels. Resolutions are now being talked about in "megapixels" with resolutions going as high as 2048 × 1536 because of the advent of 3.34 megapixel CCDs.

Memory Storage   Today's digital cameras use removable storage, but these come in a variety of formats. The main advantage is that when a memory card is full, it can be removed and another inserted in its place without having to stop and load the images onto a computer. A second advantage is that the cards can be inserted directly into a computer (with the correct accompanying hardware) and treated as a disk. One of the most popular types of storage is the camera that uses a standard floppy disk (for example, the Sony Mavica). Everyone has access to these, and they are inexpensive. They do have limitations because they can only store up to 1.44 MB (megabytes) of data.

Three other popular memory storage cards are CompactFlash, SmartMedia, and Sony's Memory Stick. The amount of storage on each varies because the cards are produced with different storage capacities. The memory capacity of the card must be coupled with the resolution of the images being captured to determine how many images will fit on one card. For instance, a 32 MB CompactFlash memory card will hold 56 "good" quality (*quality* determines how much an image is compressed to save space) 640 × 480 resolution images in a Kodak DC210 camera, but only 19 "best" quality at an 1152 × 864 resolution.

Connectivity   Most cameras provide the option of connecting directly from the camera to a serial port into an image-download software application. However, this requires power from the camera, is a slow procedure, and can drain batteries very quickly. If you are going to download in this fashion, use the AC adapter that normally comes with the camera, and save your batteries.

Different devices are available in which to insert the memory card and then connect it to the computer to download the images. These consist of parallel and floppy connections in which the card is inserted into an adapter as well as USB (Universal Serial Bus) connections. A USB connection can transfer data three times faster than a serial connection.

Camera Features   Almost every digital camera has an LCD (Liquid Crystal Display) panel, which allows you to preview and arrange pictures without having to transfer the images to a computer. It also is the interface to adjust camera settings, such as resolution selection, and it can serve in place of the viewfinder as well. You will want to examine how the LCD works because it is different on each model. If the LCD is the only viewfinder (and not just a supplement to the customary one), you should also consider that LCD panels are hard to see in the direct sunlight.

Check to see if the camera has a fixed- or auto-focus lens. With a fixed-focus lens everything from a few feet on will be in focus. This won't help if you need to photograph something close-up. Most have some kind of zoom capability, which may be two or three predefined settings or gradual zoom action. If the ability to take close-up pictures is critical to your project, you will want to be sure that this feature is included. Two different types of zoom are available: optical and digital. Optical zoom is similar to the type of zoom in a regular 35mm camera; when you zoom, the physical lens moves in and out. With a digital zoom there are no moving parts and the camera's "brain" digitally zooms in or out. The quality of a digital zoom is not as good as an optical because a digital zoom tends to look "pixelated," that is, individual pixels that make up the image are visible to the human eye.

Battery life is a very important component of research. There is a wide variation in how long a camera will last with one set of batteries, and a single camera can vary depending on whether you leave the LCD in preview mode or do most of your image selection and arranging in the camera rather than after the images are transferred to the computer. Different cameras use diverse modes of transfer, and some of these are memory hogs. If you are going to use batteries consistently, then invest in rechargeable ones, which, although more expensive up front, will save you money in the long run.

Another feature is the flash capability. Find out what the range is, whether there is red-eye reduction, and if you can override the flash if you choose to do so. Many cameras also have a self-timer that allows you to get yourself into the picture.

Some digital cameras are now available with the ability to capture short video clips that can be stored in MPEG-1 (Moving Picture Experts Group, a video-compression standard) format (discussed in chapter 5). If you just need a few seconds of video, this can be more cost effective than purchasing a digital camcorder.

File Formats   What format choices does the camera offer? If you are going to use the camera for Web projects, then it is very handy to have JPEG (Joint Photographics Experts Group) as one of the choices because this format is supported on the Web. If the camera captures images only in its native format, how easy is it to export it to the format you require?

Accessories   Depending on the types of images you want to create, you may also want to consider acquiring a tripod to ensure that your images are sharp. A tripod is beneficial when photographing things such as architecture. It will be essential for making a virtual reality tour, where you would be photographing a 360° view of a room. Although many cameras come equipped with a case and strap, don't forget to ask about these essential accessories also.

Camcorders

If you are planning to incorporate video into your project, you must realize that video editing is the most resource-hungry task that can be done on a computer. Video production requires a fast computer with plenty of RAM and hard disk space. In addition, you will probably need to install an expansion card to provide a way to input the video from a camcorder into the computer. This card is known as a *video capture card*.

Most of today's camcorders come equipped with features such as LCD monitors and zoom lenses. The main distinctions to be made between models are compatibility with a video cassette recorder (that is, the tape can be directly played in a VCR), maximum recording time, and (this should come as no surprise) resolution. The main decision to make is whether to use an analog or a digital camcorder. Most people are familiar with the traditional analog camcorder, and you may have one already available for use. However, you should be aware that you'll never have 100 percent accuracy when transferring from analog to digital. Just as with a photocopy, the quality of each reproduction is reduced.

Several different analog formats are available in camcorders. Analog camcorders include the tape format with which most people are familiar, VHS (which can be played on a VCR but has low resolution). Other formats include VHS-C (compact VHS, which plays in your VCR with an adapter), S-VHS (Super VHS with better resolution than VHS), 8mm (which has a longer playing time but can only be played from the camcorder), and Hi-8 (higher resolution than 8mm).

Each of these formats has features and limitations, but since they all need to be converted from analog to digital, a chief consideration is how effectively you can convert the video into a digital format. Selecting the right video capture card is one factor in how well your conversion will work. When converting analog video to digital, it must be compressed to reduce the size of the file. An algorithm, or specialized computer program, known as codec (compressor/decompressor) controls the amount of compression. Common codecs are M-JPEG, MPEG-1, MPEG-2, and DV (Digital Video). Different codecs are more appropriate for some tasks than for others. For instance, M-JPEG is best used when you are outputting the file back onto a tape for playback, but is not a good choice for multimedia on the Web. At this point, a better codec for that is MPEG-1, which is designed to pack a large quantity of video into a small file and is a low-loss compression technique. MPEG-4 is a codec standard under development that is specifically designed for the delivery of interactive multimedia on the Web. It will include specifications for video, audio, and interactivity. If you are interested in learning more about codecs, visit Codec Central at http://www.terran-int.com/CodecCentral.

Some of the codecs are "lossy," meaning that frames (the individual still images in a video sequence) are dropped to decrease file size. This can result in a choppy looking video. If you are using a high-quality tape, the loss may not be as evident as if you use a low-resolution tape (such as VHS). Some capture cards are more liable than others to drop frames, so it is worthwhile to locate reviews that rate different cards. Other factors that can cause frames to become dropped include whether your computer's processor can digitize fast enough or if its hard drive can spin fast enough to record at the rate selected.

When you consider which analog video capture card to select, be aware of the input/output ports you have. You will want to make certain that the card you choose has an input port that is compatible with the type of analog camcorder you are using. Also determine what codecs the card supports so that you get a card that will use the type of compression you have selected.

It's evident that there are many challenges to overcome when you work with analog tapes. That is one main reason to consider using a digital camcorder because importing digital video into your computer is a much easier undertaking and will result in a higher quality video. A digital camcorder records images digitally on a mini-DV cassette. It has better resolution than analog—500 lines versus a maximum of 400 for the Hi-8 format or 250 for VHS. A digital camcorder has built-in compression before images are written to the tape. The DV codec is a lossless algorithm, which ensures high quality images. Digital video doesn't suffer from the conversion deterioration that occurs when importing and exporting copies of analog tapes. Unlike converting analog tapes to digital, importing a digital video into a computer for editing is just like copying files from a peripheral over a high-speed connection.

The high-speed digital connection that is used is an IEEE (Institute of Electrical and Electronic Engineers) 1394 interface, a standard for connecting devices to a computer. You may hear it referred to as FireWire (Apple) or i.LINK (Sony). Digital camcorders come equipped with this port. You will need to add a digital capture card that supports IEEE 1394. Some computers are now being manufactured with this port included, but it is not yet as common as the inclusion of a USB port.

Dazzle Video Creator

An inexpensive, easy-to-use alternative to installing a video capture card is a device called Dazzle. It is easy for the novice because it has an all-external setup. It plugs into the USB port of your computer and you connect your camcorder or VCR to it. Dazzle comes bundled with all the software needed to produce MPEG-1 digital files. The minimum requirements to use this device are a 133 MHz processor and 32 MB of RAM, a much more cost-effective solution than would be needed for "traditional" video digitization. The quality and sophistication level are not going to equal a professional video production setup, but it may be a very appropriate solution for your needs. Find out more about this device at http://www.dazzle.com.

Removable File Storage

You will want to take into account how you are going to share and store your files as your project progresses. It may be that you have access to a network file server where files can be shared with everyone on your team, but usually there will be some need to transport files between computers, make backups or archives, or store large files. As you are deciding on which type of storage to select, consider the following features:

capacity (how much data it will store)

media costs (for the drive and the disks)

durability (of the storage media)

portability (ability to be moved from one computer to another)

speed (how fast the data transfers)

interface (how the device connects to your computer)

Floppy disks have limited storage capacity (usually 1.44 MB), so you may want to consider removable mass-storage options. A variety of choices are available, but be aware that most are not interchangeable with each other and that prices can vary by thousands of dollars. The best-known removable storage device today is the Iomega Zip drive. It is available in a variety of interfaces: external with parallel or USB connection or internal with ATAPI (AT Attachment Packet Interface) or SCSI (Small Computer System Interface) connectivity. Storage capacity for Zip disks is either 100 MB or 250 MB. The benefits of using a Zip drive are that it is affordable, easy to use, and widely used. The external version is portable, and the parallel connection allows it to be attached to any computer.

If you are incorporating video into your project, you may require a greater mass storage capacity than a disk that holds only a few hundred megabytes of files. High-capacity removable storage devices are available that store more than a gigabyte (GB) of data. Iomega also manufactures the Jaz Drive, one of the most popular high-capacity storage choices. It can store 20 to 40 minutes of compressed video on one of its 2 GB disks.

A medium that is becoming more readily functional and affordable is CD-Rewritable (CD-RW). Unlike the traditional CD-Writable, CD-RW drives allow you to overwrite data previously written to disk, providing a storage capacity of up to 650 MB.

AUTHORING SOFTWARE PROGRAMS

There are many different types of software applications that may be needed to produce a multimedia, interactive Web tutorial. This section presents an overview of the most common categories of authoring software that are used. Examples of each type of tool will be highlighted, but be sure to refer to the resources section at the end of this book for links to comprehensive sites to use to research each category. Your selection will be dependent upon the platform you have chosen for your development hardware, the minimum system specification required, and the types of multimedia and interactivity you have decided to incorporate into your project.

Many software applications are available for evaluation at no charge. You can find demo versions on company Web sites and can test-drive them before you make a purchase decision.

HTML/Web Editors

There are different ways to approach authoring Web pages for your project. How you decide to do it should depend upon the types of interactivity you plan to use, your team members' levels of expertise, and their preference for working either directly with the source code or using a visual method.

HTML can be written without using a Web editor at all; the most basic HTML editor is Notepad (Windows) or Simpletext (Mac). You simply input all the HTML markup code manually. However, this is probably not the most practical approach as it is quite time consuming, is prone to error, and requires a high level knowledge of HTML coding and other scripting languages. At the other end of the spectrum are simple visual editors that don't require knowledge of HTML and that operate like a word processing application. An example of this is Netscape's Composer, which is part of the Netscape Communicator suite. It works well for authoring very basic pages, but it doesn't include the functionality that will support the integration of higher-level features such as complex tables, cascading style sheets, frames, or dynamic HTML. (Each of these is defined and discussed in later chapters.)

It is best to select an application that has been developed specifically for authoring Web pages. Today these applications have matured to the point where they provide all the features necessary to build complex and advanced Web pages. Prices range from free to several hundred dollars—but don't assume that the most expensive is the best.

The two main "flavors" are code-based or visually based (WYSIWYG, for what you see is what you get, pronounced "WIZZYWIG"). Both perform the same functions, but are very different in how the author works to build a page.

With a code-based editor, the code is in plain view. (See, for example, figure 3.4.) You can see exactly which tags and attributes you are using. Unlike a plain-text editor, however, a code-based editor automates the creation of tags and often also automates the process of generating the higher-level features that will bring

FIGURE 3.4
Web Page Viewed in Code-Based Editor HomeSite

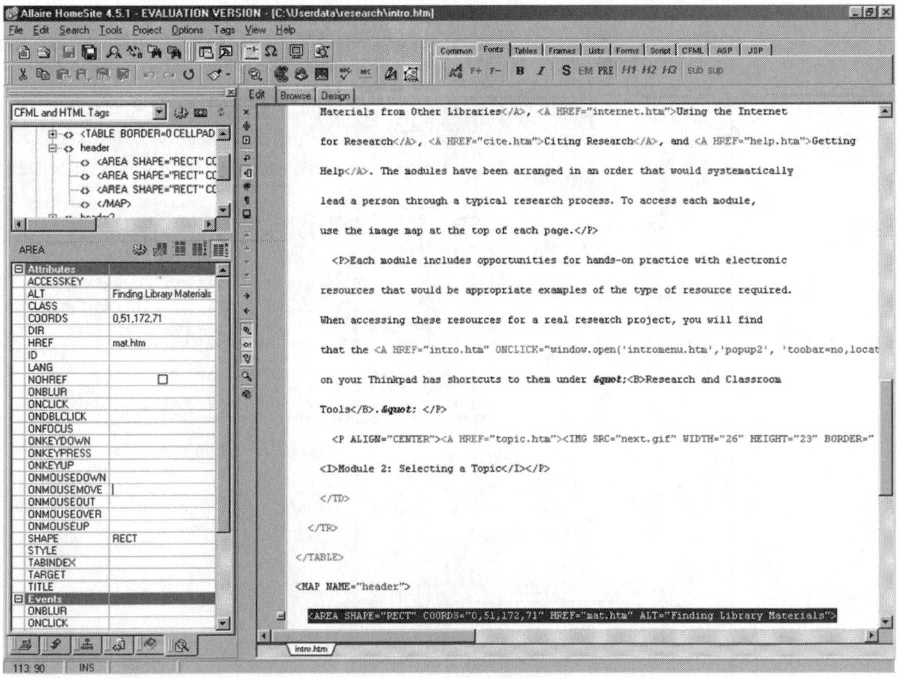

From Allaire Corp., Newton, Mass. Used with permission. Available: http://www.allaire.com/ products/homesite.

interactivity to the page. Code is color-coded so that it is easy to distinguish from the page text. Traditionally, this type of editor has been considered to be the choice for power users who don't want to give up control of the code. Two examples of this type of editor are Allaire's HomeSite (for PC) available at http://www.allaire.com/products/homesite and Bare Bones Software's BBEdit (for Mac) available at http://web.barebones.com/products/bbedit/bbedit.html.

The visual-based editor has typically been considered more user-friendly. When using a visual or WYSIWYG interface, the author is shielded from the HTML coding that is taking place and sees how the page will display to a user. (See, for example, figure 3.5.) This method allows the author to concentrate on how the content should appear, but its main drawback is that you sacrifice control of your ability to fine-tune the source code. Another obstacle to be aware of is that WYSIWYG code creation is often bloated, meaning that unnecessary code is generated. This may not make any difference in how your page displays, but it may become an issue if it is necessary to troubleshoot or reformat the page. Two examples of a WYSIWYG editor are Macromedia's Dreamweaver (for PC and Mac) available at http://www.macromedia.com/software/dreamweaver and Adobe's GoLive (for PC and Mac) available at http://www.adobe.com/products/golive/main.html.

Most of the two different types of editors provide a bridge between the two very different page construction methods. For instance, a good WYSIWYG edi-

FIGURE 3.5
Web Page Viewed in WYSIWYG Editor Macromedia Dreamweaver

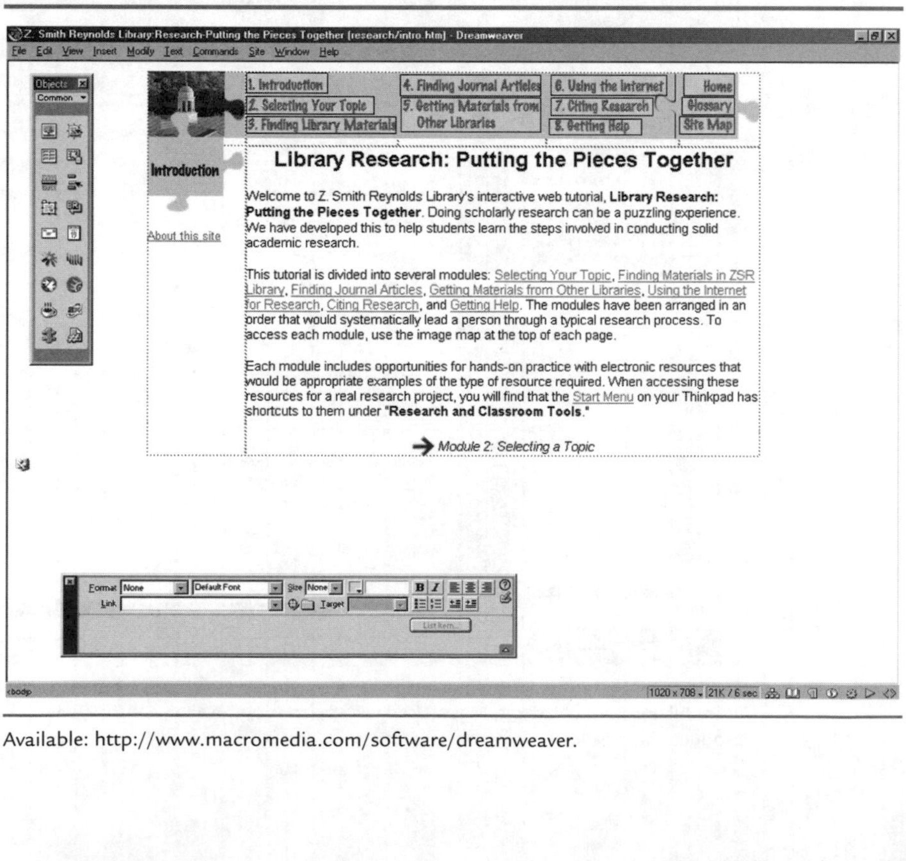

Available: http://www.macromedia.com/software/dreamweaver.

tor will have a source inspector where the author can view and edit the code directly. A well-designed code-based editor will have an interface so the author can view how the page layout will look. (See, for example, figure 3.6.)

FIGURE 3.6
Web Page Viewed in Code-Based Editor First Page with Layout View

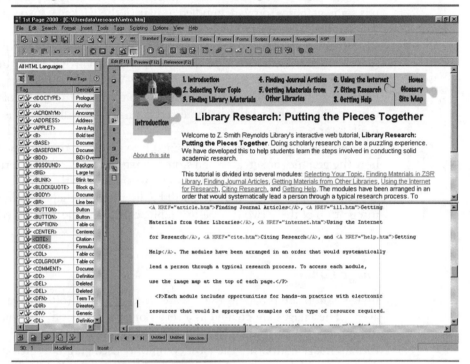

Freeware. Available: http://www.evrsoft.com.

No matter which style of editor you decide upon, there are features that you will want to look for that will help you achieve the ability to execute advanced designs and interactivity. Look for an editor that includes support for

- creation of advanced features that are discussed in later chapters
- site management
- checking the integrity of source codes
- checking compatibility with different browsers
- spell checking
- link checking
- global find-and-replace

Graphics Applications

Some sort of graphics program that creates and manipulates pictures will be a must for your project, but you will find that there is a wide range of choices (and price variations). As with other types of applications, graphics applications have been developed for both the professional artist and the novice. You will want to take into account the expertise and artistic talent of the team member who will be creating your graphics when making a decision on which applications to use. If you have purchased a scanner or digital camera for your project, it probably has some graphics software bundled as part of the package. If so, assess whether the bundled software will meet your editing needs.

Since you will be creating graphics for display on the Web, one of the basic selection criteria should be that the application provides for the most common file formats that are supported on the Web: GIF (Graphics Interchange Format) and JPEG. It should also allow you to import a variety of graphic formats. These, along with other multimedia formats, will be discussed in depth in chapter 5.

Graphic applications can be divided into two major categories that describe how the graphics are created and stored: image editors and illustration software. There are advantages and disadvantages to working with either bitmapped images or vector graphics, and these will be discussed in chapter 5. In addition, an integration of these two types is available, called an object-based editor.

Image Editors

Image editors are programs that create raster graphics (often called bitmap images). The images are created as a series of dots on a grid. Common raster file formats are BMP (bitmap), TIFF (Tag Image File Format), GIF, and JPEG. Bitmap image editors are the most commonly used graphics software. The standard with which the rest of the category is compared is Adobe Photoshop. It is the high-end editor used by most professionals and has a very steep learning curve to go along with its complex capabilities. Many other programs are also available that can produce satisfactory graphics and that require a much lower investment of time to master. Any image editor you consider should include the ability to scan in images as well as to enhance, resize, and retouch them.

Illustration Software

Illustration software includes those applications where you create drawings using lines and curves, known as *vector* graphics. Vector graphics are created through a series of mathematical statements that place lines and shapes in a two- or three-dimensional space. Common vector formats are AI (Adobe Illustrator), WMF (Windows Metafile), and CDR (CorelDRAW). Applications that are representative of this category include Macromedia Freehand, Adobe Illustrator, and CorelDRAW. (See figure 3.7 for an example.)

FIGURE 3.7
CorelDRAW Illustration Software for Vector Graphics

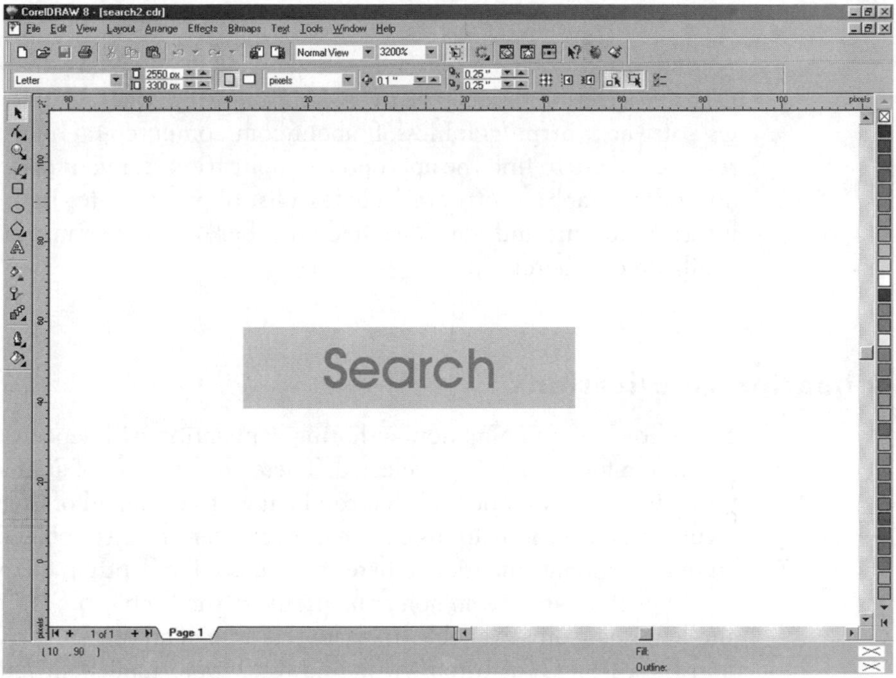

Screenshot © Copyright 2000 Corel Corp. and Corel Corp. Ltd., reprinted by permission. Available: http://www.corel.com.

Object-Based Editors

The third category of graphics software that is emerging integrates raster and vector capabilities into one package—object-based editors. This category is becoming popular for creating Web graphics. Object-based editors have greater flexibility because you can combine images with text and line art to streamline the creation of Web objects such as navigation bars, banners, and buttons. Two examples of this integrated approach are Macromedia's Fireworks (http://www. macromedia.com/software/fireworks) and Adobe's LiveMotion (http://www. adobe.com/products/livemotion) that can be used to create both graphics and animations.

There are issues to consider when creating graphics for the Web (see chapter 5), and these should be kept in mind when selecting a graphics program. Beneficial features that should be included to streamline the creation of Web graphics include

image optimization (to reduce the size of a graphic)

image slicing (to enhance the download of a larger image by slicing it into several small images)

color management and support for Web-safe color creation

batch processing of objects

built-in templates (particularly valuable for nonartists)

3-D effect creation

There are so many different choices for graphics applications available that the selection task can be overwhelming. About.com's topic site on graphics software (http://graphicssoft.about.com/compute/graphicssoft) is a good resource to use to find the appropriate applications for your project. Its section on finding graphics software includes a list of programs for both PC and Macintosh platforms and identifies free and shareware programs as well as those available commercially.

Animation Applications

Your choice of an animation authoring application will depend on the type of animation format you have selected. There are a variety of animation possibilities, but there is no one tool that can be used to create all of them. Just as with regular graphics, animations can be either raster or vector objects. The various animation formats mentioned here are discussed in depth in chapter 5.

One of the most common animations on the Web is the animated GIF. Examples of programs available to create this type of animation are GIF Construction Site, for PC, at http://www.mindworkshop.com/alchemy/gifcon.html and GIFDancer, for Mac, at http://www.paceworks.com/download/gifdancer.html. The ability to create animated GIFs is already integrated into some graphics software or can be added with a plug-in (in Photoshop), so be sure to check before purchasing a stand-alone program.

Some animation is possible via HTML scripting to manipulate page elements. Some HTML editors (Dreamweaver is an example) have this functionality already incorporated into their programs.

Vector-based animation can be created using Macromedia Flash (http://www.macromedia.com/software/flash) or Adobe LiveMotion. Flash appears to be the new standard for vector animations on the Web. Its increase in popularity has resulted in the development of third-party authoring tools that also allow you to create Flash animations or to export a file to the SWF (Shockwave Flash) format. It also supports QuickTime so that you can integrate movies into an SWF file.

Another major trend in animation on the Web uses streaming media, a technology that allows users to hear or view large multimedia files without having to wait for them to download onto their computer. RealNetworks (http://www.realnetworks.com) has been at the forefront of developing this technology. To produce real media you may want to select its product, RealProducer. However, Apple also has an authoring tool, QuickTime Pro (http://www.apple.com/quicktime/authoring/index.html), which you may want to consider. Both of these programs also support SMIL (Synchronized Multimedia Integration Language), which is a protocol for synchronizing the timed playback of multiple independent media files.

Are you considering authoring VRML (Virtual Reality Modeling Language)? VRML is the language that creates 3-D image sequences and possible user interactions within the scene. If a virtual tour of your library is high on your list to produce, you'll need to obtain software to do the VRML authoring. A wide variety of software choices are available depending on what type of project you are creating and on your level of expertise. VRML Works (http://hiwaay.net/~crispen/vrmlworks) is a good site to visit to find links to many of the available tools to author VRML. One example of authoring software that can produce interactive panorama virtual-reality scenes is Apple's QuickTime VR Authoring Studio, for Mac, at http://www.apple.com/quicktime/qtvr/authoringstudio/index.html. A second example of a reasonably priced, easy-to-use 3-D creation tool is Spazz3D, for PC, available at http://www.spazz3d.com.

Audio Software

Introducing small incidental sounds into a Web project may require nothing more than the sound recording software that is included in your operating system. However, if you plan to incorporate audio into your tutorial to any extent, you will want to explore using specialized audio editing software to record and edit sound. You can turn to RealProducer (http://www.realnetworks.com) to handle your streaming audio needs. Another digital audio editor that is well regarded is Sound Forge (http://www.sonicfoundry.com/Products/newshowproduct.asp?PID=5). There are reasonably priced editors available that are full featured: Cool Edit, for PC, at http://www.syntrillium.com/cooledit/index.html and SoundEdit 16 from Macromedia, for Mac, at http://www.macromedia.com/software/sound are just two examples. You should make certain that whichever audio editor you select supports a wide range of sound files. (See chapter 5 for further information on sound files.)

If you already have existing sound files and just need to convert them to a different format, a stand-alone batch encoder is a more cost-effective solution than purchasing audio editing software. Batch encoders are normally included as a part of a full-featured editing program. You can find shareware encoders available for download from Hitsquad at http://www.hitsquad.com.

Video Editing Applications

Once you import video into your computer, you will need some sort of software to manipulate it. It's very probable that video production software will be bundled with a digital camcorder or video capture card. If this is the case, you should make that part of your purchasing decision making. Many integrated hardware and software packages are on the market, with prices ranging from under $100 to $1,000. Well-known manufacturers include Pinnacle Systems (http://www.pinnaclesys.com) and Matrox (http://www.matrox.com). Adobe's Premiere (http://www.adobe.com/products/premiere) is the industry standard for digital video production, but because it is designed for the professional, expect a steep learning curve. If you are new to video editing, look for software that is intuitive. The editing process involves putting video segments in the order you want and then adding transitions, text, background music, and, perhaps, narration. With most software, this is a drag-and-drop process, using either a time line or a storyboard metaphor. A storyboard approach is more straightforward because each frame is represented by one thumbnail image and includes all the elements. In a time line, each separate component (audio tracks, text, video clips, or transitions) has its own track, so the author has more control. Some software packages provide both ways to deal with editing—a good solution, so that a beginner can evolve as he or she gains skill as an editor. As with other applications, you want to make sure that your video editing software supports the file format you have chosen. (See chapter 5 for more information on video file formats.)

Presentation Tools

Presentation software applications, such as Microsoft's PowerPoint, may not be your top choice to author a library instruction tutorial. Many people choose presentation software for instruction because it is easy to learn and to incorporate multimedia. The format for presentation authoring is slide creation, which lends itself to a linear progression through materials. Although most presentation software incorporates various levels of multimedia and interactivity, often those capabilities are either lost when the presentation is converted to a Web-viewable format or they do not work identically across all browser types and versions. However, some presentation software now incorporates support for Web interactivity. RealNetworks has developed a slide show product that works well to incorporate images and animated text into a streaming video slide show. If you decide to use presentation software, make sure it supports the various Web file formats, and be prepared to settle for interactivity that may include only the user's ability to select a link to continue.

Authoring Systems

Most of the authoring tools presented so far are designed to handle one aspect of a multimedia project such as the creation of graphics, animation, or sound. To combine these into an interactive multimedia program, some sort of programming is needed to make it all work together. However, a type of software called an authoring *system* has been developed so that people can develop interactive multimedia programs without having to know a programming language. This type of application allows authors to use a graphical approach to tell the program what to do by placing items in a time line, manipulating objects on a flowchart, or organizing screens into stacks (best known from Apple's Hypercard program). Although the author is looking at a graphical interface, the graphical objects are composed of underlying preset programming modules. By having preprogrammed modules, actions that might take hours to write using a programming language can be created in minutes. A few of the applications discussed under a specific category, such as Microsoft's PowerPoint, can be considered an authoring system, but usually you will hear this term used to describe more-sophisticated applications like Macromedia Director software, shown in figure 3.8. Here, a time line is used to schedule the sequence of components and interactions.

FIGURE 3.8
Macromedia Director Interactive Multimedia Authoring Software with Time Line

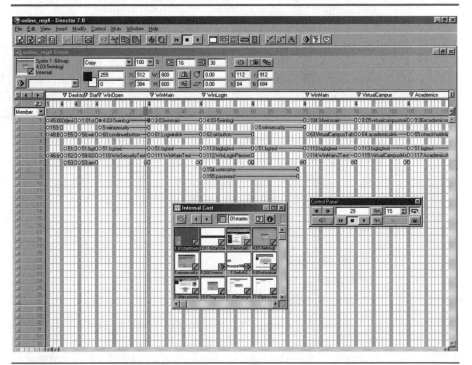

Available: http://www.macromedia.com/software/director.

Having an authoring system greatly reduces the learning curve for nonprogrammers because it requires less technical knowledge to master. However, don't think that most of these programs are so intuitive that you can sit down and be productive right away.

In addition to its user-friendliness, one of the main advantages of an authoring system is its ability to quickly prototype an application. This feature can be very helpful for making quick mockups to be shown for feedback prior to producing the site in detail.

The major disadvantage of most authoring systems is the limitation that results from having an application with predetermined programming. It reduces the flexibility to go beyond what is built into the system. Many systems allow for flexibility by including external scripting functionality for the power user. Another limitation is that programs developed on proprietary authoring systems often require a specialized plug-in so they can be played on the Web. For example,

Macromedia's Authorware requires Web Player. Finally, high-end programs like Authorware can be very expensive (more than $2,500).

Course Shells

Course shells are programs that are designed to deliver education on the Web. Many institutions are turning to these to provide a way for professors to build interactive online courses or supplement traditional classroom teaching quickly and easily. Courseware software does not reside on your computer; rather, it is located on a server. With an institution that already has a courseware product selected and in use, it may be a simple matter to initiate a course for your library instruction. For those that do not have their own servers, courseware companies exist that will host your course on their server, some at no charge. If you decide to select a course shell to build your course, there are many companies to choose from and many features available. You should look for a program that includes

asynchronous communication (threaded discussions and e-mail)

synchronous communication (real-time chat and whiteboards on which users can write or draw)

collaboration via group formation

survey and quizzing capabilities

content creation

file exchange

user tracking

course statistics

Some of the major players in this market are Blackboard (see figure 3.9), WebCT (http://www.webct.com), Top Class (http://www.wbtsystems.com), and Learning Space (http://www.lotus.com/home.nsf/tabs/learnspace).

Specialty Tools

Specialty tools are programs that serve to create very specific components of a Web site. For instance, there is software that allows you to create an online quiz, and another type can record a sequence of screens from your computer display. (Chapter 6 focuses on many specialized authoring programs to assist with the creation of interactive components.)

Web Programming and Scripting Tools

If you don't have a programmer on your development team, many of the authoring tools discussed previously have integrated components into their products that permit you to write scripts without having to know a programming language.

FIGURE 3.9
Blackboard's Free Service to Create an Online Course

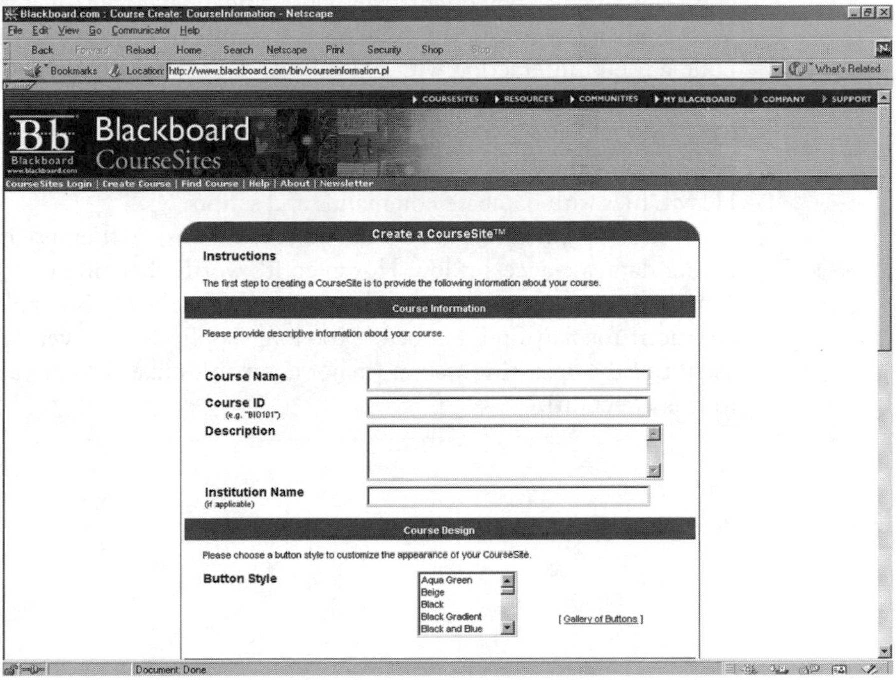

From Blackboard CourseSites. Available: http://blackboard.com.

However, if you are fortunate enough to have a team member with a programming background, authoring tools are available that facilitate writing the various languages of the Web (examples are Java, Perl, JavaScript, and Python, which will be discussed in chapter 6). These tools allow a programmer to concentrate on the development task rather than the underlying language syntax. Much like the HTML editor, these scripting tools automate much of the process of code creation. The Web Developer's Virtual Library (http://wdvl.internet.com/Software/Tools) is a good resource to use to find links to development tools for different languages.

Integrated Application Server and Authoring Tools

If you are planning to incorporate dynamic delivery of information assembled on the fly (as opposed to prewritten static Web pages) into your tutorial via a database, you could explore the feasibility of installing a Web application server. (Potential uses for a database will be discussed in chapter 6.) An application server is a program that handles transactions between a Web browser on a client computer and an institution's back-end (behind the scenes, usually on the server) applications or databases that reside on a server. For example, it processes data contained in a database and delivers that content to the user's browser in

HTML. It supplies many of the same functions that you can achieve with manual scripting, but this fairly recently developed tool is designed to tightly integrate the various components through a single development interface. With a Web application server, the developer does not have to reinvent the wheel to build a robust interaction with a database. An example of an application server with which many people are familiar is ColdFusion (http://allaire.com/products/ColdFusion). There are two separate components that work together, ColdFusion Server and ColdFusion Studio, which create applications by combining HTML files with database commands and scripts.

Because application servers can be very expensive, their use may be overkill if your database access is low. However, it's worth checking with your information technology department to determine if one already is installed at your institution. You may find that before too long, application servers will be included as part of the operating system (major companies like IBM are already heading in this direction).

4

Designing the
User Interface

The user interface, the graphical link between the student and a computer program, encompasses every aspect of a user's possible interaction with a computer. To the students who use your Web tutorial, the interface *is* the tutorial. Without a doubt, designing and creating your library instruction user interface is one of the major challenges in the preproduction/production stages. Your goal in creating Web instruction is to produce an instrument that will engage students and motivate them to actively learn in an independent environment. The successful creation of the interface requires that a wide variety of elements be brought together so that they mesh to present the instruction in the most effective manner, requiring the least explanation.

The subject of what constitutes good user interface design has been well studied and discussed. Many of the themes that are being presented here are the result of work accomplished by prominent researchers in the field of human-computer interaction; in particular the work of Ben Shneiderman (http://www.cs.umd.edu/users/ben) and Jakob Nielsen (http://www.useit.com). These pioneers have been instrumental in establishing best practices for making computers and the Internet more usable for all of us.

The purpose of this chapter is to examine the important usability factors to consider and incorporate into a winning interface. We will take a detailed look at

user-centered design

instructional design and content

basic guidelines and principles for user-interface design (adapted for the Web)

navigation

screen layout and presentation aids

visual design considerations

user accessibility

page optimization

USER-CENTERED DESIGN

From the beginning, the design process should be focused on your users, or audience. You are going to be creating a teaching tool for a population that traditionally does not have a high level of comfort in the "library world." To many students, the library is a mysterious place, organized with puzzling numbering schemes and a foreign language of library jargon. Acquiring a thorough understanding of the user is a must.

One of the first steps to be taken in the preproduction phase is the audience needs analysis that was discussed in chapter 2. The results from this analysis will be the starting point for involving the user in the design process. From the analysis you should know

who will be using the tutorial

their preferred learning styles

their previous experiences using libraries

their prior exposure to library instruction

their base of knowledge in the specific subject area being taught

the level of their computer competence

what type of hardware and software they have at their disposal

their skill using the Web

what their expectations are from the instruction

Involving the user doesn't stop with what you discover from the initial needs assessment. To ensure maximum usability of your program, users should be drawn in throughout the development process. How can users' preferences and opinions be gathered? Assembling a focus group as you begin the design process is one way to hear from users about what they like or don't like about Web site design in general, previous library instruction experiences, and various instructional methods. The one drawback to this sort of user encounter is that users can give opinions only about what they already know. If they have not experienced innovative library instruction methods or engaging interactive Web instruction, then they won't realize what is possible. Nevertheless, a focus group can provide a basic picture of what your audience thinks it wants.

Next you will want to develop a wire-frame prototype and have users try it out and provide feedback. A wire-frame prototype is a simple preliminary model of the site, without artwork, that identifies the main navigation and content. Adopt an iterative design process, and use testers' reactions about each updated version to make design adjustments. Several methods that work well for testing usability are discussed in depth in chapter 7.

INSTRUCTIONAL DESIGN AND CONTENT

When initiating a discussion about interface design, it's not uncommon to think primarily about screen layout and visual elements. This is important, of course, but it shouldn't be separated from the main goal of the project—to deliver content effectively. The instructional design of the tutorial is the place to begin.

Instructional Design

Instructional design is more than filling a page with content and throwing in a few hyperlinks. We are all used to this model of the Web; pages full of information with links that allow us to follow nonlinear paths. However, providing information isn't the same as *delivering* instruction. Instructional design is defined as the systematic process of translating general principles of learning and instruction into plans for instructional materials and learning. Ritchie and Hoffman (1997) identified the following sequences that are considered essential to the instructional process:

Motivating the learner. Visual and multimedia elements can contribute to the motivation factor, but incorporating such components as problem-solving opportunities, critical-thinking exercises, and an established relevance to the learner's needs are strong stimuli.

Identifying what is to be learned. Establish clear objectives at the beginning. Let the students know what outcomes are expected.

Reminding learners of past knowledge. Many students have had some exposure to libraries in their past or to the subject being studied; offer a review to establish their existing knowledge.

Requiring active involvement. Active involvement is more than clicking on a hyperlink to move through the site. Interactive exercises that relate to a specific assignment that the students must submit lets them actively engage in the learning process.

Providing guidance and feedback. Incorporate ways to let the students know if they are on the right track. Skill checks at crucial points throughout the instruction can give students a tool to assess their understanding of the material.

Testing. Testing is still the most common way for the instructor to know if students have learned what has been taught.

Providing enrichment and remediation. Offer a way for students to revisit parts of the instruction if they have a problem and to contact the instructor for help.

Open versus Closed Structure

One goal of instructional design is to keep the student focused on what is being taught. The very nature of the structure of the Web tends to work against this goal. The Web is an open system that can take students off on a completely new tangent with the click of a mouse. Keep this in mind as you design an instructional site. For example, you may wish to illustrate points or show examples by taking students to an external site. You want to offer this flexibility for the student, but in a controlled manner. You don't want to provide links in your instruction that will take students completely out of your site so that they have difficulty finding their way back. Proper planning of navigation and window structure is important to keep your instruction contained. Using frames is a popular way of maintaining control over the Web environment. The advantages and disadvantages of using frames will be covered later in this chapter in the navigation section. Controlling window placement and appearance is another appropriate way of making sure that your users can return to the right spots in your tutorial. Following are two different ways to make windows work in this endeavor.

Opening a Second Browser Window

Many Web users have become accustomed to having second browser windows open to take them to a new site while leaving the original window open so it can be returned to easily. It's very simple to make a second window open when a user clicks on a URL. Just add the attribute **target="_blank"** to the end of the URL. For example, **<a href="http://zsr.wfu.edu/" target="_blank">Online Catalog</a>** takes the user to a second window. A second full-sized window will open and display the new site. For the users who are comfortable moving back and forth between windows via the taskbar, this can be an easy solution. However, if a user is oblivious to new windows opening (and many still are), provide instruction on what to do so that the user knows how to return to the tutorial and doesn't end up with scores of windows open.

Opening Smaller Pop-up Windows

Most Web surfers are familiar with the little pop-up windows that often appear filled with advertising or a survey request. In that context they can be very annoying, but when used properly they can be an effective way to give access to external sites or additional information without having users leave the page where they are working. Figure 4.1 shows a pop-up window that takes users to additional information without leaving the tutorial.

Many Web editor software programs can create these pop-up windows without having to know a specific script. If your Web editor software doesn't have this capability, CNET's Builder.com (http://www.builder.com/Programming/Kahn/092497) has a tool called Window Builder that lets you fill in specifications for your window and then writes the code for you. (See figure 4.2.) You copy and paste the generated script into the head and body of your HTML document. It allows you to control how the window will appear, including if it will have a menu or tool bar, a location field, or scroll bars or be resizable. The size and placement of the window can be configured also.

FIGURE 4.1
Pop-up Window to Present Additional Information

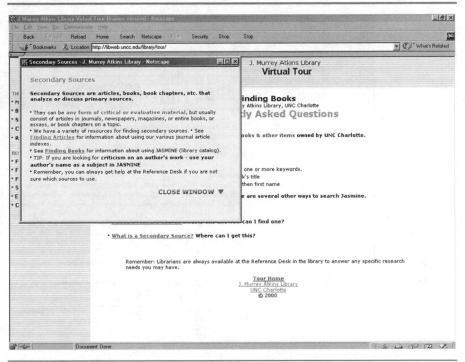

From J. Murrey Atkins Library, University of North Carolina at Charlotte. Available: http://libweb.
uncc.edu/library/tour.

Writing for the Web

Writing content for the Web requires a different mind-set than writing for print.
Morkes and Nielsen's research (1997) has shown that on the Web

reading is 25 percent slower than from paper

most users scan text rather than read word-for-word

Web content should be 50 percent of the length of its paper equivalent

How should this influence how content is written? Morkes and Nielsen offer the
following guidelines:

Be concise. People are not as comfortable reading from a computer screen as
they are reading from a print source. Reading from a screen can be tir-
ing to their eyes, and although screen readability is improving as monitor resolutions become enhanced, it will be a long time before everyone
has access to high-resolution screens. Also, users don't like to scroll
down a page to read text. By keeping the text succinct, a page of information can be restricted to fit on a screen so scrolling is unnecessary.

FIGURE 4.2
CNET's Window Builder Tool to Make Pop-up Windows

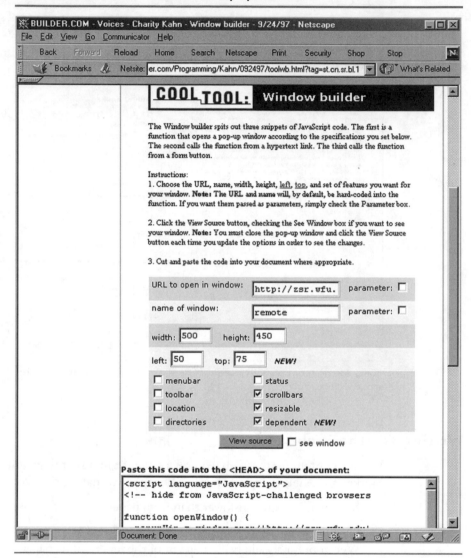

Charity Kahn, 1997. JavaScript Does Windows, Reprinted with permission from CNET, Inc., Copyright 1995–2000, www.cnet.com. Available: http://www.builder.com/Programming/Kahn/092497.

Write for scannability. Because people don't like to read text on a screen, they tend to scan a page to pick out key words and ideas. By planning to present content so that it is scannable, you will ensure that students will have a better chance to encounter the most important points. To enhance the scannability of text

- use meaningful headings that will tell the reader what content is to be covered

- highlight keywords via hyperlinks, color, or making the type bold

- incorporate bulleted lists
- restrict each paragraph to one idea
- restrict each page to one topic
- use graphics to illustrate key points and provide a distinctive caption
- include a table of contents or site map

Notice in figure 4.3 that scannability has been increased by using headings, bold text, highlighted keywords, and bulleted lists.

FIGURE 4.3
Page Optimized for Scannability

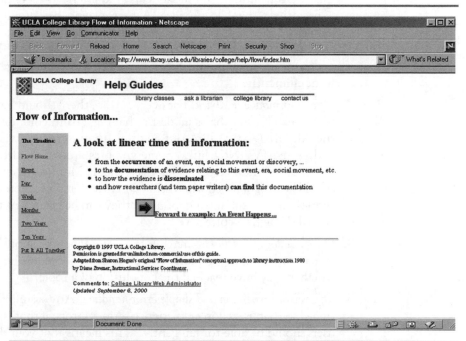

From UCLA College Library Instruction: Flow of Information. University of California, Los Angeles. Available: http://www.library.ucla.edu/libraries/college/help/flow/index.htm.

Use an inverted pyramid style via hyperlinks. Using a concise writing style doesn't mean that in-depth content has to be sacrificed. By using an inverted pyramid organizational style, users can start with the main points, the conclusion in essence, and use hyperlinks to continue deeper to secondary pages for more-detailed information.

BASIC GUIDELINES AND PRINCIPLES FOR USER-INTERFACE DESIGN

Many of the best practices for user interface design (UID) on the Web have evolved from Ben Shneiderman's eight golden rules of interface design (1998).

These principles apply to most interactive systems, and Web designers have adapted them to relate to the Web environment.

1. *Strive for consistency.* Consistency can mean many things. There is consistency of actions, navigation, screen layout, and terminology. Providing consistency helps the user to know what to expect and to learn the interface more quickly. Consistency can also be discussed as it relates to other Web sites. Experienced Web surfers have come to expect certain functionality from Web sites and recognize certain objects as having particular meanings. Straying too far from the consistency of how a typical Web site works may frustrate and disorient the user.

2. *Enable frequent users to use shortcuts.* Experienced users have different expectations than do novices. A person who has previously worked through a tutorial may want to quickly get to specific sections for remediation or to follow hyperlinks to a deeper level. These more-experienced users should have access to shortcuts to get what they want efficiently.

3. *Offer informative feedback.* For every action, there should be some sort of response. This may be as modest as having a third color designation for the ALINK (Active Link) in addition to ones for nonvisited (LINK) and visited (VLINK) links. Some graphics are designed to give visual feedback as the cursor passes over them. More-substantial feedback should be programmed when asking users to complete more-complex activities, such as submitting forms, so they can be confident that they executed the action correctly.

4. *Design dialogs to yield closure.* Information sequences should be grouped to have a beginning, middle, and end. Users shouldn't be left guessing whether they have reached the conclusion of a topic.

5. *Offer error prevention and simple error handling.* Any system should be designed so that users don't experience serious errors; if that is not possible, users should be able to "fail gently." This means that your design should anticipate potential error-causing incidents and provide corrective measures. Error correction should be worded in a straightforward, constructive, and positive manner so that users don't feel as though they have done something wrong. If a link has become outdated, provide specific directions for handling it. If higher-end technologies are being included, provide instructions for system and plug-in requirements at the start so users know what they need to use the tutorial; don't make them wait until they try to access an unconfigured file type on the introductory page. Provide links to the sites where additional software can be downloaded.

6. *Permit easy reversal of actions.* Users should be able to undo any action without dire consequence. In a Web form, include a reset button. Navigation should allow users to back out of a screen and return to the previous one.

7. *Support internal locus of control.* Skilled users of the Web want to feel that they are in control of their experience. Program in enough flexibility so that these users don't feel they are being held back. One simple tool for freeing savvy Web users is to provide a search engine or site map to allow them to move through the tutorial with greater freedom.

8. *Reduce short-term memory load.* Humans can process only a limited number of chunks of information in short-term memory. (Seven plus or minus two is the rule.) Concise content, short screens, and use of real-world metaphors can help minimize information overload.

NAVIGATION

Navigation of an instructional site is second only to content in importance to the success of the instructional design. In fact, navigation can be an organizational tool for designing your content delivery. Without effective navigation, users can become lost, and content may become inaccessible. This section looks at various types of navigation and related issues.

Qualities of Successful Navigation Systems

Research shows that successful navigation shares certain qualities (Fleming 1998). Effective navigation should

- be easily learned
- remain consistent
- provide feedback
- appear in context
- offer alternatives
- require an economy of action and time
- provide clear visual messages
- offer clear and understandable labels
- be appropriate to the site's purpose
- support user goals and behaviors

With a good navigation system, the site's users will always know where they are, where they can go next, and where they have already been. Always highlight the current location so it tells the user "You are here." Use a visual placement marker to highlight the present position of users. For example, the tutorial shown in figure 4.4 has as a location marker the title across the top of the screen, "Searching Blais by Title." Indicators of the current location should also include such information as your organization name just in case the user has entered your tutorial from a back door instead of at the top level.

FIGURE 4.4
Tutorial with Location Marker

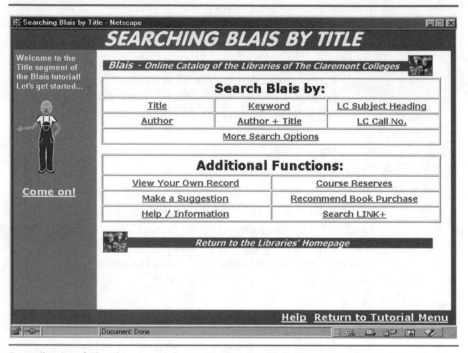

From Libraries of The Claremont Colleges, Claremont, Calif. © Claremont University Consortium.
Available: http://voxlibris.claremont.edu/research/tutorials/blais/new_title/title_frameset.html.

Types of Navigation Systems

Depending on the size of the site that the navigation is designed to serve, setting it up can range from straightforward to extremely complex. A site with breadth (many pages at the same level) and depth (multiple levels) may require more than one navigation system. Let's take a look at the types of navigation systems that might be appropriate.

Hierarchical Systems

The information structure hierarchy for your tutorial can be a principal navigation system. It can supply a picture of the information contained in your site in the context in which it was organized. Keep in mind that a hierarchical method of organization is familiar to most people because they have used similar systems that start at the top level and move down the line to more specific details. An example of a typical way to translate the hierarchy of your site into a navigation tool is to use a table of contents. A basic site map can also provide a hierarchical view of the content.

When you are planning your hierarchical navigation in terms of your information structure, don't go overboard with too much breadth (number of options at each level of the hierarchy) or depth (number of levels in the hierarchy).

Remember the rule of seven-plus-or-minus-two, and don't overload the user with too many choices from any one menu.

Global Systems

A global system is a sitewide navigation device. It provides access to areas of your site beyond the specific tutorial or module you are using. This type of navigation device can be useful if you have a number of instructional modules available for students or if your current tutorial is multimodular in structure with each module or topic standing as a self-contained unit.

Local Systems

If you consider your overall tutorial the main site, think about each individual topic or module as a subsite. Local navigation systems provide a way to maneuver through the subsite. Because users prefer to have information delivered one screen at a time and to read scannable text, it may be necessary to present one element of a particular topic on each screen. With a local navigation mechanism present, users can see what additional elements are included and can get to them efficiently.

Local navigation systems should be used in tandem with global systems. There should always be a way for users to return to other areas of the site. Most likely you will find that a combination of navigation systems is required to give users the best navigation experience. Figure 4.5 is an example of a multiple nav-

FIGURE 4.5
Multiple Navigation System Example

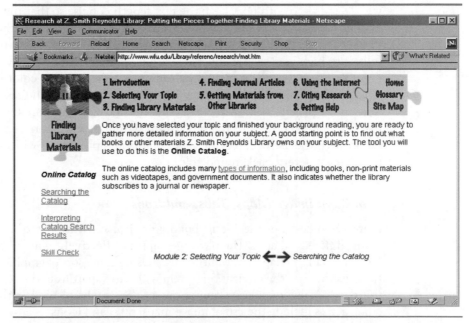

From Z. Smith Reynolds Library, Wake Forest University, Winston–Salem, N.C. Available: http://www.wfu.edu/Library/referenc/research/mat.htm.

igation system. The image map across the top of the screen serves as a global navigation system that provides links to other modules in the tutorial. The text menu down the left side of the screen acts as a local navigation system within the current module. The link to the site map at the top right of the screen will take the user to a hierarchical view of the content.

Ad Hoc Systems

Sometimes links to additional information on your site do not fit nicely into any of the previous three systems. Often you will find these links embedded into the text of the page. Because they are not overt navigation tools, they are easily missed as users scan through the text. If the link is going to some incidental piece of information, then this may be an acceptable solution. However, if you are trying to emphasize the importance of the link, figure out a way to bring it into prominence by creating a bulleted list so that it stands out to the reader.

Navigation Methods

There is no single way to create the various navigation systems. Limited only by their imagination, Web designers have produced different methods that serve the same purpose. Following are some of the most popular methods and their advantages and disadvantages.

Text

Using text links as navigation is simple to do and can be read by any browser. If you decide to go with text, keep the text length concise so that the link doesn't overlap into a second line, and use some sort of mechanism so that users will know they are looking at a navigation tool. One method that is used successfully is to highlight each menu item with a small graphic that serves as a bullet point or offset the menu by highlighting it with a different color background. This sort of visual clue sets the navigation text apart from the rest of the content on the page. Usually, a table of contents and a site map are text-based navigation tools. The text for the navigation system in the tutorial in figure 4.6 is set apart by the use of carets for bullet points and placement within a table cell that has a different background color.

Tool Bars: Image Maps, Tabs, and Icons

Many Web designers decide to build graphical navigation tool bars that take many different shapes. (Employing graphics effectively will be discussed in greater detail in chapter 5, Multimedia.) Using some sort of graphics for navigation ensures that the navigation system will stand apart from the text content of the page. A few popular permutations of the graphical toolbar that you may come across include the use of image maps, tabs, and icons.

An image map is a graphic object that is defined so that when users click on a portion of it, it takes them to a different destination. The flowchart in

FIGURE 4.6
Text for a Navigation System

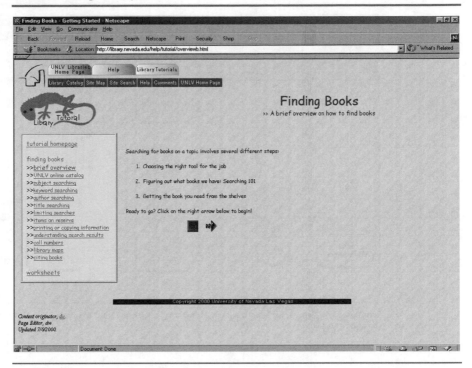

From the University of Nevada, Las Vegas Libraries. Available: http://library.nevada.edu/help/tutorial/overviewb.html.

figure 4.7 illustrates the literature review process and was created as an image map. When students clicked on one of the process steps, they were taken to the section of the tutorial that discussed that particular topic. Additional information about this diagram and its use as a navigational device can be found in an article by Jean Caspers (1998).

Tabs have become a very popular way to separate content into different categories. An example of tabs is shown at the top left of figure 4.6.

Icons are small graphics that are meaningful representations of particular topics, functions, or actions. Users are comfortable with using icons as navigation devices because icons are pervasive in a Windows and Web environment to represent common actions such as print or return home.

Menu Trees

A menu tree, or nested navigation, is a way, through scripting, to display a collapsible menu that can contain several levels. When completely closed, the user sees only the top level of the site hierarchy. By clicking on the + to the left of the text link, the next level down is displayed. To close the menu, the user clicks the −, and that branch of the tree collapses. Figure 4.8 is an example of navigation using a folder menu tree. Users can expand or contract the tree to show or hide links.

FIGURE 4.7
Flowchart Example

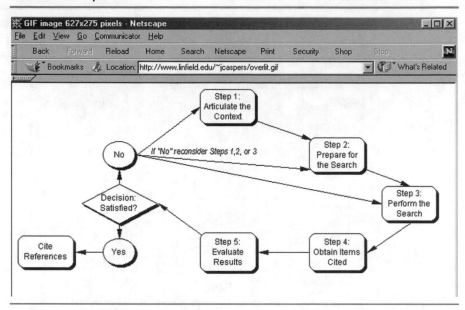

From Jean S. Caspers, Linfield College, McMinnville, Ore. Available: http://www.linfield.edu/
~jcaspers/overlit.gif.

FIGURE 4.8
Menu Tree Example

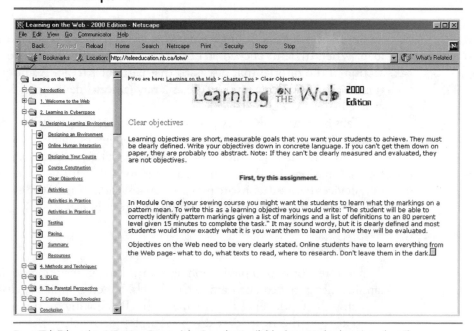

From TeleEducation NB, New Brunswick, Canada. Available: http://teleeducation.nb.ca/lotw.

Drop-Down Menus

Drop-down menus illustrate a way to supply navigation without taking up much real estate on the screen. Most users are familiar with these by now and know to click on them to get a list of options. Drop-down menus are fairly easy to assemble by using a script. Many script libraries (which will be discussed in chapter 6) have free scripts that you can adapt to use for your menu. The virtual library tour in figure 4.9 uses a drop-down box that allows the user to select a preferred method to navigate through the site.

Breadcrumb Trails

A breadcrumb trail shows the hierarchical structure of a site so that users know where they are in relation to the overall site. In figure 4.8 note the use of a breadcrumb trail at the top of the content frame to tell users where they are in the hierarchy of the site. It pinpoints their location in the context of the entire site,

FIGURE 4.9
Drop-Down Menu Example

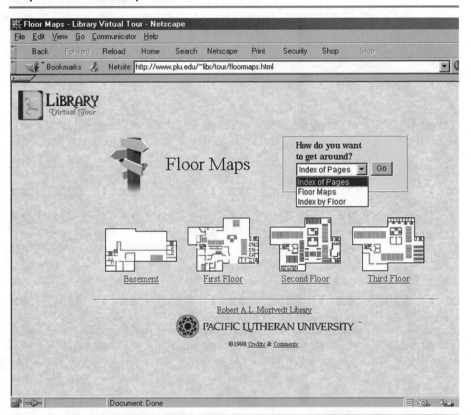

From Robert A. L. Mortvedt Library, Pacific Lutheran University, Tacoma, Wash. Available: http://www.plu.edu/~libr/tour/floormaps.html.

showing the hierarchical path from the top layer to the current page. Breadcrumb trail navigation is best suited for a large, complex site and so may have limited applicability in a tutorial setting where a guided navigation may be more appropriate. However, if you are planning an intricate instructional site, breadcrumb trails are a simple-to-construct, space-conserving way to show navigation to the user.

Arrows

Users associate an arrow on a screen with the action that will move them forward or backward one screen. Including arrows on the screen of your tutorial permits users to move sequentially through a section of the tutorial in a linear fashion. In figure 4.5 the arrows at the bottom of the screen allow the user to move sequentially through the module screen by screen. The inclusion of arrows to proceed through a subsite supplies an extra level of navigation.

Search Engines

Although normally the instructional design for a tutorial will be planned to proceed in a particular sequence, a search engine that locates terms on Web pages can be very useful to help users who return to the tutorial to revisit a particular point or concept. They can search for a term or concept without having to proceed step by step through the entire instruction. This type of flexibility passes some control to the user.

Placement of Navigation Tools on the Screen

Navigation tools are incorporated into most Web sites today. Because most people read from left to right and from top to bottom, the left and top of the screen are the areas that are most suited for navigation. If you place your navigation tools down the right hand side of the screen, unless you configure the layout to adjust to the resolution that a user has chosen, there is a great possibility that the navigation may be hidden. For example, if a screen is designed for an 800 × 600 resolution and the navigation tool is in the last 100 pixels of the screen, a user who has set his computer at 640 × 480 will not see the navigation tool without scrolling over to the right side to bring it into view. The same potential exists for navigation tools that appear at the bottom of the screen. If the content pushes the size of the screen below the "fold," or bottom edge of the initial screen, users have to scroll down to see the navigation tool. If a designer wants to ensure that what is placed on the right of the screen shows for everyone, then the design must be set to adjust by percentage (usually through the use of tables). Instead of designating a specific number of pixels for the screen by width and height, table size should be designated to be a percentage of the screen width and height. Since screens are drawn top to bottom and from left to right, it is preferable to locate navigation tools in the top or left areas of the screen to be confident that they are viewable to all.

Linear versus Nonlinear Navigation

Linear navigation takes students from point A to point Z in a step-by-step progression that guides them through the instruction in a very structured way. Students start at the beginning and only progress as they make the correct choices to show they have grasped the concept being taught. This may be appropriate for novices who have had no previous exposure to the subject being covered or if you intend that the tutorial be completed in one sitting or class period. A linear approach helps ensure that students stay on task.

However, there are risks with offering only a linear method of progression. If the instruction is of any length, students may want to stop for a while, come back later, and pick up where they left off. If they have to enter through the first screen and work through every screen to get back to where they stopped, they'll rapidly become annoyed. What about students who want to return to the tutorial to review a particular section or concept? They will want quick, easy access to just that information. If you intend for your tutorial to be used in this fashion, then a nonlinear navigation scheme is more appropriate. Figure 4.6 is an example of a way to provide a nonlinear navigation. Users can enter the tutorial from any of the topic areas in the menu.

LOBO, Library Online Basic Orientation, from North Carolina State University Libraries, has a linear navigation design. As shown in figure 4.10, students move through the instruction by clicking on the arrows at the bottom of the screen to move forward or backward. The exit button takes the students to a screen that instructs them to exit in a way that will mark their point of departure. When they return to the initial screen of the tutorial, a link allows them to continue at their point of departure from the previous session. If you decide that a linear mode of navigation best suits your instructional goals, be sure to provide some way for students to exit and return to their departure point.

Frames as a Navigation Device

Frames are used to subdivide the browser window to display multiple, independently controllable pages simultaneously. One of the most popular uses for frames is to provide a stationary navigation page that stays in view while new pages load in the second frame. This provides a uniform navigation tool without having to re-create the tool bar or menu on each page.

Whether to use frames or not is a subject that initiates passionate discussion. Web usability guru Jakob Nielsen's (1996) recommendation is "frames: just say no." Why does he think that frames should be avoided?

1. The URL that displays at the top of the browser is actually the address for the frame set, the document that specifies the size and location of each frame. The URL for the pages that are actually displayed does not appear to users. If a page from an external site is displayed in one of the frames and users try to bookmark it, they will end up with a bookmark to the original frame set document.

FIGURE 4.10
Linear Navigation Design Example

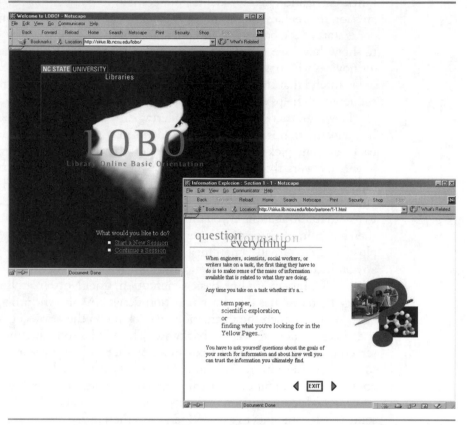

From North Carolina State University, Raleigh. Available: http://sirius.lib.ncsu.edu/lobo.

2. Printing a page from a frame can be difficult for users because they must know to click on the desired document to activate the frame for printing. If they have used the navigation frame to pull up content in the second frame and simply issue the print command, the navigation page will print because it was the most recently activated frame.

3. To ensure that important information is displayed in full, most frames are normally specified to be a particular size. This can work fine if users can accommodate a large display, but it can cause difficulty for users with small screens. The navigation frame may display fine, but the content frame may end up lacking sufficient display space.

The tutorial in figure 4.11 illustrates some of the potential pitfalls of incorporating frames. The site is nicely designed for display on either an 800 × 600 or a 1024 × 768 screen (as shown on top), but it is not as user friendly on a 640 × 480 screen (bottom) because both vertical and horizontal scrolling are required to view the content. Users who try to bookmark Metacrawler will run into difficulty. However, the site's designer has provided a good tool to overcome some of the possible problems by providing a link to "Print This Tutorial"

FIGURE 4.11
Frame Displays

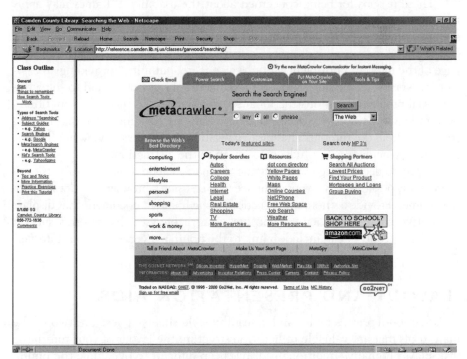

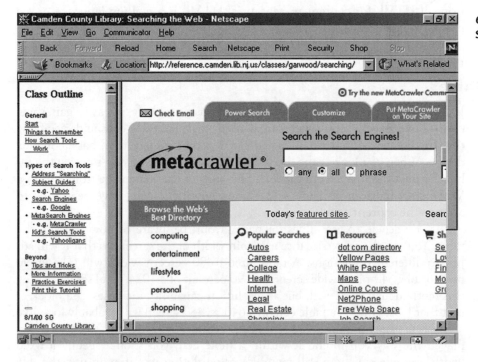

From Camden County Library System, N.J. Available: http://reference.camden.lib.nj.us/classes/garwood/searching.

(on left side of screen). This document combines all of the tutorial's screens into one easy-to-print file that includes the URLs to the external sites.

These reasons for being concerned about the usability of frames may apply more to a regular Web site than to a contained tutorial. The need to bookmark a specific content page within a tutorial is not as widespread as it may be in a general site, and most users will probably want to set the bookmark to the starting page of the tutorial. Printing may not be a concern, but if it is, providing an easy-to-print version of the site, as was done in figure 4.11, is one option to solve this potential problem. In an instructional setting, frames can serve the function of becoming a way to provide access to external resources without having students stray away from the tutorial. The static navigation menu stays in view at all times, providing a simple way for students to return to the instruction.

If you do decide to go with a frames format, include a nonframes version if there is any possibility that your audience may be using a browser that doesn't support frames. Provide a <noframes> section in the frameset document that displays alternative content to viewers who are using a browser that doesn't support frames. This content can include a link to the nonframe version of your tutorial.

SCREEN LAYOUT AND PRESENTATION AIDS

This section discusses tables and cascading style sheets. These are two of the main tools that are valuable to help you structure the layout of your tutorial so it displays optimally. Traditionally, it has been difficult to overcome the limitations of HTML for content presentation. HTML is a markup language, not a page-layout language.

Layout Tables

It didn't take long for Web authors to turn to using tables as a way to gain some control over page layout. By putting content inside of table cells and specifying that the borders be invisible, it is possible to produce a page that has a complex design. When you look at the top screen in figure 4.12, you don't notice the tables because the borders are hidden. The view of the same page from within a Web editor (bottom of figure 4.12) shows how table cells have been used to arrange the content.

If you decide to use tables for page layout, be aware of how you size the table. You can choose to size it to a certain width of the screen, so that it will adjust to different resolutions. A table sized to 90 percent width will take up 90 percent of a 640-pixel-wide screen and 90 percent of a 1024-pixel screen. Using this method may work well, but as resolution capability increases, the block of text that looks good in a table cell on a 640×480 screen will probably look like a one-line paragraph on a 1200×1024 screen. To ensure that the text is displayed the way you intend it within a table cell, you should specify a fixed width. Because there are still many lower resolution monitors in use, the safe maximum width for a table is about 600 pixels. (You want to allow for pixels lost to the browser window frame, page margins, and user taskbars.) Align the table

FIGURE 4.12
Tables Used as Layout Tools

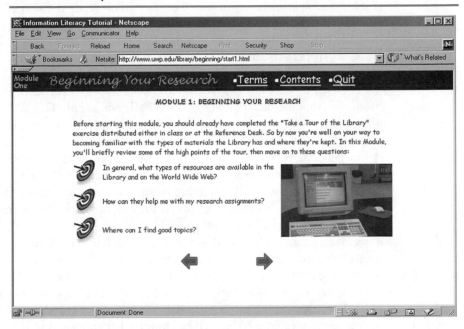

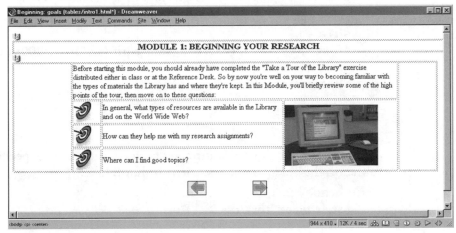

From University of Wisconsin–Parkside Library, Kenosha. Available: http://www.uwp.edu/library/beginning/start1.html.

in the center of the page so that the extra "screen space" is the same on the left and right of the table.

If you are using tables, be aware that the content of any given table will not appear until the ending table tag </table> is downloaded to the browser. This means that if you are using nested tables (tables within tables) to control page layout, the user will see a blank page until the final tag of the container table is read. An alternate approach is to use a series of individual tables that consist of one table row each. The page will start to display as soon as the first table is completed.

Cascading Style Sheets

Tables may help with page layout, but they aren't really the officially sanctioned answer to all layout problems. Tables have been put to use in a way not originally intended in an effort to address a problem that had no solution. The need for more-sophisticated control has been recognized for some years, and cascading style sheets (CSS) have been developed to handle the presentation of Web documents. CSS is a style-sheet language that allows the separation of presentation from the informational content of an HTML document. The World Wide Web Consortium (W3C), a group of more than 400 member organizations, made its first style sheet recommendation, CSS1 (Cascading Style Sheets, Level 1), in 1996. By 2000, both CSS Levels 1 and 2 were in use, and CSS3 was under development. CSS1 addresses style, while CSS2 builds on CSS1 and addresses layout. CSS3 will be used for styling interactive and dynamic aspects of a Web page.

With CSS, a Web author can control style and layout elements such as font, type size and color, margins, indentations, line spacing, and more. CSS provides separate style rules that are used to format HTML elements. Instead of trying to control formatting from within an HTML element, which has to be specified each time the attribute is used, CSS allows the author to specify the style once, and it is automatically applied to the HTML element each time it is used. For instance, using the customary formatting in HTML, if you wanted the headline for your page to be an Arial font that is green and in italics, you would code your headline tag like this every time you used a headline:

```
<h1>
<font face="Arial, Helvetica, sans serif" color="#009900">
<i>
<b>Headline</b>
</i>
</font>
</h1>
```

A style sheet allows the attributes for the headline to be specified one time, either in the header of the document as shown here:

```
<head>
<style type="text/css">
<!--
h1 {font-family: Arial, Helvetica, sans serif; font-size: x-large;
font-style: italic; line-height: normal; font-weight: bold; color:
#009900}
-->
</style>
</head>
```

or in an external file (ending with the file extension .css) that resides on the Web server. In the latter case, you enter the path to that file in the head of your document:

```
<head>
<link rel="stylesheet" href="../tutorial.css">
</head>
```

The obvious benefit of using an external file to store your styles is that you have to make changes in only one document to execute sitewide modifications.

It's not necessary that you pick just one way to apply styles. Cascading style sheets are called this because more than one style sheet can be used on a document, with different levels of importance assigned depending on the location of the style designation. If you define different styles for the same element, the style that is closest to the HTML tag prevails. For example, the style specified in the tag takes precedence over one designated in the head of the document. The style in the head of the document is more important than the one located in the external .css file. This comes in handy when you want to make one-time adjustments to an element on a particular document or a section of a document but prefer that the original style stay in place over the rest of the site. Detailed information about cascading style sheets can be found on the W3C's Web site at http://www.w3.org/Style/CSS.

Browser support for CSS is increasing, but don't expect to see support in versions older than 4.0 of Internet Explorer and Netscape Communicator. If you implement style sheets for your design control, be aware that users whose browsers don't support CSS will be able to see the content, but the browser will ignore the styles. This can affect the presentation of your content, so you may want to postpone using styles until you are certain that all of your audience members have browsers that can handle CSS.

VISUAL DESIGN CONSIDERATIONS

Visual design involves the artistic or aesthetic considerations of designing a site. A visually appealing tutorial will attract more interest from your audience. Guidelines for designing a visually appealing site exist, of course, but because of the wide spectrum of tastes and creativity, they are open to a much more flexible interpretation than are UID guidelines. This section presents some of the main visual design elements that should receive attention when designing your tutorial.

Simplicity and Clarity

No matter what other choices you make, your final result should be visual simplicity. You have seen Web sites that are so cluttered that the intended message is lost; you want to avoid this at all costs. Your goal is to get the meaning of the instructional content across to your audience as clearly as possible. If users have to wade through excessive text, links, and graphics to find the main focus of the screen, the tutorial won't be successful. Only include what needs to be there, and take out the rest.

White Space

The proper use of space can help achieve a simple, clear design. Known as white space, this is the open space on a Web page between design elements. In figure 4.13 white space works to emphasize the different visual elements on the page. In this tutorial, the white space that separates the navigation, banner, and content helps users easily differentiate between the different components of the page. On a Web page, white space isn't necessarily "white" but whatever color or texture the background has been designated. Well-designed white space can help guide the users' eyes from one screen element to the next. The space helps define the different elements on the page by acting as a cushion between them. On a computer screen, white space also provides a "rest area" for our eyes. Reading from a computer screen is more visually demanding than reading from print, and white space provides us space to absorb what is on the page before proceeding further.

FIGURE 4.13
Effective Use of White Space Example

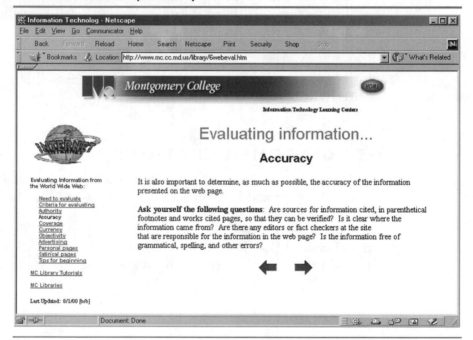

From Montgomery College Libraries, Montgomery County, Md. 2000 © Montgomery College. Available: http://www.mc.cc.md.us/library/6webeval.htm.

Color

Color is one of the most powerful visual elements that you will have in your design. It can be used to help your design in a variety of ways. Color can

- accentuate, highlight, and guide the eye to essential points or links
- identify recurring themes or be used to differentiate between elements
- trigger feelings and associations

People respond immediately to color, and the scheme you choose will set the mood for the tutorial. Color will elicit some sort of response even before users begin to read the content. You want to ensure that the colors you select will draw them into the learning experience.

Color Symbolism

Because colors mean different things to various populations, it is important to consider your target audience before you decide on the color palette for your tutorial. You should be cognizant of the different meanings of colors between cultures and of the various psychological responses that colors bring out. Figure 4.14, adapted from M. E. Holzschlag's (1999) article, categorizes color meanings and perceptions around the world.

FIGURE 4.14
Color Meanings and Perceptions

COLOR	PSYCHOLOGICAL RESPONSE	NOTES OF INTEREST
Red	Power, energy, warmth, passions, love, aggression, danger	Changes meaning in the presence of other colors: with green, it becomes a symbol of Christmas; when combined with white, it means joy in many Eastern cultures
Blue	Trust, conservatism, security, technology, cleanliness, order	Used in the U.S. by many banks to symbolize trust
Green	Nature, healthy, good luck, jealously ("green with envy"), renewal	Doesn't do well globally: problems are associated with green packaging in China and France
Yellow	Optimism, hope, philosophy, dishonesty, cowardice, betrayal	A sacred color to Hindus
Purple	Spirituality, mystery, royalty, transformation, cruelty, arrogance	Appears very rarely in nature
Orange	Energy, balance, warmth	Signifies an inexpensive product
Brown	Earth, reliability, comfort, endurance	Food packaging in the U.S. is often colored brown with success; in Colombia, brown discourages sales
Gray	Intellect, futurism, modesty, sadness, decay	The easiest color for the eye to see
White	Purity, cleanliness, precision, innocence, sterility, death	Signifies marriage in the U.S., but death in India and other Eastern cultures
Black	Power, sexuality, sophistication, death, mystery, fear, unhappiness, elegance	Signifies death and mourning in many Western cultures; in marketing, conveys elegance, wealth, and sophistication

Adapted from M.E. Holzschlag, Satisfying Customers with Color, Shape, and Type. Web Techniques. Nov. 1999. Available: http://www.webtechniques.com/archives/1999/11/desi.

Our response to color is strongly influenced by our cultural background. For example, the color green in the United States indicates both "go" (safe) at traffic lights and environmental awareness, but in some tropical countries it is associated with danger. In Western cultures black means death and mourning, but in Eastern cultures, white is the color for death and mourning. In the United States, white means purity, but in India, red is associated with purity. Understanding these differences will ensure that your tutorial won't send the wrong message to diverse audiences through its choice of color.

Color also brings emotional responses from people. (See figure 4.14.) We are all familiar with the concept that red connotes the feeling of warmth while blue gives the perception of cold. Red, orange, and yellow hues can induce excitement, aggressiveness, and stimulation. Blues and greens can suggest security and peace.

Combining Colors

The combination of colors that you choose can also have an effect on your audience. Some colors, when combined, complement each other while others contrast. The use of a complementary color scheme may create a mood very different than if contrasting colors are used. Learning to choose the most effective color scheme is a process that can be a career in itself. However, many resources on the Web can teach you the basics of color theory so that creating an effective color scheme doesn't become an overwhelming task.

If you are like many people, you last studied color in elementary or high school. Before you start to work out your color scheme, you should reacquaint yourself with some color basics (Kennedy 1999).

There are three primary colors on the color wheel: red, yellow, and blue. When you combine two of the primary colors, your result is a secondary color: violet (a combination of red and blue), green (blue and yellow), or orange (red and yellow). A primary color combined with an adjacent secondary color produces an intermediate color: red orange, red violet, blue violet, blue green, yellow green, and yellow orange. These make up a basic twelve-color wheel. (See figure 4.15.) To complete the picture, include the neutral shades: white, black, and gray. White reflects all light, while black absorbs all light. Gray is an impure white.

With just these twelve hues and the three neutral ones, you can have an almost unlimited choice of colors. This is possible by variations to the basic group of tint, shade, tone, value, and intensity.

Hue is color with no black, white, or gray added.

Tint is a hue plus white.

Shade is a hue plus black.

Tone is a hue plus gray or a hue plus a complementary color.

Value is how light or dark a color appears.

Intensity is how bright or dull it appears.

Figure 4.15 also shows a few proven approaches to take when deciding on a color scheme.

FIGURE 4.15
Color Wheel and Color Schemes

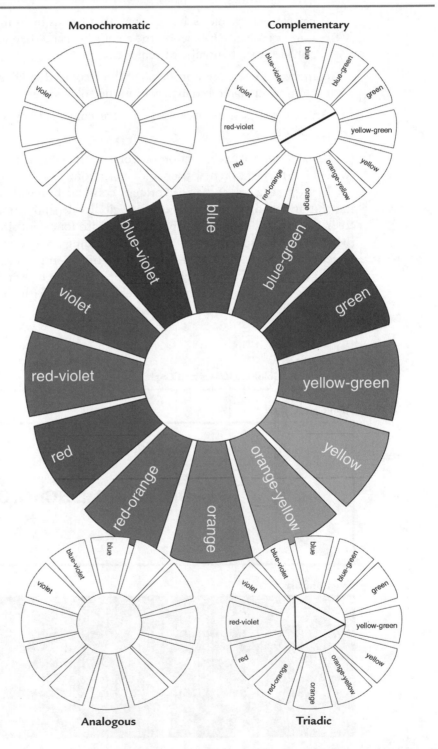

Monochromatic is a scheme that uses one color in combination with some of its tints, tones, and shades.

A *complementary* color scheme is one that begins by using two colors that are opposite each other on the color wheel and then incorporates tints, shades, etc., to finalize the colors.

A *triadic* color scheme is made up of three colors that are selected by drawing an equilateral triangle within the color wheel.

An *analogous* scheme uses two or more colors side by side on the color wheel.

Refer to the resources section on color at the end of this book for several good places to start or renew your color education.

In selecting a color scheme, a primary consideration will be the legibility of the text against the background color. Legibility depends on many factors, but color is one of the important aspects, along with font, font size, and word style (which will be discussed shortly). When deciding on a color combination to increase readability, it is safest to go with a high-contrast combination. Black text on white background has high contrast, while red text on blue background has a very low contrast. Figure 4.16 illustrates (even with the gray scale used here) that the high contrast is more easily read.

FIGURE 4.16
High and Low Color Contrasts and Legibility

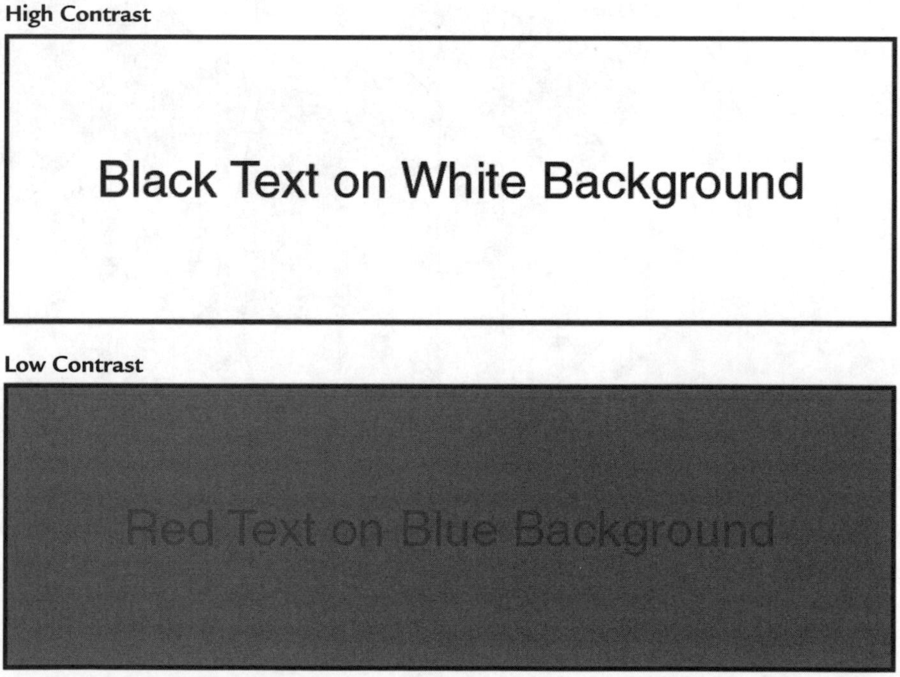

High Contrast

Black Text on White Background

Low Contrast

Red Text on Blue Background

Using Colors to Show Similarities and Differences

Color can be a useful tool to help users see relationships among screen elements as well as to differentiate between tutorial components. For instance, color-coding titles and subtitles can help users see the levels of importance and organization of information. Navigation systems can be enhanced with the proper use of color also. The key to using color coding effectively is to use these visual clues consistently throughout the site. For example, the colorful tutorial shown in figure 4.17 on Internet patent searching incorporates a combination of blue, yellow, and orange. The navigation system along the left side of the screen is blue, and the individual menu items change to yellow as the mouse passes over them. The chart in the middle of the content frame uses blue to highlight the headers in the table.

FIGURE 4.17
Effective Use of Color Example

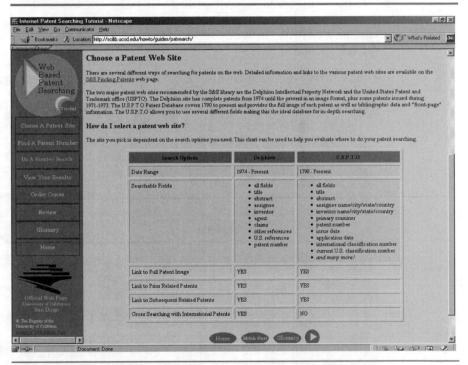

From University of California, San Diego Libraries, La Jolla. © The Regents of the University of California. Available: http://scilib.ucsd.edu/howto/guides/patsearch.

Browser-Safe Colors

Even though there appear to be millions of colors to choose from, that's really not the case on the Web. Color on the Web can be very complex and frustrating. The unfortunate truth is that the color you see on your monitor through your browser may not be what another person sees on a different monitor. Colors display in a different way on dissimilar monitors, browsers, or operating systems. Although this may not be a problem in a number of years, right now many people are using monitors that display only 256 colors. The outcome of all of this inconsistency is that unless you are very careful, the colors you intend for your audience to see may dither. Dithering is the attempt by a computer program to approximate a color from a mixture of other colors when the required color is not available.

To circumvent this problem, Lynda Weinman published a 216-color palette (http://www.lynda.com). Weinman was the first researcher to identify that out of the possible 256 colors, only 216 show almost identically on PCs and Macs. By sticking with this "browser-safe" color palette, your site will be optimized for cross-platform color display. The version of the 216-color palette shown in figure 4.18 is arranged in hue order and shows the hexadecimal and RGB (red, green, and blue) values for each color. Because HTML uses hexadecimal numbers for color coding, make note of that value from the chart. (Hexadecimal refers to the base-16 number system, which consists of 16 unique symbols: the numbers 0 to 9 and the letters A to F).

FIGURE 4.18
Browser-Safe Color Palette

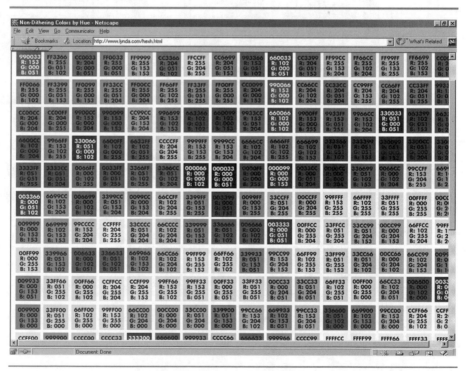

From Lynda Weinman, founder, lynda.com, Ojai, Calif. Available: http://www.lynda.com/hexh.html.

Many graphics programs include the browser-safe palette as part of the package, but if your program doesn't, use the palette (which is available from many different sites) to select your colors. There are also many free color utilities available on the Web that can help you convert colors into their hexadecimal values and identify Web-safe colors. Figure 4.19 is an example of one of the many free color utilities available on the Web.

FIGURE 4.19
Free Color Utilities Example

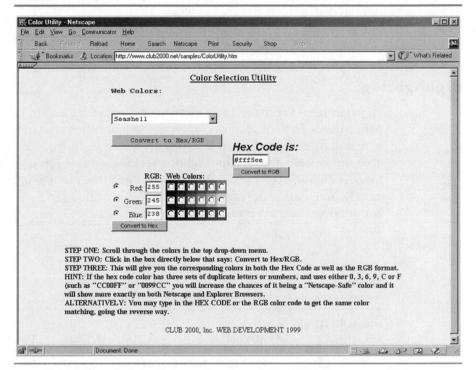

From Club 2000, Inc., Web Development, Pleasanton, Calif. Available: http://www.club2000.net/samples/ColorUtility.htm.

How Many Colors?

Although it may be tempting to include many colors, using too many can be distracting and overwhelming to users. You'll do best if you stick to Ben Shneiderman's (1998) guidelines, "use color conservatively" and "limit the number of colors." Many design guides suggest limiting the number of colors to four. Like other visual-design guidelines, this is not set in stone, but it provides a good basis to work from.

Link Colors

The first hyperlinks were all blue that changed to purple once they had been visited. As the art of Web design evolved, many Web authors began to tie their link colors in with the overall color scheme of the site. Some usability experts feel very strongly that the only appropriate colors for links are the original blue/purple because these colors are recognized and understood by most Web surfers. There is little confusion by users on this point. If the link is blue, they haven't been there yet. If it is purple, they have.

This concern is understandable when one is discussing people accessing Web sites worldwide. An instructional tutorial is different, however, because it is primarily a closed structure. Students will be remaining in the same environment for the most part and will quickly assimilate what the link colors mean. It is more important to be consistent and keep the same link colors throughout the tutorial than to limit the links to blue/purple.

Highlighting

Highlighting refers to various methods used to make critical information prominent to users. In Web design, colors or patterns are often used to bring attention to text or objects, but they are not the only way to highlight information. Figure 4.20 shows some different highlighting techniques that you may consider and lists their advantages and disadvantages. It's important to use highlighting judiciously. You want to use highlighting to bring something to the user's attention but not overpower other objects on the page.

FIGURE 4.20
Advantages and Disadvantages of Highlighting Techniques

HIGHLIGHTING TECHNIQUE	ADVANTAGE	DISADVANTAGE	USE FOR
Color-coding	Show relationships among screen elements	Some people have difficulty distinguishing colors. Use redundantly with another highlighting method	See section on "color"
Blinking	Gets users' attention	Distracting, illegible, annoying	Don't use
All uppercase characters	Easily recognized as a headline	Not as easy to read as mixed case	Use for table labels and some headings
Underlining	None	On a Web page, underlining means a hyperlink	Don't use
Oversized characters	Gets attention easily	Takes up a great deal of screen space	Use for headings
Center and right alignment	Gets attention quickly	Difficult to read long blocks of text	Use for headings and accents

Backgrounds

Page backgrounds are used to create a mood for the site. A background should contribute to the purpose of the site and enhance the content. Be conscious that it can have a positive or negative effect based on how it is designed and used.

Backgrounds can be either a color or an image. If you decide to specify a color as your page background, select it using the color issues discussed earlier in this chapter.

If an image is your preference, there are some additional considerations to think about. A background image is a .gif or .jpg file (see chapter 5, Multimedia) that is tiled across and down the screen. Because of this, you should consider the following:

Keep the file size small because the browser will have to download it to display the image. Think in terms of pixels. A background image that is 50 pixels by 50 pixels will be small enough to download efficiently at most connection speeds.

Select a pattern that will tile seamlessly horizontally or vertically so that it seems to be one continuous pattern.

Choose a subtle pattern that won't interfere with the readability of the content.

Try not to use one large image as your background. Since backgrounds tile, if you design your image to display on an 800×600 screen, it will tile on a large screen and not be viewable in its entirety at a smaller resolution. An image of that size will also be very large.

The starting page for a tutorial from UNC Libraries shown in figure 4.21 uses a small .gif file as its background. Although it looks like one large textured image, it is actually a 50-pixel by 50-pixel image that tiles horizontally and vertically across the screen (as displayed in the smaller browser in the lower left corner). Its pale gray color and subtle pattern don't interfere with the instructions on the screen and help set the tone for the site.

Typography

Type has always been an important component of graphic design because it contributes greatly to setting the tone or mood of a design. However, it has typically been a frustrating experience to effectively control type on a Web page. The following subsections discuss typography on the Web and some of the issues you will encounter. Let's start by reviewing some of the common terms you will hear.

Fonts and Typefaces

You will see the terms *font* and *typeface* used interchangeably many places. They really have different definitions, and it helps to understand these. A font is a complete set of characters in a particular style *and* size. Times New Roman in 12 point

FIGURE 4.21
Textured Background Image

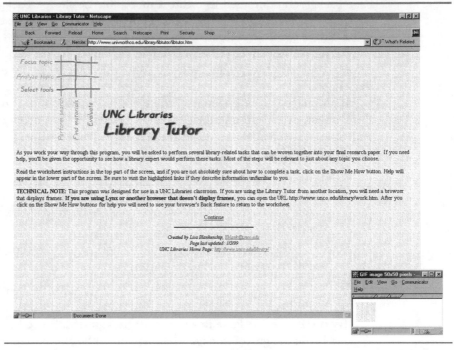

From University of Northern Colorado, Greeley. Available: http://www.univnorthco.edu/library/
libtutor/libtutor.htm.

is a font. A typeface contains a series of fonts. An example of a typeface would be
Times New Roman in 8-point, 10-point, 12-point, etc., size. Additionally, within
each typeface there can be many variations, such as normal, *italics,* and **bold.**

You should be aware that type sizes aren't standard. A point size in one typeface is not necessarily the same dimension as the same point size in another typeface. Figure 4.22 shows that different typefaces of the same point size are not
actually the same size. This is because the point size is the distance between the
bottom of the lowest descender (e.g., *j* or *y*) to the top of the highest ascender

FIGURE 4.22
Comparison of Typefaces at Same Point Size

This is 14-point Helvetica.
This is 14-point Futura Lt.
This is 14-point Optima.
This is 14-point Times.
This is 14-point Garamond.

(e.g., *l*, *d*, or a CAPITAL letter) with a little bit added on. This ensures the prevention of lines of type touching each other when set with no additional space.

Typeface Categories

There are different categories of typefaces. The most popular ones are the following:

Serif: These typefaces have little strokes or "feet" that decorate the letters. Times (Times) and Garamond (Garamond) are both examples of serif typefaces. This is a more formal style of type. Serifs serve a helpful purpose in providing a visual barrier to the tops and bottoms of letters, creating a horizontal emphasis that moves the eye as it travels along the line of text. For this reason, many feel that a serif typeface is the most readable.

Sans serif: These letterforms have no strokes or "feet" and are more contemporary looking. Popular sans serif typefaces are Helvetica (**Helvetica**) and Avant Garde (Avant Garde). Some experts believe that a sans serif typeface is easier to read on a computer screen than a serif. Because of the low resolution on many computer screens, there aren't enough pixels to give the detailed definition to the serifs on each letterform.

Monospace: In monospace typefaces, each letter takes up the same amount of space, similar to the old typewriter fonts. In other words, an *i* is as wide as an *r*. An example of a monospace typeface is Courier (`Courier`).

Decorative: This category includes just about everything that doesn't fit into the other categories. With the wide variance of styles, decorative type can evoke a wide range of moods. These typefaces work best for titles and other accent text and shouldn't be used in body text because they are often more difficult to read. Zapf Chancery (*Zapf Chancery*) and Bauhaus Bold (**Bauhaus Bold**) are illustrations of decorative type.

Combining Typefaces

A combination of typefaces makes a more appealing visual design, but just as with color, it's not a good idea to overdo it. Pick out two typefaces, one serif and one sans serif, to use. If you use the serif for your body text, then select a sans serif for the headings. And if you decide on a sans serif for your text, use a serif for its companion. Using two different serifs or two different sans serifs will look careless and indistinctive.

Text Alignment

Text should be left aligned because it is easier to read. This doesn't mean that center and right alignment shouldn't be used, but they should be reserved to accent and highlight.

Text Case

Mixed uppercase and lowercase letters are much easier to read and understand than are all capital letters. According to Nielsen (2000), it takes readers 10 percent longer to read a block of text that is in all capitals.

Text on the Web

When text is transported from the printed page to a computer screen and the Web, challenges arise. What holds true in print isn't necessarily so on a screen display. How to handle text on the Web also is dependent on whether your audience has the latest browsers or not. If they do, you will want to turn to cascading style sheets to control your text. If they have browsers that don't support CSS, then some of the following "older" solutions may be helpful.

HTML Font Sizes versus Point Size   Since the beginning, HTML hasn't used point sizes to designate how large to display a font. It has really been left to the browser developers to decide the relationship of HTML font size to actual type size. In this spirit, until HTML Version 4.01, font sizes have been specified using 0 to 7. If no font size is specified, the default size is 3. The browser developers decided what point size 3 equaled. With the latest HTML specifications, these controls have been deprecated, meaning that they have been outdated by newer concepts and may become obsolete in the future. For now, they are still interpreted, but the use of controls through CSS is being encouraged. Cascading style sheet specifications for fonts are accomplished through setting a series of font properties that include family (for example, Helvetica, sans serif), style (for example, normal or italic), variant (for example, normal, small caps), weight (for example, normal, bold, bolder, lighter), stretch (for example, normal, wide, narrower), and size (for example, small, medium, or large). For detailed information on CSS2 specifications for fonts, visit http://www.w3.org/TR/REC-CSS2/fonts.html#font-specification.

Browsers and Fonts   Older browsers don't interpret instructions about which font to display. If a browser can't interpret the instruction, it will display the default font for the browser. For most browsers this is Times Roman (Times on a Macintosh) at a 12-point size. The HTML <font face> attribute was developed several browser versions ago to give designers some control over what font is displayed to the audience. By tagging text with

> **<font face="Arial, Helvetica, sans serif">**
> **Text Here**
> **</font>**

the author could tell the browser to display an Arial font, or in its absence, look next for Helvetica. Finally, if neither of those is installed, the browser is instructed to use any available sans serif font. It was just an interim solution, however, and has also been deprecated. Again, CSS is the preferred recommended method for specification of font family.

User-Controlled Font Display   No matter what text typeface you decide to use, most browsers allow users to override your choice and select their own font style and size. This may not be what you had in mind, but it is an important bit of user control that allows your audience to get to your content using their browser's preferences.

Font Availability   No matter what font you designate, if that font is not installed on the user's computer, it will not appear. For this reason, it is wise to use fonts commonly found on most computers (unless you are going to use embedded fonts, to be discussed shortly). Common Windows fonts are Arial, Verdana, Helvetica, Times New Roman, Georgia, Courier New, and Comic Sans. Common Mac fonts include Arial, Geneva, Helvetica, Chicago, and Times. Because you have no way of being sure what fonts are on every user's computer, you should always specify more than one font when coding using either <font face= > or with {font-family: } when using CSS. If your first choice of font is one found commonly on one platform but not the other, then make sure your second choice is a font commonly found on the opposite platform. The final choice should always be either generic font designation, serif or sans serif, so you give the browser some indication of the kind of font you want displayed.

Platform Display Differences   Text is rendered 33 percent larger on a Windows computer (figure 4.23, top) than on a Macintosh (bottom). Both of the screen captures shown were taken of a 1024 × 768 screen resolution. The Mac OS uses 18 pixels to render 18-point text, while Windows uses 24 pixels to display the same text. This is because Macintosh assumes a display at a resolution of 72 dpi, but Windows assumes 96 dpi. The result is that the same size text will appear much smaller on a Mac than on a PC.

Text and Screen Resolution   It should come as no surprise that screen resolution affects text size appearance. When you are selecting a typeface size, test it at different resolutions. What is very legible on a 640 × 480 screen may be very difficult to read at a high resolution. The top display in figure 4.24 shows the text at a 640 × 480 resolution. The bottom display resolution is 1280 × 1024.

Images as Text

Because of the limitations of rendering typefaces on the Web, Web designers often turn to graphics to guarantee that the style of type they have chosen displays exactly as intended. By creating a text graphic, you can introduce more "personality" into your design. However, the downside to this solution is that your audience will experience a longer download time to display the graphics. (See chapter 5 for a detailed discussion.) If you decide to use graphics for some of your text, be sure to include the ALT attribute so that the text is accessible to those who turn off graphics or are visually impaired.

FIGURE 4.23
Comparison of Windows and Macintosh Displays

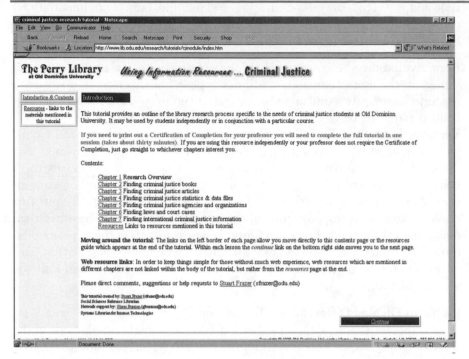

Windows
Display

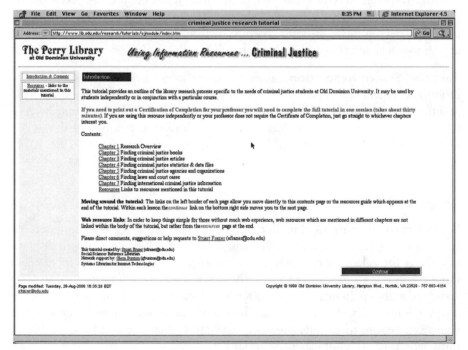

Macintosh
Display

From Perry Library, Old Dominion University, Norfolk, Va. Available: http://www.lib.odu.edu/research/tutorials/
cjmodule/index.htm.

FIGURE 4.24
Comparison of Resolution and Text Size

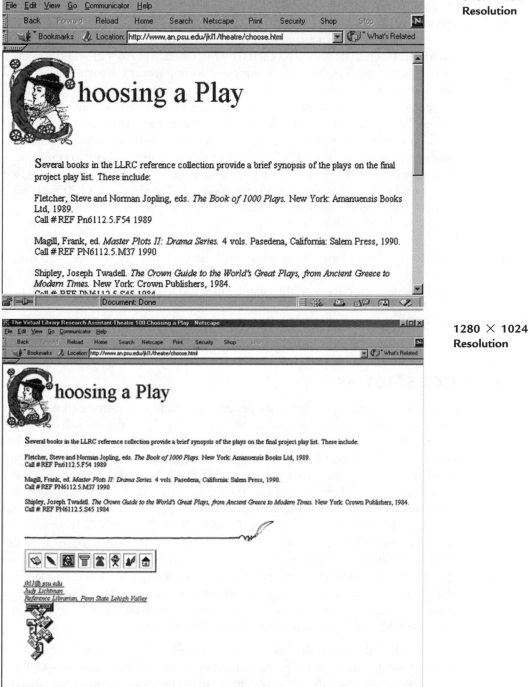

640 × 480
Resolution

1280 × 1024
Resolution

From Penn State Lehigh Valley Library, Fogelsville. Available: http://www.an.psu.edu/jkl1/theatre/choose.html.

Dynamic Fonts

A more-recent solution to the Web typography problem has been established. Now Web authors can bundle fonts and send them along temporarily with their HTML pages. This means that you can select whatever fonts you desire from your font library, and your audience will view your pages on their screens with your intended font formatting intact. Currently, there are two competing technologies, Open Type (being promoted by Microsoft and Adobe) and Bitstream's TrueDoc (adopted by Netscape). Font embedding works only with version 4.0 browsers and above, and each of these technologies functions differently and is supported in varying degrees by the rival browsers. For detailed information on Open Type, visit http://www.adobe.com/type/opentype and to learn about True-Doc go to http://www.truedoc.com/webpages/intro. Both technologies work using portable font resource (PFR) files that store the font information until it is requested via coding in the HTML document. The TrueDoc site provides free fonts on its site. If you prefer to create your own, TrueDoc has a font authoring system that allows you to make PFR files from any fonts that are installed on your computer and then host them on your own site.

Dynamic fonts have many benefits over previous methods of typeface control on the Web. First, the fonts are fully scalable to any size and resolution, which permits users to resize them on their screens to their preference. In addition, because they are text, they can be indexed in a search engine, unlike text graphics. Finally, the size of the file is smaller than a GIF or JPEG containing the same typeface.

USER ACCESSIBILITY

An integral part of your tutorial's design should address ensuring that it meets standards for access by disabled users. Unfortunately, as the Web has become more graphical and multimedia laden, it has become less accessible to those who have visual, auditory, motor, and cognitive impairments. If you are mindful of this need as you plan your project, it really isn't hard to design an accessible site. As part of its Web Accessibility Initiative Standard, the W3C has compiled the Web Content Accessibility Guidelines 1.0 (Chisholm, Vanderheiden, and Jacobs 1999) at http://www. w3.org/TR/WAI-WEBCONTENT. To make content more available to all users, the consortium has developed fourteen guidelines with sixty-six checkpoints that have each been assigned one of three priority levels. Those that have been assigned a priority 1 level are considered to be essential for accessibility to a document. As you begin the construction of your tutorial, it will be valuable for you to visit the preceding link and become familiar with this guide. The fourteen guidelines follow:

1. *Provide equivalent alternatives to auditory and visual content.* Provide a text equivalent for every nontext element, including images, graphical representations of text, image-map regions, animations, applets, ASCII art, frames, scripts, sounds, audio files, and video. Doing such

things as using ALT attributes for all graphics and image maps and providing transcripts for video clips make the content available through assistive devices such as screen readers or talking Web browsers. Providing nontext equivalents of text can also be beneficial to some users.

2. *Don't rely on color alone. Ensure that text and graphics are understandable when viewed without color.* Approximately 5 percent of Web users experience some degree of color blindness. Many have problems distinguishing shades of color. If your site depends on color solely to provide visual clues or uses low-contrast colors, it may be inaccessible to many users. To test the text you have selected for color accessibility, try this applet from the Internet Technical group: http://www.InternetTG.org/newsletter/mar99/color_challenged_applet.html.

3. *Use markup and style sheets, and do so properly.* Using markup incorrectly hinders accessibility. This usually refers to using markup for presentation effects such as font size or layout tables.

4. *Clarify natural language usage.* Use markup that facilitates pronunciation or interpretation of abbreviated or foreign text. Identifying this helps devices switch to the new language. For example, when using a word containing a diacritical mark, use the proper markup to display it rather than pasting the symbol into the document from a word processing document. (That is, the proper markup to display ê is &ecirc.)

5. *Create tables that transform gracefully.* Tables should be used to mark up tabular information and should have their row and column headers labeled correctly. Using tables for layout makes it hard for users with assistive tools to navigate through the page. If you are going to use tables for layout, provide an alternate version.

6. *Ensure that pages featuring new technologies transform gracefully.* If using newer technologies that may not be supported by all browsers, alternative methods should be included so that the page still works.

7. *Ensure user control of time-sensitive content changes.* Some disabilities prevent users from reading moving or scrolling text. Make sure these can be paused or stopped.

8. *Ensure direct accessibility of embedded user interfaces.* Elements that are embedded into an HTML page should be directly accessible or compatible with assistive technologies.

9. *Design for device-independence.* Users should be able to interact with their preferred input device, whether it is by mouse, voice, keyboard, etc.

10. *Use interim solutions.* Some older assistive technologies and browsers do not interpret page elements correctly. Some elements that cause difficulty are pop-up windows, tables, forms, and adjacent links. Until these can be handled by newer technologies, consider avoiding their use or provide alternative versions.

11. *Use W3C technologies and guidelines.* Many non-W3C formats (such as Shockwave or PDF [Portable Document Format]) require viewing via a plug-in or stand-alone application. Some assistive technologies can't view or navigate through these.

12. *Provide context and orientation information.* Group different page elements, and provide contextual information. This guideline applies to frames in particular. Be certain to title each frame to help users navigate.

13. *Provide clear navigation mechanisms.* Navigation should be clear and consistent. Incorporate site maps and tables of contents. Make text links meaningful.

14. *Ensure that documents are clear and simple.* The key to this is consistent page layout, easy-to-understand language, and identifiable graphics with text alternatives.

The W3C also has compiled a page of links to tools that can be used to evaluate, repair, and transform pages to meet accessibility rules. It is available at http://www.w3.org/WAI/ER/existingtools.html. An example of one of these tools is Bobby. (See figure 4.25.) Bobby is a free Web-based tool that can be used to analyze the accessibility of your site.

FIGURE 4.25
Bobby Accessibility-Check Tool

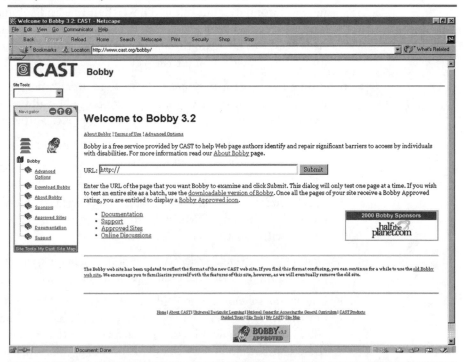

From: CAST, Peabody, Mass. Available: http://www.cast.org/bobby.

PAGE OPTIMIZATION

An important part of your students' experience with your tutorial is whether the pages load in a timely fashion. Users become impatient if they have to wait several seconds for a page to display. Slow-loading pages hinder the focus on the learning that is your main goal. Graphics can be one of the biggest hindrances to quick-loading pages. Solutions will be discussed in more detail in the next chapter. You should be aware that there are other things that can slow down a page display. Even extra spacing can contribute to a bloated page. However, there are ways to reduce this slowness through page optimization, the process of minimizing HTML file size to maximize page-display speed.

Visual-Based Web Editors

As discussed in chapter 3, visual-based (WYSIWYG) Web editors are more user friendly than are code-based ones. You don't need to know HTML to produce professional-looking Web pages. The down sides to this type of editor are that it does not always create code efficiently and it often leaves unnecessary code behind during the editing process. WYSIWYG editors may be the biggest cause of code bloat.

Tables

You've read about some of the pros and cons of using tables in HTML. Unfortunately, tables slow down page display because browsers need to understand a table's structure before they can render tables on the screen. So if you have used large or nested tables for layout, the page-download time can be seriously hindered. Optimally, make the switch to CSS2, and use its positioning power to get table-like layout at much greater speed. However, if you feel that tables work best for layout because your audience is running older browsers, try to use lots of little tables instead of one big, many-rowed table. Also, make sure you use the width attribute of the <table> and <td> tags properly. The widths defined in the <td> tag need to add up to equal what is specified in the <table> tag, or the browser will become confused. A note of interest: WYSIWYG editors are notorious for bloating tables through inefficient code.

Optimization Tips

There's no reason you can't optimize manually if you are a code buff. Following are a few examples of some adjustments you can make by hand. These ideas and additional tips are available in Andrew King's article on HTML optimization (2000).

Remove comments. Although they may be helpful to the author, they take time to download and are meaningless to the user of the page.

Simplify tables (see above).

Substitute style sheets for font tags. Designating style elements in one place in the head of the document or in a separate file can greatly reduce the size of the file.

Use attribute defaults where possible. (For example, the horizontal rule defaults to a width of 100 percent and align = center. If this is what you want to display, there's no need to specify it.)

Use named colors rather than hex, when shorter (e.g., bgcolor = white rather than bgcolor = #FFFFFF).

Get rid of unnecessary closing tags, spaces, returns, tabs, and quotes within the tags in the code.

Optimization Tools

Some software programs are designed to automate the optimization process. Most work in a similar manner by removing excess spaces, tabs, quotes, unnecessary attributes, etc. Some provide you with a report of what changes were made and the percentage of file reduction.

An example of a Macintosh optimization program is VSE Web Site Turbo, available at http://vse-online.com/web-site-turbo. A similar application for Windows is HTML (Un)Compress at http://gallery.uunet.be/Jacobs.Jan/htmlcomp/index.htm.

NOTES

Caspers, J. S. 1998. "Hands-on Instruction across the Miles: Using a Web Tutorial to Teach the Literature Review Process." *Research Strategies* 16, no. 3: 187–97.

Chisholm, W., G. Vanderheiden, and I. Jacobs. 1999. Web Content Accessibility Guidelines 1.0: W3C Recommendation 5 May 1999. Cambridge, Mass.: World Wide Web Consortium. Retrieved 4 March 2001 from http://www.w3.org/TR/WAI-WEBCONTENT.

Fleming, J. 1998. *Web Navigation: Designing the User Experience*. Cambridge, Mass.: O'Reilly & Associates.

Holzschlag, M. E. Nov. 1999. Satisfying Customers with Color, Shape, and Type. Web Techniques. Retrieved 4 March 2001 from http://www.webtechniques.com/archives/1999/11/desi.

Kennedy, J. R. Mar. 1999. Introduction to Color: Color Theory 101. Web Design Clinic 1, no. 1. Retrieved 4 March 2001 from http://www.webdesignclinic.com/ezine/v1i1/color/index.html.

King, A. 2000. Extreme HTML Optimization. Darien, Conn.: Internet.com. Retrieved 4 March 2001 from http://www.webreference.com/authoring/languages/html/optimize/index.html.

Morkes, J., and J. Nielsen. 1997. Concise, Scannable, and Objective: How to Write for the Web. Retrieved 4 March 2001 from http://www.useit.com/papers/webwriting/writing.html.

Nielsen, J. Dec. 1996. "Why Frames Suck (Most of the Time)." Retrieved 4 March 2001 from http://www.useit.com/alertbox/9612.html.

———. 2000. *Designing Web Usability: The Practice of Simplicity*. Indianapolis, Ind.: New Riders.

Ritchie, D. C., and B. Hoffman. 1997. "Incorporating Instructional Design Principles with the World Wide Web." In B. H. Khan, *Web-Based Instruction*. Englewood Cliffs, N.J.: Educational Technology Publications.

Shneiderman, B. 1998. *Designing the User Interface: Strategies for Effective Human-Computer Interaction* 3d ed. Reading, Mass.: Addison-Wesley.

5

Multimedia: Using Graphics, Sound, Animation, and Video

Multimedia is the integration of text, graphics, sound, and video/animation in a computer-based environment. Since the Web is a multimedia environment, it is easy to envision incorporating multimedia into an instructional tutorial to enhance the learning experience. This chapter examines the various medias and issues surrounding their use.

MULTIMEDIA AND INSTRUCTION

When you contemplate how and when to incorporate multimedia into online instruction, there are various considerations to be made. This section examines the benefits and limitations of multimedia, explores some of the appropriate uses of multimedia for instruction, and discusses multimedia issues that can influence its effective use.

Benefits and Limitations of Multimedia

Why is multimedia good to use in an online learning experience? Students have different learning preferences, and for that reason alone, offering information in more than one medium is beneficial. Newby and others (1996) compiled a list of advantages and disadvantages of including multimedia as a part of instruction.

Advantages
- Better learning and retention
  Multimedia engages students and provides multiple learning methods.
- Addresses different learning styles and preferences
  Multimedia provides opportunities for teaching individuals and incorporating their preferred learning styles. Some students learn best

through an auditory channel (lecture), while others learn best through visual channels. Multimedia can provide both.

- Realism
  Multimedia can introduce an element of realism that may be missing in a lecture presentation. Instead of simply reading information, students can hear and see things in context.

- Motivation
  Studies show that learners consistently show positive attitudes toward multimedia (particularly interactive multimedia, which will be discussed in chapter 6).

Disadvantages

- Equipment requirements
  The hardware and software required for multimedia development may be a burden on organizations that are limited in their abilities to install and maintain them.

- Start-up costs
  The initial costs for resources to support multimedia development can be prohibitive.

- Complexity and lack of standardization
  Much multimedia today is still proprietary. It is often very difficult to configure various components so that they can work together.

Appropriateness

Multimedia can offer an enhanced learning experience, but only if it is used properly. It should be used only when it can contribute something to aid the student. Using it just because it is "cool" is not a suitable reason. Some viable reasons for including multimedia are identified in the following sections.

Navigation

The importance of navigation was discussed in the previous chapter. Using images to build a navigation tool bar is a popular design approach. Images can serve to highlight the navigation scheme for the tutorial. Regular Web users are accustomed to looking for navigation icons and images that will direct them through a site.

The global navigation in the tutorial shown in figure 5.1 from the University of Arizona Library incorporates image buttons. The color changes from blue-on-white to white-on-blue to indicate what area of the tutorial you are in.

Establish a Theme or Mood

Setting the appropriate tone for a particular learning event helps to engage the student. Images, audio, or animation are all possible means to create just the right setting. The tutorial shown in figure 5.2 from Z. Smith Reynolds Library

FIGURE 5.1
Images Used for Navigation

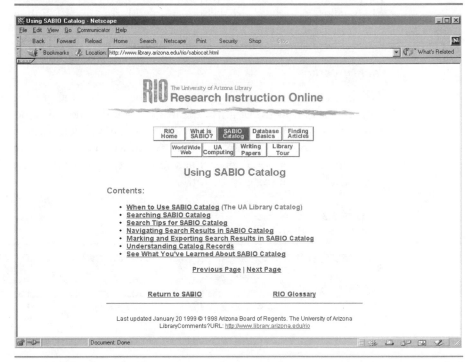

From University of Arizona Library, Tucson. Available: http://www.library.arizona.edu/rio/sabiocat.html.

FIGURE 5.2
Graphics Used to Set a Mood

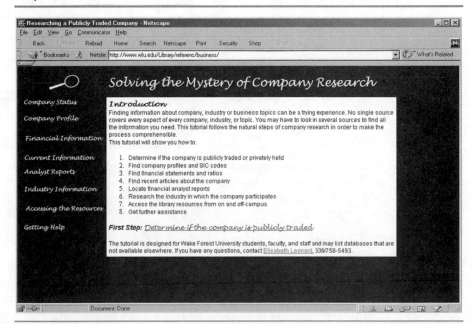

From Z. Smith Reynolds Library, Wake Forest University, Winston–Salem, N.C. Available: http://www.wfu.edu/Library/referenc/business.

illustrates the use of graphics to set a mood. Business research is often a daunting prospect to students, and the script-text graphics set a casual tone. The magnifying glass provides a visual connection with the theme, "Solving the Mystery of Company Research."

Identification

The inclusion of a library logo or some other identifying graphic helps ensure that students know the origin of the instruction. If someone comes into your tutorial at a point other than the starting page, having identification helps to orient him or her to the current location. As shown in figure 5.3, the University of Houston Libraries' logo appears at the top of each screen. There's no doubt about the origin of this instruction.

FIGURE 5.3
Logo Used for Identification

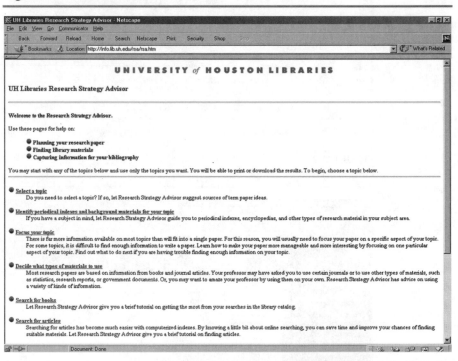

From University of Houston Libraries. Available: http://info.lib.uh.edu/rsa/rsa.htm.

Tell a Story

As they say, one picture is worth a thousand words. In many situations an image provides information much more effectively than do words. One common use of images and illustrations is in conjunction with virtual library tours. Pictures of the different areas of the facility and floor maps help familiarize potential library users and give students a good way to become acquainted with how the building is organized. In figure 5.4, the Milner Library virtual library walk includes photos of public areas and a floor map to help orient students to the facility.

FIGURE 5.4
Photo and Map in Virtual Tour

From Milner Library, Illinois State University, Normal. Available: http://www.mlb.ilstu.edu/vtour/vtour2.htm.

Illustration

Another case of a picture being able to help convey an instructional point more efficiently than text is that of using illustrations or screen captures. For instance, you can describe what students will see when they conduct a search, but showing a screen-capture image of what is being described allows students to associate the description with a representation of the screen they will see. In figure 5.5 students from Irwin Library at Butler University see a typical results list in EBSCOhost's Academic Elite database.

Demonstration/Simulation

Often, the best way to get a concept across is through demonstration or simulation. One typical type of demonstration is how to conduct searches using particular search software. In figure 5.6, this demonstration is accomplished through the screen-recording application ScreenCam from Lotus. Students can view a movie that takes them step-by-step through a typical search process. A more interactive approach is to set up a simulation where students are instructed to enter

FIGURE 5.5
Screen Capture Used in Searching Tutorial

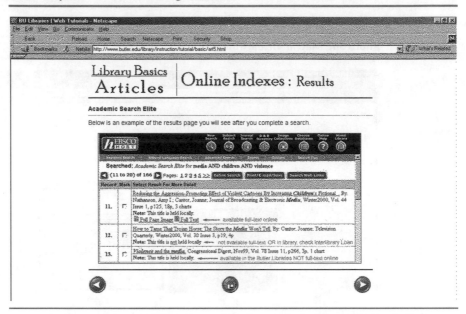

From Irwin Library, Butler University, Indianapolis, Ind. Available: http://www.butler.edu/library/instruction/tutorial/basic/art5.html.

FIGURE 5.6
Lotus ScreenCam Demonstration Used in Searching Tutorial

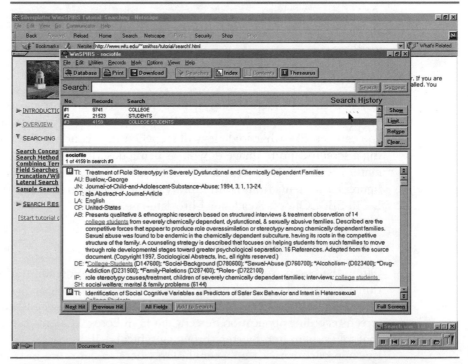

From Z. Smith Reynolds Library, Wake Forest University, Winston–Salem, N.C. Available: http://www.wfu.edu/~smithss/tutorial/searchf.html.

FIGURE 5.7
Screen-Capture Demonstration Used in Author-Search Tutorial

From Libraries of The Claremont Colleges, Claremont, Calif. © Claremont University Consortium. Available: http://voxlibris.claremont.edu/research/tutorials/blais/new_author/author_frameset. html.

information and receive feedback as they successfully accomplish tasks. Figure 5.7 is a simulation of an author search using screen-capture images of the catalog and additional programming to deliver a level of reality to students.

Visualization

Visualization is a way to help students grasp difficult concepts and ideas. By including graphics, charts, diagrams, animation, and even 3-D objects, designers can help students visualize to make content more understandable. One concept that students commonly have difficulty understanding is Boolean logic. Figure 5.8 shows how an animation can help students understand this idea. The three different sets of terms enter the screen (top left screen) and move toward each other until they are joined together by an AND (bottom right screen) to illustrate a Venn diagram.

Multimedia Considerations

As you are deciding on what types of multimedia to integrate into your tutorial, always keep your audience's best interests in mind. You will want to consider each of the following elements.

FIGURE 5.8
Animation Used for Visualization of Boolean Logic Concepts

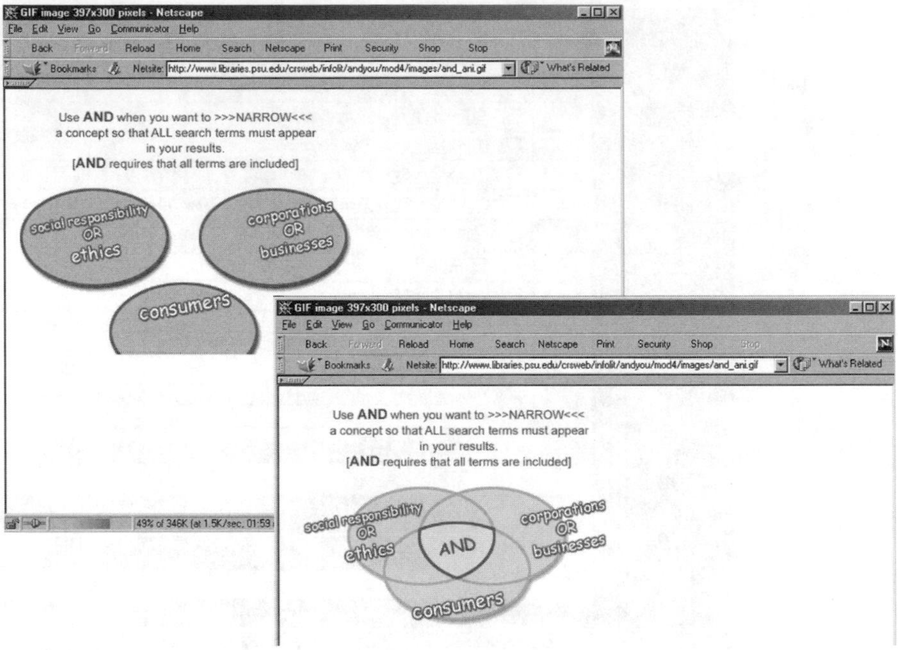

From Pennsylvania State University Libraries, University Park, Pa. Available: http://www.libraries.psu.edu/crsweb/infolit/andyou/mod4/comb.htm.

Bandwidth

Bandwidth is the amount of data that can be transmitted in a certain amount of time. Any type of multimedia requires additional bandwidth. Webmonkey's Adam Powell compares moving multimedia through the Internet to sucking a bowling ball through a garden hose (http://hotwired.lycos.com/webmonkey). Even when students have a good connection, every multimedia file has to be downloaded, and this takes time. Keep the size of multimedia files as compact as possible by using file compression. Ways to do that will be discussed later in this chapter. If you are incorporating files of any size, communicate that fact to the user. It will help prevent the frustration of long download times.

Plug-ins

Plug-in applications are separate programs that are installed and run as part of your browser. Many of today's latest multimedia technologies require a plug-in so the media can be viewed or heard. Once installed, plug-ins permit multimedia to become integrated into the browser environment, but most people don't make the effort to download and install them until faced with the need to view a page that requires one. Be kind to your students. State at the beginning of the tutorial what plug-ins are required, and provide a link to their download sites.

Hardware and Software Requirements

It's worth mentioning again that your use of multimedia should not exceed your audience's capacity to access it. Before you invest a great deal of time and money in developing sophisticated multimedia elements, be certain your users have the hardware and software capabilities to play and view what you create. If you have a diverse user group, consider making a "high tech" and a "low tech" version of your instruction.

TYPES OF MULTIMEDIA

The basic divisions between types of multimedia with which most of us are familiar include graphics, sound, animation, and video. However, in the world of computer multimedia, the lines of distinction often blur. For instance, animations can include text, sound, and video. Videos can include text, animation, and still images. As you explore the various types of multimedia, be on the lookout for formats that overlap other categories and have more than one function. You will also see several references to interactivity capabilities, which are discussed in greater depth in chapter 6.

Graphics or Images

When the Web was first popularized, the combination of text and images constituted multimedia on the Web. Now, however, images are almost a given on any particular Web page. Nevertheless, creating graphics for the Web is different from creating them for print. The following subsections examine some of the basics of computer imaging and how to work with Web graphics.

Raster (Bitmap) versus Vector Images

Computer graphics come in two different flavors: raster (also called bitmap) and vector. It is helpful to have some understanding of what each type is and to understand their differences and the benefits and drawbacks of each type.

Raster (bitmap) images are made up of small squares called pixels that are arranged in a grid. Each pixel is a tiny unit of color that comes together with the other pixels to form the images you see on your screen. When you create a raster image, you set the number of pixels that will be in the grid, and this determines the resolution, measured in dots or pixels per inch (dpi and ppi). When you view raster images at the size they were created, you will not see the pixels. However, if you zoom in on an image with a photo-editing application, the individual pixels appear. (See figure 5.9.)

Raster images are resolution dependent. If you increase the size of a raster image, the pixels are simply enlarged and the edges appear jagged. Computer screens typically display at 72 or 96 dpi. That is why an image scanned in at 300 dpi looks so large on a computer monitor. If you are creating a raster image that

FIGURE 5.9
Zoom-in View of Raster Image Pixels

will be displayed only on a computer monitor (and is not intended for printing), there is no reason to create it any larger than 72 dpi.

Because they are created on a grid, raster images are rectangular in shape. Some raster formats support transparency, which designates some of the pixels to be invisible to the eye, giving the illusion of a nonrectangular shape. Transparency permits one color to be specified as "see through." This capability allows the rectangular raster image to appear to be other shapes because it permits a Web page's background color to show through the transparent pixels. Because they are resolution dependent, it is difficult to resize raster images without degrading the quality. Making the graphic smaller forces your imaging program to throw away pixels. Resizing the image to a larger size forces the program to create new pixels, and it will have to guess what new pixels to create.

Resizing is different from scaling. Scaling takes place when you adjust the image size by dragging the corners of it in a page-layout program. This does not permanently change the image, but it does change how it displays. If you enlarge an image via scaling, the result will be pixelated much as the example in figure 5.9. It's best to create raster images at the size you plan to use them. Since scanners and digital cameras both produce bitmap images, you can control size creation from the image-editing software. For a discussion of potential imaging programs, refer to chapter 3.

Vector images are made up of mathematically described objects. The objects can be lines, curves, and shapes and have attributes such as color, fill, and outline. Vector graphics are resolution independent: They are scalable and can be manip-

FIGURE 5.10
Vector Images

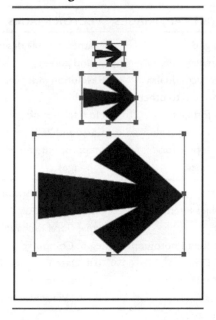

ulated without losing qualities as illustrated by the arrow in figure 5.10 that has had its size reduced and enlarged. A font is an example of a vector object.

Unlike bitmap images, vector images are not restricted to a rectangular shape, so they are much more flexible when combining with other objects. One major advantage of vector images is that their file size is small because the file really represents an equation the operating system uses to re-create the object. Another advantage is the ease with which a vector image can be edited and resized. The major disadvantage is that they are not suitable for photo-quality images. They are best suited for line drawings. Vector images are normally created using illustration software such as Adobe Illustrator.

As you will discover in the next section, most graphics on the Web today are raster images. However, most illustration programs include the capability to convert a vector image to a raster image so that it can be viewed on the Web. Just be certain that the image is sized correctly before converting it. For a summary of raster and vector features and file formats, refer to figure 5.11.

Current Web Graphics Formats

Although there are a multitude of formats that can be used to create computer graphics, only a limited number of them are supported by browsers for display on the Web. The two standard Web image formats are GIF and JPEG, both of which are raster images. At this time, these are the only two image formats that can be displayed in all browsers without resorting to a plug-in. However, several newer formats are being proposed for use on the Web. Their potential is discussed later in this chapter.

GIF (.gif)   The Graphic Interchange Format (GIF, pronounced "jif") was defined in the late 1980s by CompuServe. It incorporates a compression scheme that keeps file sizes at minimum with no loss of data (lossless compression) while preserving sharp detail. The compression used is LZW (which stands for its inventors Lempel, Zev, and Welch), a scheme that efficiently compresses large fields of homogeneous color. GIF files have a palette limited to 256 colors (8 bits). There are actually two GIF standards: 87a and 89a (supports transparency). The GIF format also supports interlaced images; every eighth row in an image is displayed, then every fourth, then every second. This allows users to view emerging images as they are being downloaded to their computers, a particularly attractive technique if your audience includes some people who use modems to access your tutorial.

FIGURE 5.11
Comparison of Raster and Vector Images

	RASTER (BITMAP) IMAGES	VECTOR IMAGES
Key points	Pixels in a grid	Mathematically described lines
	Resolution dependent	and curves
	Resizing reduces quality	Resolution independent
	Easily converted to other	Scalable
	bitmap formats	No background
	Restricted to rectangle	Cartoon-like
	Minimal support for	Inappropriate for photorealistic
	transparency	images
Common file formats	.bmp, Bitmap	.ai, Abobe Illustrator
	.gif, Graphics Interchange	.cdr, CorelDRAW
	Format	.cmx, Corel Exchange
	.jpeg, jpg, Joint Photographic	.cgm, Computer Graphic Metafile
	Experts Group	.dxf, Data Exchange Format
	.png, Portable Network	(Autocad)
	Graphics	.wmf, Windows Metafile
	.pict (Macintosh)	
	.tiff, .tif, Tag Image Bitmap File	
	.psd (Adobe Photoshop)	

From S. Chastain, Vector and Bitmap Images. Graphics Software. New York: About.com. Retrieved 4 March 2001 from http://graphicssoft.about.com/compute/graphicssoft/library/weekly/aa000327a.htm.

GIFs are most useful for images that have a limited number of colors or large areas of solid colors, as is the case with line art and cartoons. This format works nicely with logos and illustrations with type. Vector images convert well to GIF because of its lossless compression and ability to support transparency. You can also use the GIF format to create animated images, which will be discussed shortly.

JPEG (.jpeg, .jpg)   JPEG (pronounced JAY-peg) stands for Joint Photographic Experts Group, the committee that developed the standard in the late 1980s and early 1990s. The JPEG image format is designed to compress full-color or gray-scale realistic images. The JPEG format supports 24-bit color, or more than 16 million colors. Because it provides significantly more image information than does a GIF format (with a 256-color limit), JPEG is better suited for photographs and scanned artwork. It is, however, a lossy compression, meaning that some data is discarded during the compression process. This loss may or may not be discernible to the naked eye depending upon the quality of the original and the amount of compression you select. The ability to specify degree of compression with JPEG, giving you the control over the balance of size versus quality, is an advantage of this image format. JPEG has the capability to provide up to a 20:1 compression of full-color data without visible loss. This can make a significant difference in download time while still presenting intact image information.

The JPEG format offers a counterpart to the interlaced GIF. Progressive JPEG allows the image to download in stages instead of all at once, so viewers get a low-resolution preview until the image completely arrives.

There is one caution worth mentioning about JPEG. Because it is a lossy compression, the information that is discarded is gone forever. Always maintain an uncompressed original of the image and work from it.

For a comparison of the two most popular Web graphics formats, refer to Figure 5.12.

Emerging Web Graphics Formats

Although GIFs and JPEGs dominate the Web, they are not the only formats available nor are they necessarily the best in every circumstance. This section takes a look at some of the emerging image formats.

PNG (.png)   PNG (pronounced "ping") is the Portable Network Graphics format, designed to be the successor to the GIF format. Interest in an alternative to

FIGURE 5.12
Advantages, Disadvantages, and Uses of GIF and JPEG Formats

	GIF	JPEG
Advantages	Can be indexed to a set color palette (helps with browser-safe color determination)	Supports 24-bit true color
		Preserves broad range and subtle variations in brightness and hue
	Lossless compression scheme	Can specify degree of compression
	Supports transparency	Supports progressive download
	Superior when compressing a few distinct colors	
	Supports interlacing	
	Supports animations	
Disadvantages	Limited to a 256-color palette	Has difficulty with sharp edges (which come out blurred)
		Lossy compression scheme
		Doesn't support transparency
Use for	Line art	Full-color or gray-scale realistic images
	Logos	
	Cartoons	Images with lots of complex, gradient color variations
	Type and fonts	
	Black-and-white images	
	Images with large areas of solid color	

GIF increased when the company that owns it announced that programs implementing GIF would require royalties. The PNG compression was developed expressly to be royalty-free and contains a number of improvements over the GIF format. It was developed in 1995 and issued as a W3C recommendation in October 1996. You might wonder why, if it has been around so long, it is not more established, but it has taken some time for it to gain support in most browsers and authoring software. Most of the major browsers and imaging programs now support the format, so it is probable that you will see an increase in its use.

PNG supports three main image types: true color, gray scale, and palette-based. Since JPEG supports only true color and gray scale, and GIF supports only palette-based, PNG can offer a potential alternative to both of these formats in certain circumstances.

Like GIF, PNG is a lossless compression, but unlike GIF, it is not restricted to a 256-color palette. Since PNG supports up to 48-bit color, it is possible to display complex color schemes with no loss of data. When it is done properly, PNG has a higher compression rate than GIF.

PNG also supports transparency, but once again, it improves on what GIF can offer. While GIF supports transparency of one color, PNG allows for up to 254 levels of partial transparency with a normal Web image.

Interlacing is also incorporated into PNG. Where GIF uses a one-dimensional interlacing scheme, PNG uses a two-dimensional scheme, which results in a faster viewable image to the user. With only $\frac{1}{64}$ of a PNG downloaded, a viewer gets a preview of the entire image, compared with only $\frac{1}{8}$ of a GIF image.

Should you use PNG? If your authoring software supports PNG and your audience's browsers also do, then PNG may well be a worthwhile format. If you know that many of your users are viewing your tutorial through older browsers, you will probably want to postpone experimenting with the PNG compression. For more information on this promising Web format, visit the PNG home site at http://www.freesoftware.com/pub/png.

SVG (.svg)   All of the Web graphic formats discussed so far have been raster (bitmap). Because vector graphics have some benefits over raster images, developing a standard for supporting display of them over the Web has been a priority for some time. Currently, there are a number of proprietary vector graphic formats being used on the Web, but these require plug-ins. This prevents their use in all the places that raster Web graphics can be. Because no single format is widely supported for either viewing or graphic creation and there is little cross-platform support, W3C has taken on the development of a vector graphic standard. Called SVG (Scalable Vector Graphics), it is a language for describing two-dimensional graphics. The language issues instructions to describe how a figure should appear by assigning attributes to SVG elements. In other words, it is coded in plain text that resides within an HTML document with no other files involved. SVG allows for three types of graphic objects: vector graphic shapes (e.g., paths consisting of straight lines and curves), images, and text. SVG drawings can be dynamic and interactive. It is an open standard that has development support from more than twenty organizations, including major players such as Sun Microsystems, Adobe, Apple, and IBM.

Some advantages of SVG over the "traditional" Web graphic formats are

scalability: Because it is a vector format, SVG can be scaled to any resolution without degradation of quality.

smaller file size: Of course, this translates to faster download time.

scripting and animation: SVG has the capability to render dynamic and interactive graphics.

plain-text format: SVG language is written in plain text. This makes it possible to use a variety of tools to read and modify an SVG file. It also contributes to a smaller file size.

ability to apply styles: Unlike bitmapped images, which are "frozen" once they are created, with SVG you can make changes to appearances through the use of cascading style sheets. This means, for instance, that you can easily change text in objects to a different font or color.

selectable and searchable text: With SVG, the textual content of a graphic becomes searchable, can be indexed, and can be displayed in multiple languages. This has great benefit for disabled users.

open standard: It is an open recommendation developed by a cross-industry consortium.

As of January 2001, SVG is a "Candidate Recommendation" through the W3C, meaning that the development community is being called upon to develop applications implementing the standard. Within the next year, it is expected that its status will be increased to either a "Proposed Recommendation" or "Recommendation." What does this mean to you? Look for SVG to become a major factor in Web graphics. For detailed information on SVG, visit the W3C's SVG site at http://www.w3.org/Graphics/SVG.

Icons

An icon is a small picture intended to represent something. On the Web, icons are small graphic elements on a Web page that represent a topic or additional information on another page or, once clicked, a function for the user. Icons are quickly becoming a common tool on commercial sites; for instance, most people know what the shopping cart icon means. Appropriate icons on an educational site can be valuable also. A good icon contains a visual image that a user may recognize more quickly than written text. Figure 5.13 illustrates some of the well-known Web icons that have potential usefulness in a tutorial.

Clip Art

Clip art is "canned" artwork that was originally designed for use in desktop publishing. It was prepared in a standardized form for nonspecific use and wide distribution. With the popularization of the Web, clip art libraries have become a common means for both artists and nonartists to incorporate art into their Web pages quickly and economically. Clip art includes visual elements such as

FIGURE 5.13
Useful Web Icons for Tutorials

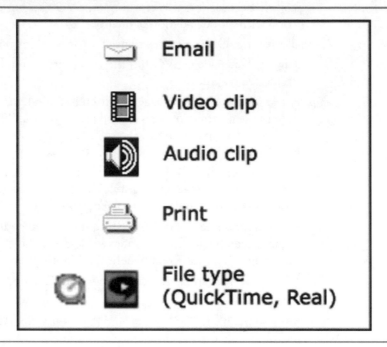

bullets, lines, and arrows as well as subject-related illustrations on almost any topic under the sun.

Clip art is available commercially from many companies, but there are also plenty of clip art libraries on the Web. It is a very simple matter to download clip art from the Web, but it is important to know that you can't assume that all clip art is freely available for download and use. Be aware that clip art may be copyrighted and that many clip art sites have terms and conditions for the use of their art. It is your responsibility to familiarize yourself with specified rules and to comply with them.

Finding clip art on the Web is not difficult. You can use your favorite search engine or Web directory to find resources similar to these: Clipart.com at http://www.clipart.com or About.com's Web Clip Art site at http://webclipart. about.com/internet/webclipart.

Image Map

As mentioned in chapter 4, an image map is a graphic that is defined so that users can click on different areas of the graphic to go to various destinations. These areas are called *hot spots* and are constructed by defining the x and y co-ordinates (the horizontal and vertical distance from the left-hand corner of the picture). The two different types of image maps are server-side and client-side. The server-side map stores the map data on the server, which means a longer response time for the user since the client has to query the server for the map destination. With client-side maps, the map data is embedded in the HTML document and is interpreted by the browser program on users' computers. Response time to the user is faster with a client-side image map, so use this type if at all possible.

Image maps are often used as the main menu on an introductory page. However, with some imagination, there are applications for them in an educational tutorial. For instance, Figure 5.14 shows the construction of an image map to make a simulation of an online catalog search.

Image maps can be created in many Web editors, as illustrated in figure 5.14. Hot spots are selected by drawing one of three shapes (circle, rectangle, or polygon) and assigning a destination to that spot. In the top screen in figure 5.14, the local catalog button and the Author/Title/Search button have both been made into hot spots. The map coordinates are coded into the HTML document, as is shown in the lower righthand window.

Rollover Images

A rollover (also known as a mouseover) is a JavaScript technique that allows a Web author to program a page element change when a user's cursor passes over something on the page. The page element is usually a graphic, and rollovers are often used in navigation tool bars. Rollovers invite a feeling of user interactivity because changes take place in response to the user's activity. To view a rollover, visit Irwin Library's tutorial (see figure 5.5). The navigation button at the bottom of the screen uses rollover scripting. Another common use is the remote

FIGURE 5.14
Creating an Image Map with Dreamweaver

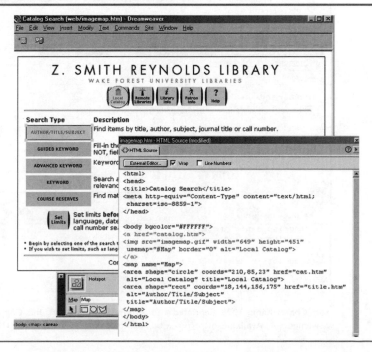

rollover, which causes a previously invisible graphic element to appear when the user passes the cursor over a certain page element.

To make rollovers, create two graphics that have the same dimensions. (If you are doing a remote rollover, you'll prepare a third.) One will load when the page first displays. The second will swap places with the first when the cursor passes over the original image. The third will appear in a different location along with the second image. Don't hesitate to use rollovers just because you don't know how to write JavaScript. Many Web editors include behind-the-scenes scripting for the creation of rollovers. In addition, it is easy to find free rollover scripts on the Web. You may also want to try out the Mouseover Machine from CNET Builder.com. (See figure 5.15.) This free utility creates a rollover script in response to information you put into fields. Then you simply cut and paste the script into your HTML document.

Image Optimization

Even though GIFs, JPEGs, and PNGs are compression formats, there are other steps you can take to ensure that your images are optimized for faster download times.

FIGURE 5.15
CNET Builder's Mouseover Machine

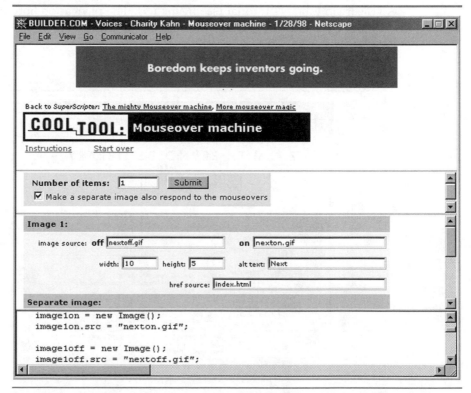

From Charity Kahn, 1998. Reprinted with permission from CNET, Inc. Copyright 1995–2000, www.cnet.com. Available: http://www.builder.com/Programming/Kahn/012898.

Use only meaningful graphics; remove everything else. This tip bears repeating because it is so easy to get carried away using graphics.

Select the correct format for the type of graphic you are using. Figure 5.12 can help you decide which type is best.

Size the images correctly.

Keep the resolution to 72 dpi. If you are not printing the image, there is no need for any higher resolution.

Always use the width and height attributes. This allows the browser to render the rest of the page while the graphic downloads so users have something to read while they wait for the image.

Make the width and height of the image the exact size that will display. Don't use the width and height attributes of the <image> tag to resize the image so it displays at a size other than its real size. If you use those attributes to increase the display site, the image will appear jagged. If you use them to constrain the display size, you are wasting bandwidth because the actual image still has to download.

Crop images to discard extra space around the image's subject matter.

Reduce the number of colors (bit depth) in the image as much as possible in those formats that are palette based (GIF and PNG). This means that you can use a graphics optimizer program and play with the color palette to take out unnecessary color. If done correctly, this reduction is invisible to the naked eye.

Optimize JPEG files through a degree of compression. The less compression that is selected, the higher the quality of the image and the larger the file. Utilities such as JPEG Wizard (available at no cost from http:// www.jpg.com/products/freewizard.html) will display your image at different compression degrees so that you can see which compression best reduces file size while retaining image quality.

Stick to the 216-color Web-safe palette to ensure that the file size isn't bloated due to color.

Repeat the same graphic. Since browsers cache files as they download, images that are repeated throughout your tutorial will appear quickly because they don't have to download every time they are displayed. If the browser recognizes a file name, it will look to the cache to retrieve it rather than pointing to the originating server.

Store your images on the same server on which your tutorial resides. This helps minimize the slight lag that an extra domain name server lookup entails.

If you don't have access to an optimizing application, utilities are available on the Web. One example is GIF Lube, available through Netscape Netcenter's Web Site Garage. This utility will examine a graphic (GIF, JPEG, or PNG) by pointing to a specific URL or by uploading the file from a disk and provide several options for reducing the file size through color reduction. It also predicts download time and lists the percentage of file reduction. (See figure 5.16.)

FIGURE 5.16
Netscape Netcenter's Web Site Garage GIF Lube Image Optimizing Utility

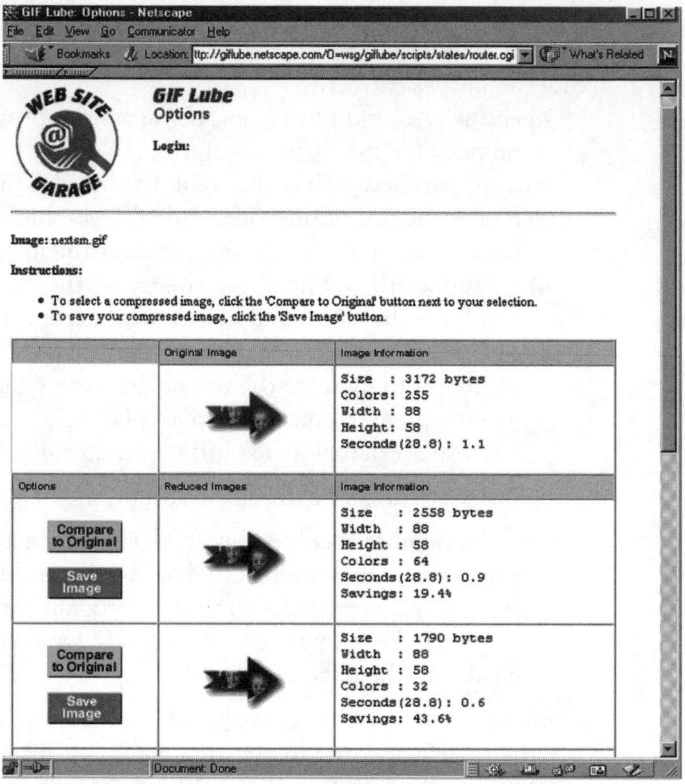

Netscape Netcenter's Web Site Garage screenshot © 2000 Netscape Communications Corp. Used with permission. Available: http://giflube.netscape.com.

Image Slicing

Image slicing is a technique that combines image editing with HTML. It allows large images to be sliced into a number of pieces, which are then reassembled in an HTML table. Illustrated in figure 5.17 is an original image (top) and the same image after it is sliced in an imaging application. Each numbered rectangle becomes a table cell. Although it seems as though the main benefit of image slicing would be to facilitate faster download times, in reality no bandwidth is usually saved. It does, however, give the illusion of a quicker download, which sometimes can be just as important to the user. Slicing has some benefits worthy of consideration.

Each sliced section can be individually optimized, which may result in a smaller overall size after all. For instance, if a graphic combines areas that are best suited to be GIFs and others that would warrant being optimized as JPEGs, with slicing you can define the sections so that each section can be treated separately.

FIGURE 5.17
Image before and after Slicing

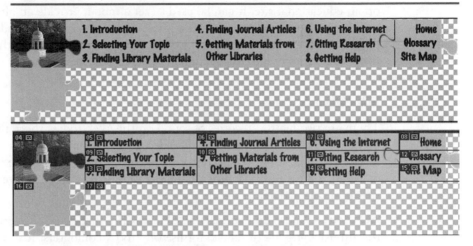

From Z. Smith Reynolds Library, Wake Forest University, Winston–Salem, N.C.

Blank areas of an image can be eliminated altogether so that the background color shows through. This would also save download time that would have been used for that part of the graphic.

Slicing can be used to make graphic elements individual links. Although this can be accomplished via image maps, separate images for each link result in better compatibility when a page is viewed with the graphics off (using the ALT attribute) and makes updating links easier.

The ability to create rollover images for navigational elements by slicing is possible.

Large areas of identical image color can be sliced into smaller identical images that, when named the same file name, can be cached and displayed much more quickly than if it were just one larger file.

Slicing allows the animation of a portion of a large image.

Labeling Images

The ALT attribute provides an alternative way for your images to "display" to those who can't view graphics or choose not to do so. HTML code that utilizes the ALT attribute looks like this:

```
<img src="intromenu.gif" width="540" height="399" alt="Start Menu">
```

Users with visual disabilities or those who have turned off image loading in their browsers will hear (via a screen reader) or see the text alternative. If this attribute is ignored or overlooked during the authoring process, the result will be a site that is not accessible to all.

Audio   Although the Web is a very visual medium, as it has matured, the use of audio has become much more common. Proper use of audio can serve many purposes on an educational site. It can be used to set a mood, provide an alternate communication channel apart from the visual material, or give an audible clue for different actions within the interface. As with other multimedia, the important thing to remember is to use audio for a specific purpose and not to overdo it.

File Formats

There are two main categories of sound on the Web today: those that are "self-contained" (and have to be downloaded to the computer before they can be heard) and streaming audio. The following subsections explore the first category of audio file types. Streaming audio is examined within the presentation of streaming media later in the chapter.

AU (.au)   Audio File Format, or AU, was the first audio file format used on the Internet and was intended for use on UNIX computers. It is also the standard sound format for the Java platform. This format supports a 2:1 compression ratio, which gives the format a relatively small file size of about 8 KB per second of audio. It is probably the closest to a nonproprietary audio standard available on the Internet and so can be found in quantity from sound libraries. Because the quality of AU files is not very high, they work well for short clips and sound effects but would not be the first choice for a project that relies heavily on sound.

AIFF (.aiff, .aif)   Apple developed the Audio Interchange File Format for the Macintosh platform. The AIFF file format is an uncompressed one, so the files can be very large. Its sound quality is better than the AU format.

WAV (.wav)   Developed by Microsoft, the Waveform Audio File Format is the PC/Windows equivalent of Apple's AIFF. Because it is the native sound file format for the platform that has the overwhelming majority of presence on the Internet, it is common to see. However, it, too, is an uncompressed format, and just 60 seconds of WAV audio can take up more than 10 MB of disk space. WAV has a comparable sound quality to AIFF.

   All three of these sound file types store recorded sound that originated as analog and was converted to digital. The next file type is quite different.

MIDI (.midi, .mid)   The Musical Instrument Digital Interface is a protocol that was adopted by the electronic music industry for controlling music synthesizer devices (both keyboards and sound cards). It doesn't represent music sounds directly (as is the case with AU, AIFF, and WAV), but instead, it transfers information that tells the synthesizer what to play to produce a musical composition. In a way, MIDI might be compared with vector art in that both file types consist of instructions or commands. Like a vector file, the MIDI file sizes are smaller than their counterparts because the instructions consume much less data. One drawback to the MIDI format is that it will only play instrumentals; it doesn't record voices.

MPEG   MPEG (Motion Pictures Experts Group) is both an audio and a video compression format. Refer to the video section of this chapter to learn about it.

MP3 (.mp3)   MP3 (MPEG-1 Audio Layer-3) is the most talked-about audio format on the Web today. Although it is most famous for the illegalities involved with downloading MP3s, actually MP3 is just a very efficient audio compression format. The compression ratio is 12:1, yet the original sound quality is preserved. It is an open (nonproprietary) standard, which, combined with its small file size, is the reason that it has skyrocketed in popularity on the Internet. Expect to see its use expanded to educational purposes as well.

File Download versus Inline

Linking to a sound file is the simplest way to include sound in a Web page. This method is the most appropriate to use when supplying certain types of files such as sound clips that accompany other material. Providing a link puts the control of the sound into the user's hands. When using a link, remember to include all the information about the file that is important to the audience: type of file format, file size, and estimated download time. A typical link might look like this:

<a href="boolean.wav">Hear about Boolean Logic</a>

When the user clicks on this link, either a player or a plug-in will be invoked depending on the browser and its configuration.

Sounds may also be embedded, that is, be put in line so that they are a part of your page resulting in sound playing automatically in the background when the page loads. To handle this, Netscape developed the <embed> tag, while Internet Explorer (IE) developed the <bgsound> tag. The <embed> tag is now recognized by IE browsers, while <bgsound> isn't used by Netscape. The <embed> tag offers control functionality that the <bgsound> tag doesn't, so if you choose to embed sound files in your page, stick with <embed>. Be aware that the <object> tag in HTML 4.0 has replaced this tag, but if you want to support older browsers, you'll need to remain with the deprecated tag.

If you decide to include background sound, do your audience a favor and give them the controls to turn the music on and off. What sounds great to one person's ears may sound like fingernails across the blackboard to others. Part of the coding of the <embed> tag allows the specification of a control console. Illustrated in figure 5.18 are two different control options along with the HTML source code that created them.

A third option for including sound files can be through JavaScript. The options for interaction with sound via JavaScript include having sound play when the screen loads or having it play in response to different mouse actions.

Using Existing Sound Files

If you don't have the experience or expertise to create your own audio files, many sound libraries are available on the Web for sound clips. However, be very

FIGURE 5.18
Two Control Options for Sound Files on Web Pages

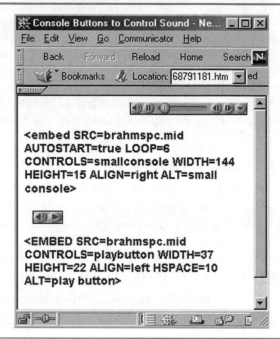

careful when downloading others' sound files; always research the copyright requirements. Copyright issues in the music industry are very complicated and are a hot topic now. Several organizations deal with various aspects of music copyright, including the ASCAP (American Society of Composers, Authors and Publishers) at http://www.ascap.com, BMI (Broadcast Music, Inc.) at http://www.bmi.com, RIAA (Recording Industry Association of America) at http://www.riaa.com, and the HFA (Harry Fox Agency, Inc.) at http://www.nmpa.org/hfa.html.

Animation

Animation can be defined as the creation of the illusion of movement. This is done through subtle changes in a sequence of stationary screen elements or images. Although motion across the screen is a primary use of animation, it also deals with any change in an object: change in brightness, color, size, shape, or into another object altogether (metamorphosis). Animation can include a variety of different media: text, vector and raster graphics, audio, and video. An animation is not just a viewable object; it can also incorporate elements of interactivity for user response.

When is animation appropriate to use? Good uses, as identified by Jakob Nielsen (2000), include to

- indicate transitions
- illustrate change over time
- show multiple information objects in the same space
- enrich graphical representations
- visualize three-dimensional structures
- attract attention

Basic Animation Concepts

In-depth instruction about animation is beyond the scope of this book. How-ever, it is helpful to become acquainted with a few key ideas so that as you look at the various animation technologies, you can recognize similarities and differ-ences in approach.

One common element of all animation is the capability to create sequential frames and then work with the timing and transition of those frames to ready them for playback. As part of this procedure, following are a few basic terms and concepts you will encounter:

Cycling (looping) This involves creating cycles of motion that end the same way they start, allowing the reuse of the cycle as many times as needed. On the Web, cycling helps keep the file size of an animation smaller, thus conserving download time.

Keyframe The animator designates specific objects at critical points on the animation time line, and the computer program then fills in the mo-tion between these frames.

Sprite This is a graphic image that can move within a larger graphic. Soft-ware that supports sprites allows the designer to create individual ani-mated images that can be combined into a larger animation.

Tweening Short for "in-betweening," this is the calculation (made by the application software) for determining the intermediate frames between two key frames to simulate motion.

Time line This is a scale measured either in seconds or frames that provides an editable, visual record of animation events. (See figure 3.8.)

The different types of animation will fall into one of two main categories: prerendered and real time. Prerendered (also called frame-by-frame) animations include those that are downloaded in their entirety to the users' computers be-fore they can be played. These typically are raster (or bitmap) in format, and so they are larger files. The real-time animations are often vector based, which means that the file being downloaded contains instructions only (meaning a much smaller file size) that the computer reads, interprets, and then renders, all on the client side.

If you are new to the world of animation, refer to the resources at the end of this book for a list of links to animation information and tutorials. In the world of computer animation, you will find that there are often overlaps of technologies. It may not be necessary to try to pigeonhole the various technologies, but be aware of the major difference between animation and video. Remember that video takes a continuous motion and breaks it down into discrete frames, while animation starts in the opposite direction with independent frames that are then put together to form the illusion of movement.

Types of Web Animation

The following subsections introduce you to some of the Web animation technologies available today. It is beneficial to have an overview of what each is designed to do because it is important to pick the right one for your purpose. Some of these animation technologies are easier to implement if you are a novice; others have a steep learning curve that requires an extensive investment of time.

Animated GIF (.gif)   Using the GIF 89a standard, a GIF image can be animated by combining several images into a single file. Animations are easy to create and are supported by most Web browsers. Because this is a GIF format, it works bests with a limited number of colors and with illustration images instead of photographic ones. There are some drawbacks; it tends to create large file sizes that don't compress very well, and it has no sound capabilities. But for small animations, it is very serviceable.

To create animated GIFs, you will need a GIF 89a generating application. Some image-editing programs include this as part of the package, or you can download a freeware or shareware application from the Web. Begin by creating several images that have identical dimensions using an imaging application. Make small changes in each image. (This is the basis for the illusion of movement.) Each of these images will become a frame in the animation. Use as few frames as possible to limit file size. Once you have opened all of your images in the GIF generating program, you will arrange them in order, set the timing for each frame, and run the optimization utility that is part of the program. The optimization program handles such tasks as generating a palette for the file based on all of the frames, applying special dithering to prevent flickering, and optimizing the frames so only areas that change from frame to frame are included. (This greatly reduces the file size.) Figure 5.19 illustrates the construction of an animated GIF from Penn State Libraries' tutorial Searching Online Databases. This animation, which is designed to help students understand Boolean logic, consists of thirty-four individual images. The individual images are displayed in the left frame, and a window for previewing the animation appears in the right frame.

MNG (.mng)   Multiple-Image Network Graphics (pronounced "ming") has been developed as the format to handle all of the multi-image capabilities that are not supported in PNG. It can be considered to be PNG's counterpart to the animated GIF. As of January 2001, the MNG specifications were upgraded and application support is starting to emerge. Its developers have included a number of features that show promise to improve on animated GIF capabilities:

FIGURE 5.19
Creation of an Animated GIF

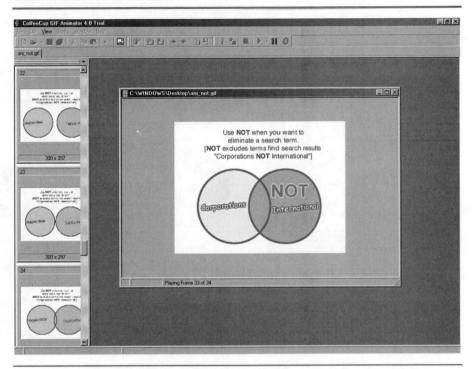

From Pennsylvania State University Libraries, Pennsylvania State University, University Park, Pa.
Available: http://www.libraries.psu.edu/crsweb/infolit/andyou/mod4/mod4main.htm. GIF Animator
by Coffee Cup. Available: http://CoffeeCup.com.

- object- or sprite-based approach to animation
- nested loops for complex animations
- integration of both PNG- and JPEG-based images
- support for transparent JPEGs
- nonpatented compression either lossless (for PNG) or lossy (for JPEG)

Although the MNG format is not a practical choice for your animation at this time because of its limited support for development and display, it is a format that you will want to keep tabs on for future consideration. For additional information, visit MNG's home page at http://www.freesoftware.com/pub/mng.

Flash (.swf)   Macromedia Flash (swf) file format has become one of the top Web animation formats. It is created by using the authoring tool Macromedia Flash software. The Macromedia Flash software is a full-featured animation authoring system. As shown in figure 5.20, the application interface has a stage to work on, a library where you store all the items that make up your animation, symbols (which are reusable entities that are stored in the library), a time line to synchronize animation frames and timings, and layers where individual items are

FIGURE 5.20
Macromedia Flash Application Interface

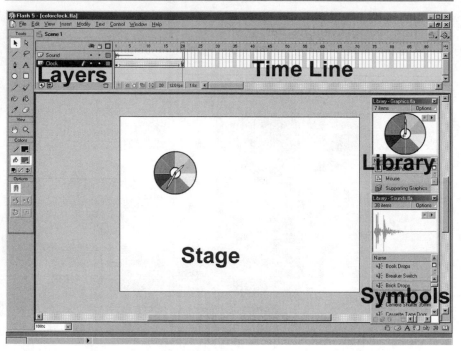

From Macromedia Flash. Available: http://www.macromedia.com/software/flash.

stacked. Flash is vector-based, which is the main reason behind its popularity. Vector-based animations are, of course, scalable and download quickly. In fact, Flash files can stream so that users don't have to wait for the entire file to download before viewing it. However, Flash is not limited to just vector graphics; it allows the incorporation of bitmaps, MP3 audio, and interactivity. Flash animations can be exported to QuickTime and RealPlayer. Flash is now an open standard rather than a proprietary one, which will help ensure its continued attractiveness. One factor that was originally a drawback was the fact that Flash files require a plug-in to play. Now the player is preinstalled on most computers and in the major browsers, so this is not as big a concern as it once was.

Flash is being used for a whole host of purposes on the Web, including educational ones. The award-winning TILT (Texas Information Literacy Tutorial) project from the University of Texas System Digital Library is a good example of the innovative animation possibilities of Flash. The engaging introduction to the subject of common Internet misconceptions in TILT is shown in figure 5.21.

Director Shockwave (.swd, .dcr)   Shockwave is designed to be highly interactive; it supports audio, animation, and video. Shockwave files are created through Macromedia's Director authoring software. Director works with the same theatrical metaphor as does Flash, with a stage, score, and cast members. Director's (and therefore Shockwave's) strength lies in its ability to create

FIGURE 5.21
Flash Animation Used in Texas Information Literacy Tutorial

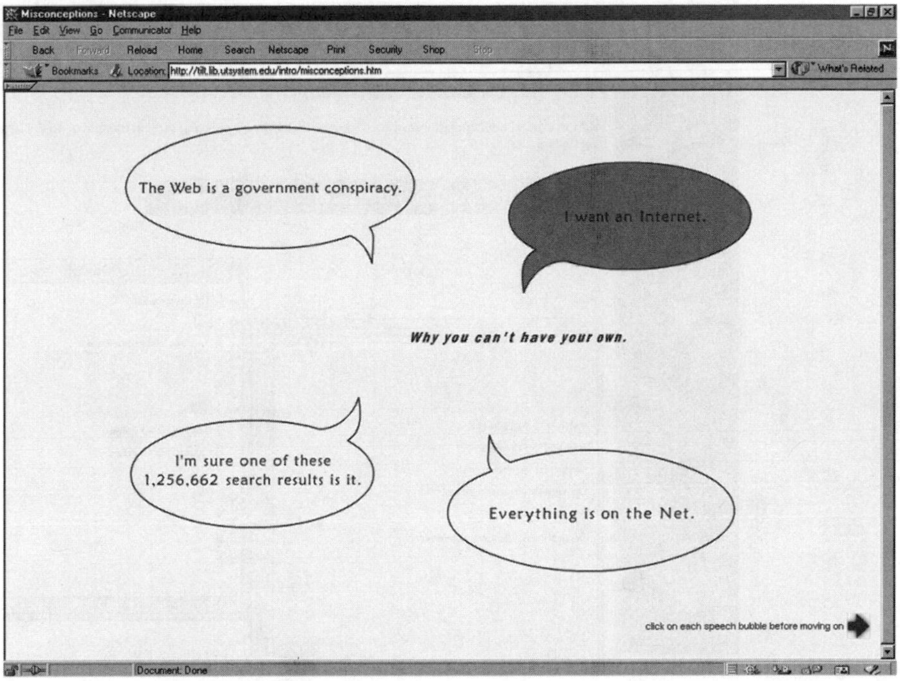

Screenshot copyright clearance received from the Digital Information Literacy Office on behalf of the University of Texas System Digital Library, Austin. Available: http://tilt.lib.utsystem.edu/intro/misconceptions.htm.

advanced interactivity. Organize and Synthesize Information, a tutorial from California Polytechnic State University, uses Shockwave to give students a high level of interactivity to reinforce the concepts being taught. The screen in figure 5.22 shows an exercise in which students organize bookmarks by moving them from one window to the other.

Which should you create—Flash or Shockwave files? Director preceded Flash and wasn't originally designed for the Web. Its main function was to create offline multimedia productions in stand-alone programs. It has a higher learning curve than does Flash and a higher price tag. However, if you are well versed in using Director, the latest versions are more Web-focused. If you are both creating for the Web and planning to publish to CD-ROM, you can do both with Director. If you are creating strictly for the Web, stick with Flash because it was designed as a Web authoring tool.

dHTML Layer-based animation (.htm, .html)   *Dynamic HTML* (dHTML) is a term used for a combination of the more recently developed HTML tags and options, including some topics that have been previously covered, such as cascading style sheets and dynamic fonts. One of the uses for dHTML is to provide animation capability. You won't be able to create the complex animation of Flash or Shockwave, but for simple animations, using dHTML works very well.

FIGURE 5.22
Director Shockwave Used in Organize and Synthesize Information Tutorial

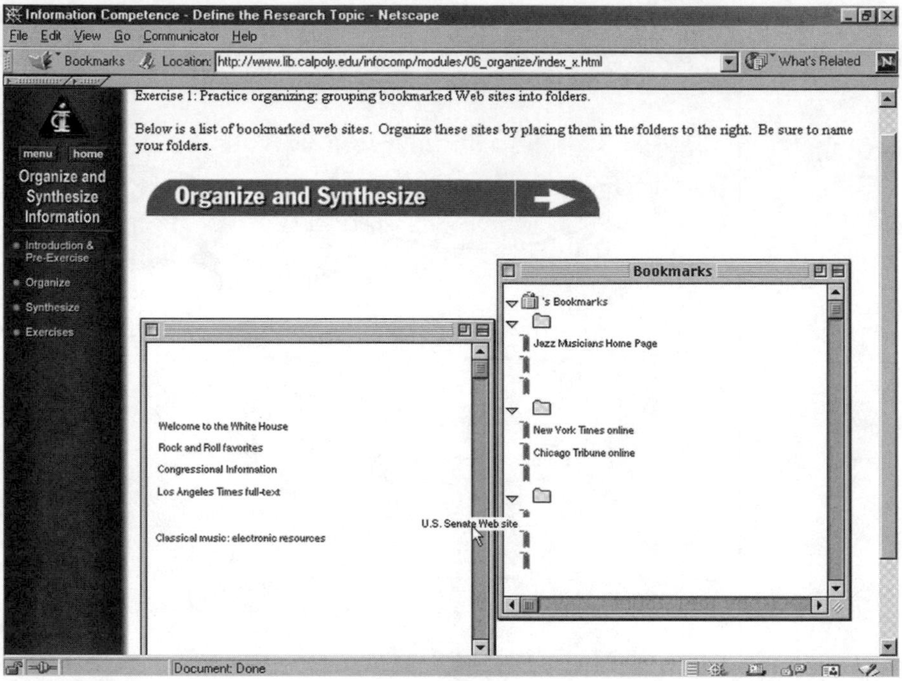

From Robert F. Kennedy Library, California Polytechnic State University, San Luis Obispo. Available: http://www.lib.calpoly.edu/infocomp/modules/06_organize/index_x.html.

Animations are created through the use of layers that can overlay other page elements and move around the screen. You can place either plain text or a graphic in a layer. Multiple layers can be created, each with its own time line and actors, behaviors, and property settings. Unless you are proficient at JavaScript, you will probably want to use a WYSIWYG Web editor to create your animations. Many Web editors incorporate this capability as illustrated by the screen shot of Macromedia Dreamweaver software shown in figure 5.23. The animation, in which one circle expands into two to highlight two important pieces of information, is constructed by placing two images, each into its own layer, and timing their entry and travel across the screen using a time line and keyframes. If you don't have access to an editor that has this capability, CNET Builder.com has an Image Mover that will build the code for you (http://www.builder.com/ Programming/Scripter/012999), but it may not supply the control you desire.

One major benefit of layer-based animation (besides the ease of authoring) is that a plug-in is not required for viewing because the animation script is part of the HTML page code. Support for layers does vary from browser to browser (layers are supported only in version 4 and above) and platform to platform, so it is important that you ascertain that your audience's browsers can interpret the

FIGURE 5.23
Macromedia Dreamweaver Used to Create Layer-Based Animation

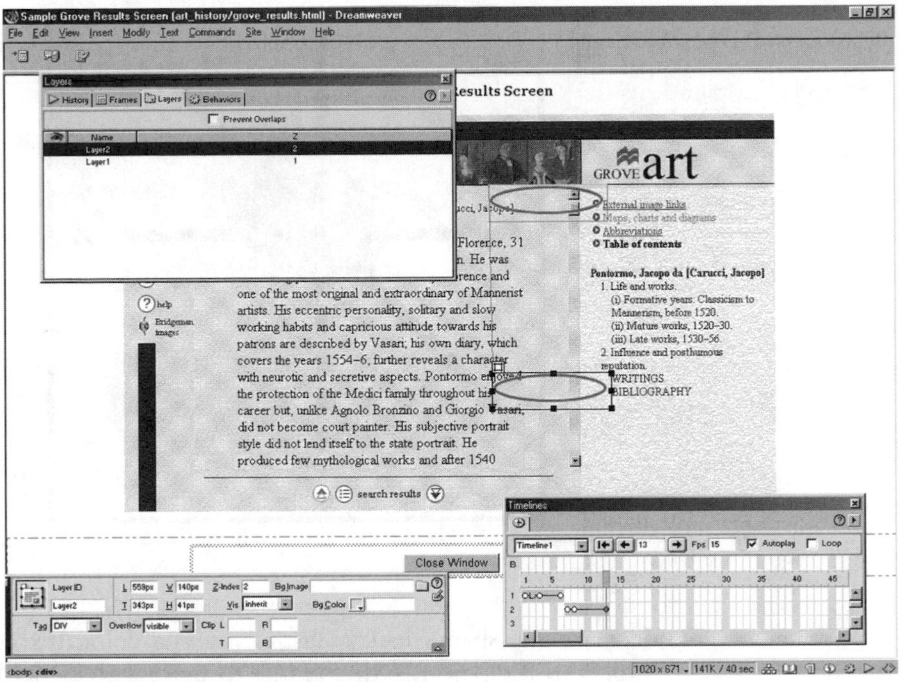

From Z. Smith Reynolds Library, Wake Forest University, Winston-Salem, N.C. Available: http://www.wfu.edu/Library/referenc/art_history/encyclopedia.htm.

code. An additional benefit of the ability to insert plain text into a dHTML animation is that the text will be able to be searched and indexed.

3-D   Three-dimensional (3-D) graphics are those that provide the perception of depth. When these graphics are animated, they can be viewed from different angles and distances. Animation is what makes 3-D objects appear real to the user. It is an effective visualization tool, but its creation requires both creativity and technical proficiency. Learning to produce 3-D objects and animations is no simple task; even with 3-D authoring software, plan on a major commitment of time. Following is a very simplistic summary of how 3-D is made:

1. Most 3-D animations start with solid geometric objects that are called *primitives* (spheres, cubes, cylinders, etc.). When thinking about 3-D, it is helpful to understand about the three dimensions of space, the x (width), y (height), and z (depth) planes. The x and y axes are the 2-D coordinates, and the z axis adds the third dimension. (See figure 5.24.) Adding the z-axis to a 2-D object is called *extrusion*.

2. Combining, resizing, or reforming the primitives can create other shapes, called *modeling*.

FIGURE 5.24
Axes of Three-Dimensional Graphics

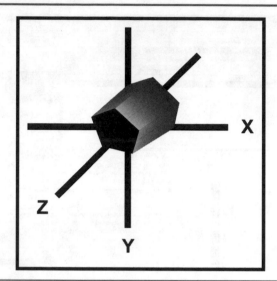

3. To make the shapes look realistic, you add color, textures, and light sources to the object. Other effects to make a shape look realistic include reflection, transparency, and smoothness.

4. You create a 3-D space by positioning the objects, light, ground plane, and sometimes a background.

5. Animation is added via a time line of movements and events.

6. The last step is to render the final scene. This is where you define the quality and type of the output.

VRML (.wrl)   Virtual Reality Modeling Language (VRML) is a screen-description language that describes the geometry and behavior of a 3-D scene or world. VRML is an open standard and is an ASCII text file, so it can be viewed in any plain-text editor. This language was originated with a goal of creating shared virtual worlds on the Internet. Using VRML, you can build a sequence of visual images with which a user can interact with a scene by viewing, moving, rotating, etc., it. VRML can range from very simple objects to complex scenes. For example, in the VRML presentation shown in figure 5.25, visitors can take a virtual tour through the IRCAM (Institut de Recherche et Coordination Acoustique/Musique) Multimedia Library. When they click on a shelf or cabinet, the call number range shelved there is displayed to the right of the scene. When they click the call range hyperlink, the individual titles are displayed in the bottom left frame.

To view VRML files, you will need a stand-alone browser or a plug-in for your Web browser. Even though it is possible to create VRML with a simple text editor, unless you are a glutton for punishment, get an integrated VRML development system that will generate the VRML for you.

FIGURE 5.25
VRML Used to Tour a Library

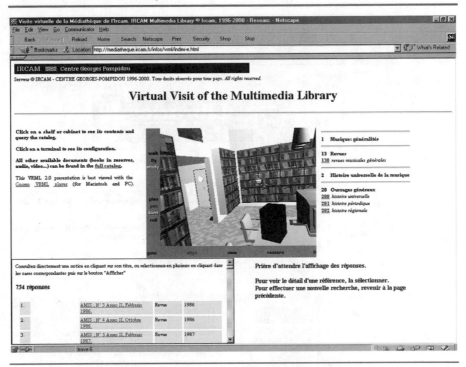

Video

Video is a multimedia format that requires careful planning to use appropriately over the Web. There are three traditional video file formats that are commonly seen on the Web: AVI (Audio Video Interleave), MPEG, and QuickTime (discussed in the following sections). All three of these are files that must be downloaded onto a user's computer before they can be viewed. Because of bandwidth constraints and the fact that video files can be quite large, it is best to incorporate video in short clips that are less than a minute long. Remember to always prepare your audience for the wait they will encounter in downloading by specifying the anticipated download time and the size of the file/playing time. For example, in the tutorial from University of Saskatchewan Libraries shown in figure 5.26, students are told at the opening screen that video clips are part of the instruction and are shown the icon that will indicate a movie is available (top screen). When students come to a screen where there is a link to the movie, they are given the anticipated download time and the length of the clip (bottom screen).

AVI (.avi)

AVI is Microsoft's proprietary video for Windows format. Because it has been a part of Windows, the majority of computer users can view it, thus its rise in pop-

FIGURE 5.26
Video File, Load-Time, and Run-Time Indicators

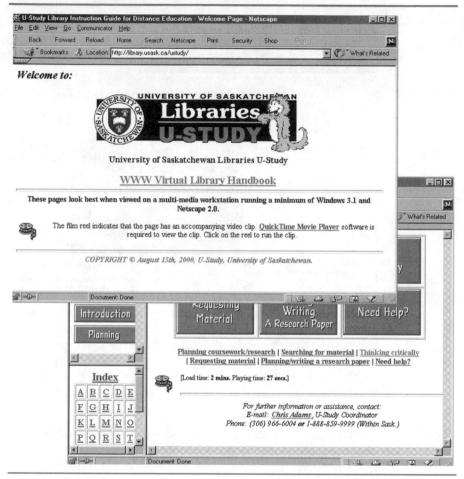

From University of Saskatchewan Libraries, Saskatoon. Available: http://library.usask.ca/ustudy.

ularity. However, although you can find plenty of AVI files on the Web, its use is declining. In fact, Microsoft is no longer supporting video for Windows and is replacing AVI with an Active Streaming Format (ASF).

QuickTime (.mov, .qt)

QuickTime, developed by Apple, is both a file format and a software architecture for multimedia development, storage, and playback. It is a technology that is extensively used by developers, and it enjoys widespread support. QuickTime movies are able to incorporate a variety of media types including audio, graphics, video, text, MPEG, vector media, VR, and 3-D—more than thirty file formats are supported (visit http://www.apple.com/quicktime/authoring/fileformats.html). This flexibility in delivery of multiple formats makes Quick-

Time very versatile. Although QuickTime was originally developed for the Macintosh, both platforms are equally well supported now. A plug-in is required for viewing QuickTime movies, but it is included as part of Netscape. IE provides its Windows Media Player, which supports QuickTime. QuickTime is now moving into streaming technology (discussed later in this chapter). Another development that is sure to keep QuickTime in the forefront is that it was selected as the format that MPEG-4 will be based upon (see MPEG later in this chapter).

QTVR

QuickTime Virtual Reality is an enhanced version of Apple's QuickTime standard. It adds the ability to tour through a virtual scene or examine 3-D objects by rotating them. A virtual scene in QTVR is a panoramic movie. Taking a series of photographs in up to a 360° range and then stitching the images together to create a photorealistic virtual reality achieves the panorama. The result is a cylinder-shaped image that surrounds the viewer, who can look in all directions, forward, backward, up, and down. Each one of these stitched photos is called a *node*, and when one or more nodes are connected, the viewer can move through the scene by clicking on designated hot spots. Harvard's Wiedener Library is a destination on the campus QTVR tour shown in figure 5.27. People can take a

FIGURE 5.27
QuickTime Virtual Reality Tour

From Wiedener Library, Harvard University, Cambridge, Mass. Available: http://www.hno.harvard. edu/tour/qtvr_tour/index.htm.

virtual tour through the library by finding the hot spot on the image or by clicking on one of seven different stops designated on the accompanying floor map. At each stop, holding down the mouse and pointing the cursor to the left or the right will offer a 360° view of the area. Navigation controls let visitors zoom in and out on each scene.

The second type of QTVR format is called an *object movie*. An object movie allows users to simulate the action of picking up an object and turning it around to view it. As with the panorama, this is done via a series of still photographs that include shots of all sides (including top and bottom) of an object. The photos are stitched together, and then they can be rotated to view the object from any direction by using a mouse. QTVR production can be expensive because it requires specialized equipment, training, and photography skills, but it can give users a very unique experience.

MPEG (.mpeg, .mpg, .mp3, .mp4)

MPEG (pronounced M-Peg) is named for the Moving Picture Experts Group, which develops standards for digital video and audio compression. MPEG is the family of standards used for coding audiovisual information in a digital compressed format. There are various MPEG codecs. Commonly used for computer videos, MPEG-1 was a standard created for use with CD-ROMs, video games, and other media that require high quality video and audio playback. It supports up to thirty frames per second (the same as a standard TV) as well as a high compression ratio. This, combined with the fact that it was designed as a digital video capture and playback technology, resulted in it becoming a popular method to deliver video content over the Web. MPEG-1 is also an audio compression standard; MP3 is part of the MPEG-1 family. MPEG-4 is being developed to become a compression standard for interactive multimedia on the Web. With MPEG-4, users will be able to interact with a scene that can be composed from real sources such as video or from synthetic ones such as vector-based objects. Authors will be able to empower users to modify scenes by deleting, adding, or repositioning objects. MPEG-4 will support scalable content. As mentioned earlier, QuickTime has been selected as the basis for starting development of the MPEG-4 standard (.mp4).

Screen-Capture Movie

Making a movie of the action that takes place over time on a computer screen is done with specialized software that acts like a video recorder. Most of this type of software also includes an audio component so that the activity that takes place on the screen can be accompanied by narration. Many of the available screen recording applications support both the AVI format and streaming technology. You may hear this type of technology referred to as "screen recording," "desktop activity recording," or "screen-capture video." One example of a popular screen capture application is Camtasia, available from http://www.camtasia.com.

Streaming Media

Streaming media is fast becoming the multimedia delivery method of choice. With streaming audio, video, and other multimedia, users can play files without waiting for a download. Streaming technology works differently from the traditional Web transaction we are used to. A normal Web transaction occurs when a user clicks on a link of some sort. The request for a file, whether it is HTML, audio, graphic, or video, is sent to a Web server. The Web server takes the request and pushes out the file as quickly as possible and then disconnects. Back at the user's end, once the client (computer) receives the file that was sent, it is disconnected from the server, and the browser and plug-ins handle the display of the file. This works fine for small files, like HTML and most graphics. However, with larger files that are the norm with audio and video, the wait for the download to take place takes too long, and users get annoyed.

With streaming media, the data is fed to the user from the server as it is viewed. So rather than a quick connect and disconnect from the server, there is a continuous connection for the duration of the delivery of the media. On the receiving side of the data feed, the computer must be able to collect the data and send it to the player as a steady stream. If the data arrives faster than required, it is stored in a buffer until it is needed.

Even though the data is being delivered in a stream and is playing as it arrives, this doesn't mean that there is no need to compress the data as it streams. A lossy compression is used to reduce file size. The result is a much smaller file size, but there is degradation in image and sound. However, the main goal of developing streaming technology was to improve access, and it does accomplish that. We will continue to see a steady improvement in the quality as the technology matures.

The basic process for creating streaming video and audio is to

- capture the video and/or audio
- digitize and edit it
- encode the digitized file with the appropriate codec
- deliver the file through a Web site

To include streaming media into a Web page, you can either provide a text or graphic link or embed the file (using the <embed> tag) into the HTML document so it is displayed as part of the Web page.

Right now, streaming technology is primarily proprietary. The three major competitors for the streaming market are RealMedia, QuickTime, and Windows Media.

RealMedia (.ram, .rpm)

RealMedia is today's leader in the streaming technology race. Its streaming media is handled through RealSystem G2 (better known as RealAudio and RealVideo) streaming-media architecture. Two different kinds of streaming are available: true streaming that requires RealServer and serverless streaming that is known as "progressive download." Using RealSystem with a server provides a much greater level of flexibility and scalability. For instance, one feature allows the creation of up to six versions of your audio and video tracks that are encoded for common user connections. RealNetworks streaming media requires a RealPlayer, which can be embedded into a Web page by the author. Real-Producer is necessary to encode streaming media. RealMedia has two versions available, one for no cost and a more highly functional one for a charge. However, some third party applications will also encode RealMedia content. Looking to the future, Real has taken an important step by becoming an early supporter of SMIL, a language designed to synchronize multimedia (discussed in a following section).

QuickTime (.mov)

Apple has arrived on the streaming-media scene later than either RealNetworks or Microsoft and so has not developed its streaming technology as fast as the others. However, QuickTime does a lot of things very well, so you shouldn't dismiss it from consideration. If for no other reason, it has potential because of the number of file formats QuickTime supports. Also, as previously mentioned, QuickTime is deeply involved with the development of the MPEG-4 standard, which will incorporate streaming technology. Streaming QuickTime is viewed through QuickTime 4. Content can be created using QuickTime Pro. As with RealMedia, QuickTime streaming media can be delivered via a server or in "pseudo" streaming form from a regular Web server. Currently, Apple has released its streaming server technology as an open source.

Windows Media (.asf, .asx)

Microsoft's entry into the streaming media mix is called Advanced Streaming Format (ASF). ASF does require a server component (Windows Media Services streaming server) for delivery of the file. However, the tools to create, serve, and play ASF content are available at no charge from Microsoft's Web site. The player that is needed to play ASF is Windows Media Player, and Windows Media Tools is the production module. Windows Media does not support as many file types as does QuickTime, but it does recognize AVI, WAV, MP3, and MPEG, which covers a good portion of the most popular formats.

SMIL   Synchronized Multimedia Integration Language (.smi, pronounced "smile") is a markup language developed by a group coordinated by W3C. SMIL is written as an XML (Extensible Markup Language) application and is currently a W3C recommendation. Its purpose is to give Web authors a way to define and synchronize multimedia elements. Until now, separate multimedia elements could be incorporated in the same page, but it was almost impossible to control the sequence and timing of when each would play. A SMIL presentation is its own document that looks similar to HTML. The head of the document contains information about the layout of the presentation. The body is a collection of components placed in a certain order. These components can have different media types such as audio, video, image, or text. They can appear sequentially or can run parallel (concurrently). Although the language has been constructed so that it can be authored in a text editor, HTML editors are now adding support for the SMIL tags so that it is no more necessary to know every SMIL tag than it is to know HTML. Vendors are also developing SMIL authoring tools. A SMIL player is required for viewing presentations, but again, players are available and both QuickTime and RealPlayer support SMIL. For detailed information on SMIL, including available development tools, visit the W3C site at http://www.w3.org/AudioVideo.

NOTES

Newby, T. J., D. A. Stepich, J. D. Lehman, and J. D. Russell. 1996. *Instructional Technology for Teaching and Learning: Designing Instruction, Integrating Computers, and Using Media.* Englewood Cliffs, N.J.: Prentice-Hall.

Nielsen, J. 2000. *Designing Web Usability: The Practice of Simplicity.* Indianapolis, Ind.: New Riders.

6

Interactivity

Research tells us that students have better retention and understanding when they are involved in active learning environments. Active learning takes place when a student is more than just a spectator and becomes a participant in the instructional process. With Web-based instruction, active learning is encouraged through the incorporation of interactivity. A very simple definition of *interactivity* is "a dialog that occurs between a human being and a computer." It's easy to see that this can encompass a wide range of possibilities when you start to ponder what forms interactive Web-based instruction can take. It can mean that the student has some level of control over the sequence, pace, and content of the instruction; additionally, on a higher level, the student can act on information and transform it into having some personal meaning. This chapter takes an in-depth look at interactivity as it applies to Web-based instruction, including

- categories of interaction
- interactivity methods
- interactivity languages and technologies
- tools for interactive development by nonprogrammers

CATEGORIES OF INTERACTION

Many different kinds of interaction possibilities on the Web are accomplished through a variety of technologies, both synchronous (same time, different place) and asynchronous (different time, different place). It is helpful to become familiar with the possible types of interactivity. Kathy Rutkowski (2001) identifies five major categories of interaction that take place on the Web: social, information transfer, remote access, knowledge building, and virtual experiences.

Social Interaction

The social category of interaction includes the various methods of communication that take place on different levels, both person-to-person (student-to-student and instructor-to-student) and in groups. Because a Web tutorial is a remote learning experience, it is important to provide avenues for participants to become acquainted and comfortable with the instructor and other students, particularly with classes that extend into multiple sessions. Social interaction can be accomplished through e-mail, online chats, and online discussion forums. The screen shot shown in figure 6.1 is from an online Internet surfing skills course. It shows how a discussion forum was used as a means for the instructor and students to introduce themselves and become better acquainted.

FIGURE 6.1
Social Interaction through a Discussion Forum

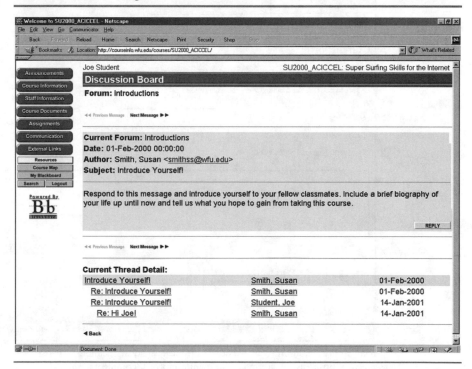

From Wake Forest University, Winston–Salem, N.C. Available: http://courseinfo.wfu.edu/courses/ SU2000_ACICCEL.

Information Transfer Interaction

Information transfer encompasses all of the ways that data, information, and knowledge are swapped. It can be a one-sided delivery of information or a two-way exchange. Information transfer can take place on an individual level or for an entire group. It can be solicited from students by the instructor via such tools as a survey, test, or request for feedback, or it can be delivered to students in the form of online lectures. For example, InfoTrekk, an information literacy tutorial, includes a feedback form on the first page of the tutorial. (See figure 6.2.) This is a straightforward way to solicit an exchange of information from the user to the tutorial developers.

FIGURE 6.2
Information Transfer through Use of a Feedback Form

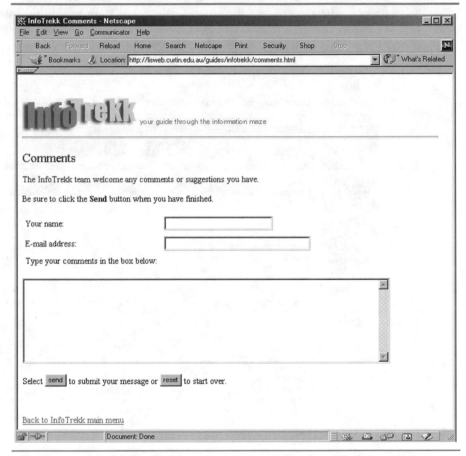

From Library and Information Services, Curtin University of Technology, Perth, Western Australia. Available: http://lisweb.curtin.edu.au/guides/infotrekk/comments.html.

Remote Access Interaction

The Web can be used to connect users to remote sites where they can interact with other systems. An example of this category of interaction is the ability to provide real-time skills practice with remote databases. In the example shown in figure 6.3, students link directly to Bell & Howell's ProQuest and can execute actual searches.

FIGURE 6.3
Remote Access to a Database

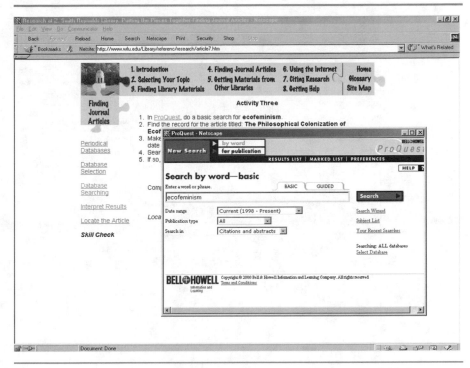

From Z. Smith Reynolds Library, Wake Forest University, Winston–Salem, N.C. Available: http://
www.wfu.edu/Library/referenc/research/article7.htm.

Knowledge Building Interaction

Knowledge building offers the opportunity for higher-level active learning experiences. In this category, students use interactivity to construct new knowledge through a variety of means. It can take place at an individual level or through interaction with a group of people. Teaching students to develop their critical thinking skills is one example of knowledge building. In the exercise shown in figure 6.4, students learn how to formulate effective search strategies by brainstorming for synonyms, alternate spellings, abbreviations, and acronyms (left column). Then the screen compares those entries with its recommendations. Knowledge building can be facilitated through the use of many interactivity methods including discussions, conferences, collaboration, and training.

Virtual Experiences Interaction

A virtual experience can be as basic as interacting in a virtual classroom, a space that is designated for people to come together for an educational purpose. Participants are distributed in different geographic areas but come together in real

FIGURE 6.4
Knowledge Building through Formulating Search Strategies

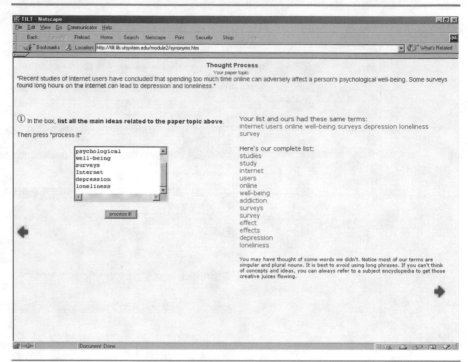

Screenshot copyright clearance received from the Digital Information Literacy Office on behalf of the University of Texas System Digital Library, Austin. Available: http://tilt.lib.utsystem.edu/module2/synonyms.htm.

time to learn. Some of the typical vehicles for a virtual experience are a chat room or a MOO. MOOs are virtual online environments designed for live interaction and collaboration. MOO stands for *multiuser domain* (which means that many users can log on simultaneously), *object-oriented* (which refers to the type of program the MOO core uses). Although MOOs are primarily text-based at this point, Web and VRML interfaces are being developed so that they are becoming more graphically oriented. Café Moolano, shown in figure 6.5, is an example of an educational MOO that provides online meeting space for instructors and students. The other major means to a virtual experience is through VRML-constructed Web spaces.

INTERACTIVITY METHODS

The decision about what level and types of interactivity to include in your tutorial will be influenced by the scope and goals of your project as well as the expertise of your development staff. However, there are simple, straightforward ways to incorporate interactivity into your instruction. The following subsec-

FIGURE 6.5
Virtual Experiences Designed for Live Interaction and Collaboration

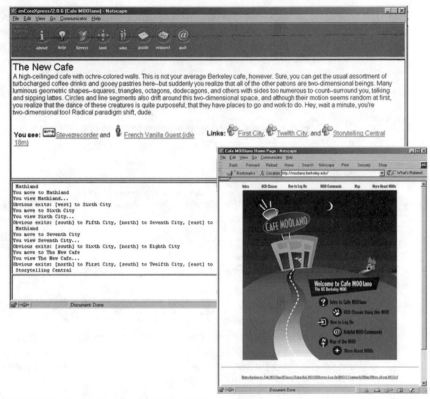

From University of California-Berkeley. Available: Web interface: http://moolano.berkeley.edu:7000; Telenet interface: telnet://moolano.berkeley.edu 8888.

tions explore some common methods that are used to integrate interactivity: basic hyperlink interaction, communication, forms, skills practice, interactive animations, image rollovers, and database connectivity.

Basic Hyperlink Interaction

At the most elementary level, point-and-click hypertext is a form of interaction. With a hyperlink, the user makes a conscious choice to go in a certain direction or take an alternate path. In a tutorial, including a clickable table of contents, navigation buttons, and text provides a low level of self-direction to the student. However, it is such a common function on any Web page that incorporating hyperlinks alone should not be considered a sufficient interactive solution.

There are ways, however, to use simple hyperlinks creatively to establish an element of interactivity. Bowling Green State University Libraries used hyper-

FIGURE 6.6
Hyperlinks to Create Interactivity in a Library Catalog Tutorial

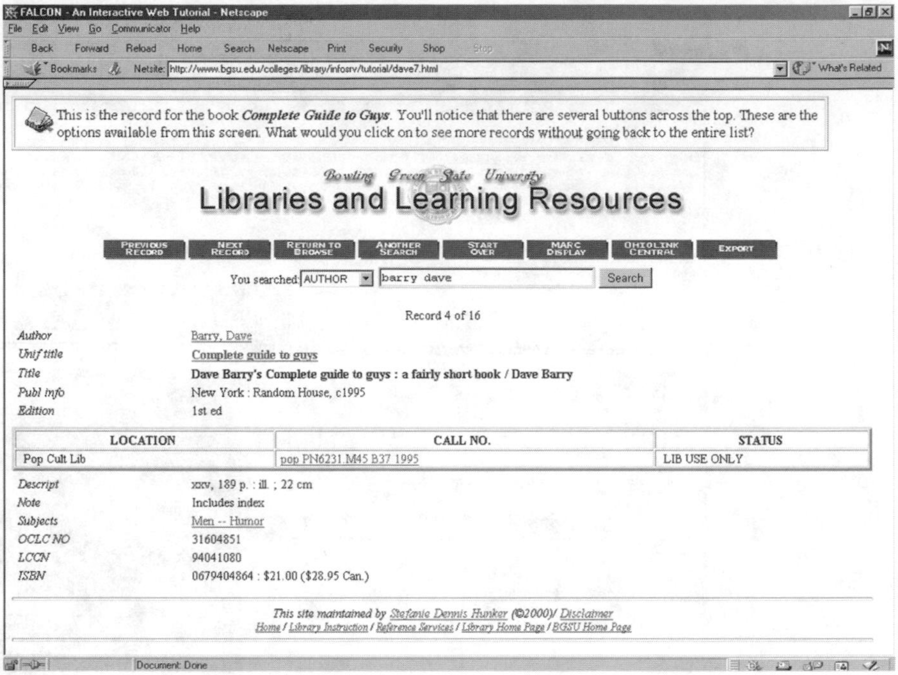

From Bowling Green State University, Bowling Green, Ohio. Available: http://www.bgsu.edu/
colleges/library/infosrv/tutorial/dave7.html.

links in their library catalog tutorial as the vehicle for movement through the
screens. (See figure 6.6.) On each screen, a question is posed, and students respond to it by clicking on hypertext or an image link. If they make the correct
choice, they are taken to the next step in the tutorial. If they select an incorrect
link, an information screen is displayed that directs them back to the previous
screen.

Another innovative example can be found in Irwin Library's Library Basics
tutorial. (See figure 6.7.) In an exercise to test understanding of call numbers,
students are asked to click on the appropriate shelf location for a certain call
number. When the student clicks on any of four possibilities, a pop-up window
opens and tells whether the choice was right or wrong.

Communication

Online communications can take different forms. This section identifies the
major types of communication that have potential usefulness in a tutorial: e-mail,
discussion forums, chat, and conferencing.

FIGURE 6.7
Image Map with Hyperlinks to Provide an Interactive Activity

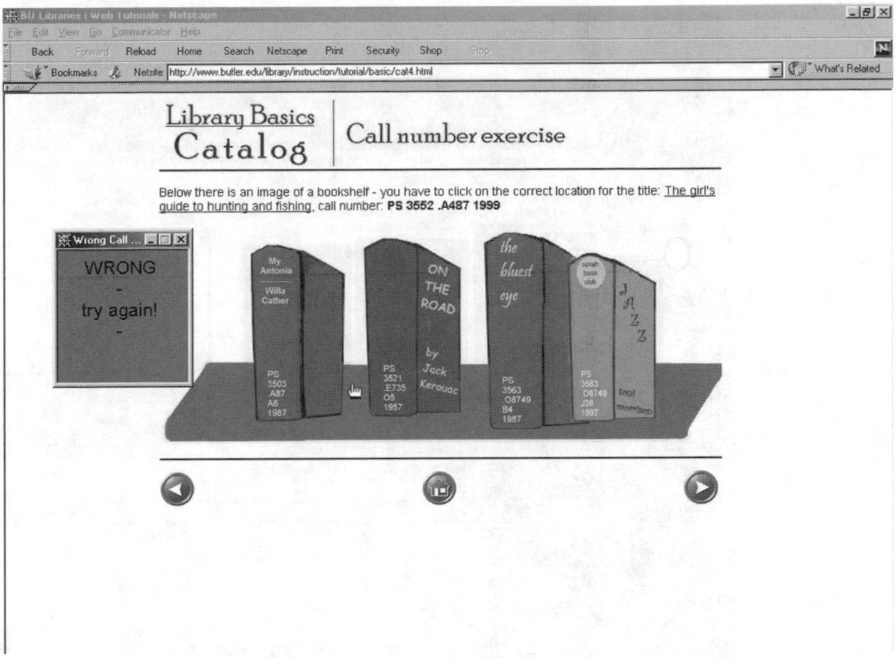

From Irwin Library, Butler University, Indianapolis, Ind. Available: http://www.butler.edu/library/instruction/tutorial/basic/cat4.html.

E-mail

E-mail is one of the most straightforward methods of online communication. With a simple *mailto:* link, students can easily establish access to the instructor. (For example, in figure 6.8 the instructor has provided e-mail links to herself in three different locations to encourage students to contact her with any questions or comments. E-mail is an asynchronous technique, meaning that students can initiate communications with instructors at a time convenient to them (often after the midnight hour). If you are creating a multiple-session course, supplying e-mail links for all the class members can help promote student-to-student interaction.

Discussion Forum

Setting up online discussion forums can be an effective method for facilitating information transfer, idea sharing, and collaboration. This sort of communication works well in a multisession course to stimulate class interaction. The instructor establishes a discussion topic, and participants respond to it and to

FIGURE 6.8
E-Mail Links to an Instructor

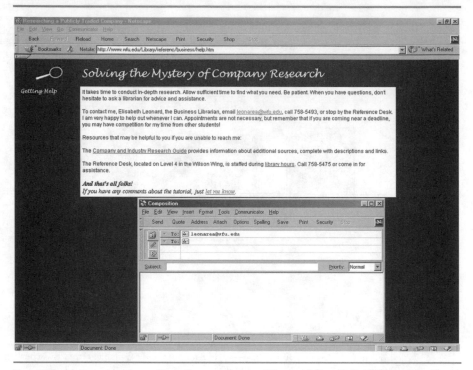

From Z. Smith Reynolds Library, Wake Forest University, Winston–Salem, N.C. Available: http://www.wfu.edu/Library/referenc/business/help.htm.

each other's responses, creating what is called a discussion thread. Figure 6.9 pictures the main screen of a course's discussion forum. Each topic of discussion is shown on the screen, and students click on one of the hyperlinks to enter a specific forum to participate. A discussion board is a built-in feature in many course shell applications such as this one by Blackboard. It is an asynchronous form of communication.

Chat

A chat program is one where two or more people are connected online via chat software and type in text that is transmitted to the other person's computer screen. There are different situations where real-time communication may be appropriate or necessary: Students who are located in different geographical regions may be involved in a group project and need to meet to talk with each other, or the instructor may determine that it is beneficial for the class members to meet with each other in a real-time situation. There is also the possibility that the instructor may want to establish "office hours" so that a student can talk with him or her. Using a chat program for these and other uses is a simple

FIGURE 6.9
Discussion Forum as a Communication Method

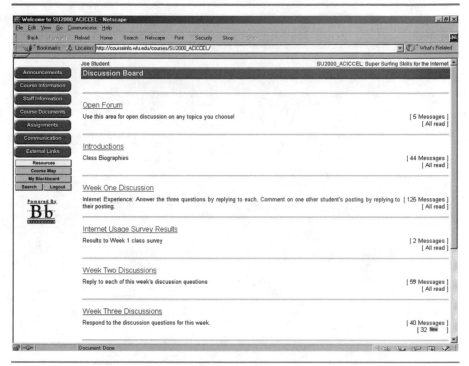

From Wake Forest University, Winston–Salem, N.C. Available: http://courseinfo.wfu.edu/courses/
SU2000_ACICCEL.

way to make it possible. For example, Florida Distance Learning Reference and
Referral Center uses a chat program to aid instruction to distance education students on specific research databases and methods. (See figure 6.10.)

Conferencing

Conferencing takes real-time communication a step farther by incorporating
audio and video capability. Some conferencing software applications also
incorporate other features that facilitate online collaboration. For instance,
Microsoft NetMeeting (http://www.microsoft.com/windows/netmeeting) includes a white board, file transfer, and the ability to demonstrate or share control of a software application.

Forms

Forms are used to provide a variety of types of interactions. They can include text
fields, buttons, check boxes, radio buttons, and drop-down lists. This variety of
choices opens the way for multiple possibilities. Online forms can be programmed
to process information that is made available to the instructor, or they can be designed to give immediate feedback to the student. Forms don't necessarily have to

FIGURE 6.10
Chat Program for Real-Time Distance Learning Communication

From Florida Distance Learning Reference and Referral Center, University of South Florida, Tampa.
Available: http://www.rrc.usf.edu/chat/index.html.

be scripted to gather and transmit information; there are many examples of forms that are meant to be printed out by students for offline work to be subsequently turned in to the instructor in the old fashioned way: hard copy. This section identifies some popular uses of forms for interaction: feedback, questionnaires and surveys, learning experiences, self-assessment, tests, and evaluation.

Feedback

Using a form to solicit feedback is a common use. (See figure 6.2.) This can be helpful for the evaluation of your tutorial. It can also provide an alternative way for students to communicate (perhaps in an anonymous fashion) about any concerns.

Questionnaires and Surveys

An online questionnaire can be a good tool to conduct a survey of your students. It can be valuable for gathering opinions and views from students. Surveys can be very helpful for assessing such things as student demographics including skill base, previous library experience, and level of subject interest and knowledge. The preinstruction survey shown in figure 6.11 was a constructive tool to assess the existing business knowledge and library and Internet research experience of students in a survey business course prior to their working through a Web tutorial to teach business research skills. Results helped the instructor to determine the knowledge base of class members.

FIGURE 6.11
Online Survey Using Forms

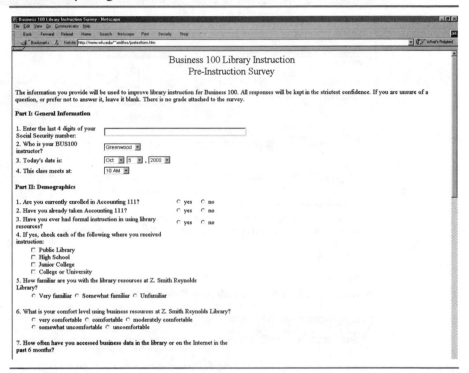

From Wake Forest University, Winston–Salem, N.C. Available : http://www.wfu.edu/~smithss/
pretestform.htm.

Learning Experiences

Many tutorials incorporate forms as a means to provide an interactive learning experience. One common use of form technology is to construct a page that mimics an actual database interface. This type of use is a fairly simple method of producing a simulation for exercise purposes, which will be discussed in greater detail in the next subsection on skills practice. For example, in the tutorial shown in figure 6.12, a form text field is used to simulate the data entry field for an author search of the library catalog.

Another use includes completing a form in a knowledge-building lesson. In figure 6.13, by completing a form, students work through an activity that will teach them to think through a research question and prepare a search strategy. In this case, there are no right or wrong answers; students use the text boxes to record their responses. Once the form is submitted, it can be printed or saved to disk.

FIGURE 6.12
Exercise Using Forms in Library Catalog Tutorial

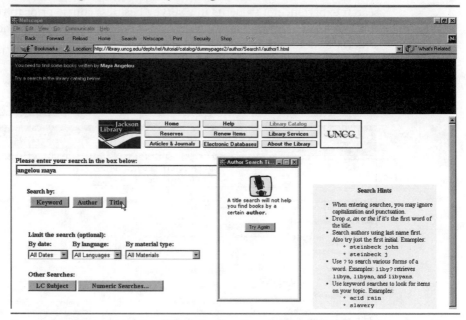

From Jackson Library, University of North Carolina–Greensboro. Available: http://library.uncg.edu/ depts/ref/tutorial/catalog/dummypages2/author/Search1/author1.html.

FIGURE 6.13
Activity Using Forms for Developing Research Strategies

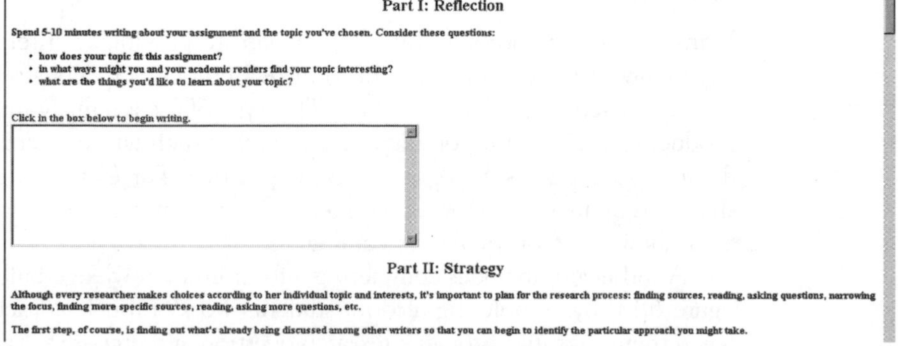

From Washington State University Libraries, Pullman. Available: http://www.systems.wsu.edu/ usered/act1.htm.

Self-Assessment

One of the most popular uses of forms is as a self-assessment tool. These forms are scripted to accept input from students and return immediate feedback to them that help them evaluate whether they have grasped the concepts being taught. With this type of form, the results are communicated only to the person taking the assessment; a score is not sent to the instructor. Often self-assessments are programmed to permit the student to retake the assessment until all questions have been correctly answered. For example, in the University of California, Santa Cruz, NetTrail online literacy courses, students are given exercises to assess if they have learned what has been taught. As shown in figure 6.14, if the student misses a question, he or she is apprised of this and afforded the opportunity to try again until the correct answer is given. The instructor is notified that the exercise was successfully completed.

Tests

Creating a test to assess student learning is another common use for a form. Often the form can be scripted so that test answers are submitted to a database, which can be programmed to grade it and track students' grades. Most of

FIGURE 6.14
Self-Assessment Using Forms

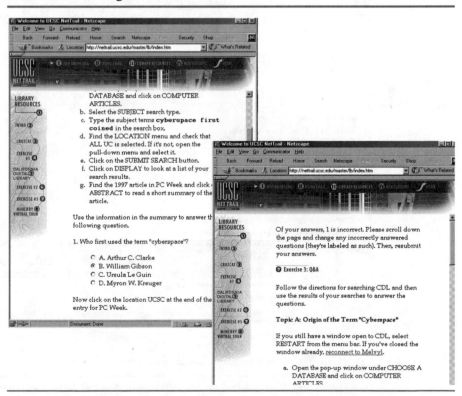

From University of California, Santa Cruz. Available: http://nettrail.ucsc.edu/master/index.htm.

the major course shells are equipped with this capability. For example, at the University of Wisconsin–Parkside, new students are required to take an information literacy tutorial and pass six quizzes to fulfill the school's general education requirement. (Part of a quiz is shown in the top window in figure 6.15.) Students can take each quiz up to five times, but a score of at least 80 percent must be achieved on each to pass. The quizzes were created and are stored in WebCT, a course shell. Once a student submits a quiz, it is automatically graded. The student can view the results and keep track of his or her score on all six modules (lower right window in figure 6.15).

Course Evaluation

A course-evaluation form can be developed as a tool to measure the success of your online instruction. As shown in figure 6.16, each module in net.TUTOR includes an evaluation form so that students can rate the tutorial. It is important to find out students' reactions to the experience, particularly if you are instruct-

FIGURE 6.15
Testing Using Forms

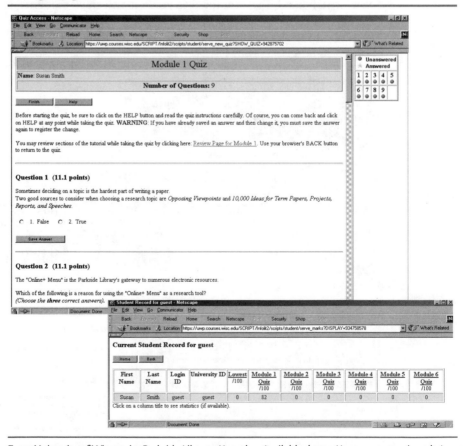

From University of Wisconsin–Parkside Library, Kenosha. Available: https://uwp.courses.wisc.edu/webct/public/show_courses.pl.

FIGURE 6.16
Evaluations Using Forms

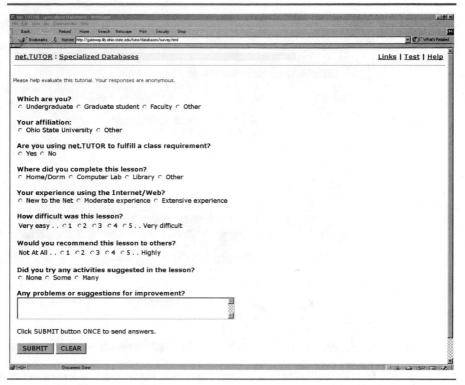

From Ohio State University Libraries, Columbus. Available: http://gateway.lib.ohio-state.edu/tutor/
databases/survey.html.

ing distance-education students with whom you have no personal contact. A
course-evaluation form is a type of feedback mechanism, but it is normally designed to be more structured than simply having a text field in which comments
can be made.

Skills Practice

One of the proven methods of promoting learning retention is to provide a
method for students to practice newly learned skills. The two most common
means of accomplishing this in a Web tutorial are programming a simulation
and establishing real-time connections to actual databases.

Simulations

Simulations work well in a variety of situations. A simulation has the look and
feel of the actual resource being studied, but it provides a controlled experience.
Simulations can be scripted to force users to make the right choice before being
allowed to proceed further in the tutorial. In the tutorial about finding journal

FIGURE 6.17
Skills Practice through Simulation of Database Searches

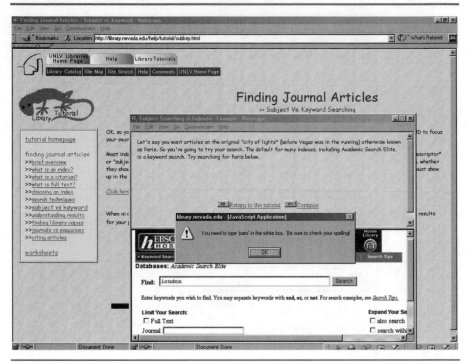

From University of Nevada Las Vegas Libraries. Available: http://library.nevada.edu/help/tutorial/subkey.html.

articles shown in figure 6.17, students are taught about subject versus keyword searching and are guided through a practice session with a simulation of conducting a search in Academic Search Elite from EBSCOhost. When students click on a hyperlink in the tutorial, a pop-up window displays. The window is divided into two frames, with directions for completing the exercise in the top frame and a simulation of the database in the bottom frame. If the wrong information is typed into the text field, a warning is displayed with a suggestion for correcting the error.

Another example of an interesting use of simulation is shown in figure 6.18. The tutorial, created using Macromedia Authorware, combines animation and interactivity to engage and guide nursing students through a simulated experience as they learn to search the MEDLINE database in EBSCOhost. Simulations are also a good choice if remote access to actual resources is not available. In this case, a simulation allows the tutorial to be used without having to worry about what access restrictions have been placed on the resources being studied. Many of the tutorials shown in the figures for searching databases include simulations.

FIGURE 6.18
Skills Practice through Simulation Created in Macromedia Authorware

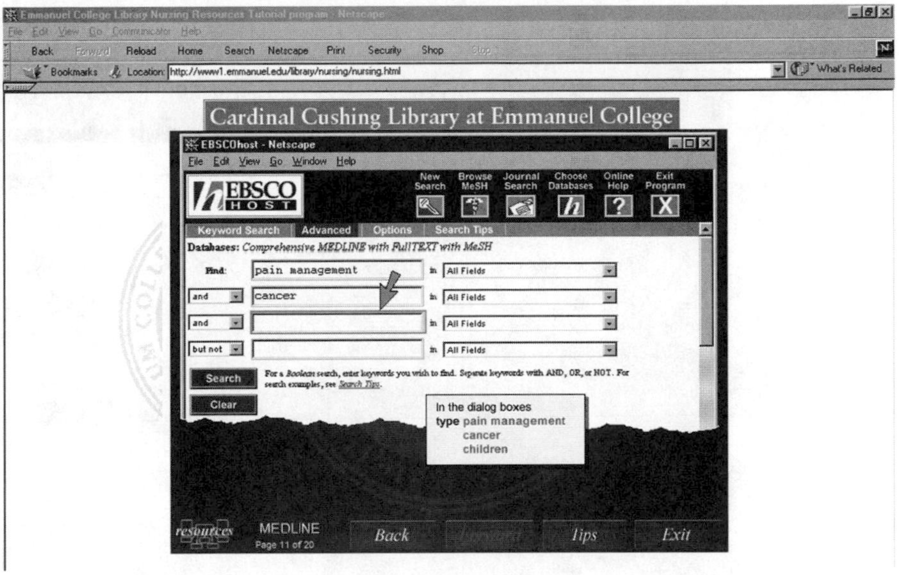

From Cardinal Cushing Library, Emmanuel College, Boston, Mass. Available: http://www1.
emmanuel.edu/library/nursing/nursing.html.

Live Access

When done properly, incorporating the ability for students to practice real-time in a live database is an effective way to provide reinforcement. When planning a live interaction, it is important to make sure that students don't become disoriented or lost by sending them out of the instruction environment totally. As mentioned in chapter 4, many designers use frames (as in figure 6.19) or pop-up windows (as in figure 6.3) to introduce external applications or resources so that students remain in the tutorial while accessing the live resources. In the tutorial on patent searching shown in figure 6.19, the designer has provided access to Delphion's Intellectual Property Network so that students can conduct an actual patent search. Instructions are displayed in the left frame, and the Delphion site is loaded in the right frame. Students can search the database and still remain inside the tutorial. When they have finished practicing, they are returned to the main tutorial when the "close" button is clicked.

Interactive Animations

Chapter 5 explored several types of animation that included interactive capabilities. Included in this category were Flash and Shockwave. These types of multimedia can add a sophisticated, engaging level of interactivity to a tutorial. They can be used to build simulations (see figure 6.18) or to create interactive

FIGURE 6.19
Skills Practice through Live Access

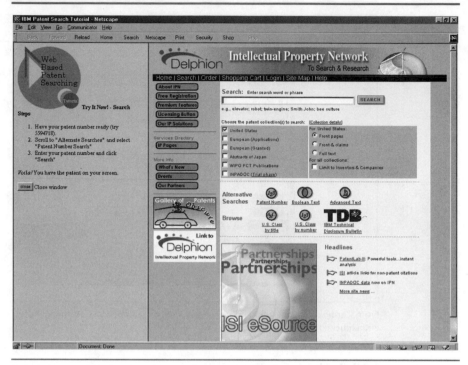

From Science and Engineering Library, University of California, San Diego. © The Regents of the University of California. Available: http://scilib.ucsd.edu/howto/guides/patsearch.

activities that help teach concepts and critical thinking. Figure 6.20 is an example of an exercise in an organize and synthesize information tutorial in which students attempt to organize information by moving notes into the correct order in an outline. They pick up the note by clicking on the mouse and then drag it and drop it into position. Students have complete control over the positioning of each note.

Image Rollovers

Although rollovers are typically used to attract attention in a navigation system, they can offer a level of interactivity for active learning exercises also. In figure 6.21, an example from the Texas Information Literacy Tutorial, rollovers are used to explain the structure of URLs. Students pass their mouse over each section of a URL, and the meaning is displayed.

Database Connectivity

Depending on the scope of your Web instruction project, you may find that you want to turn to a database solution. If you are planning on tracking test scores or

FIGURE 6.20
Interactive Movement to Organize Notes

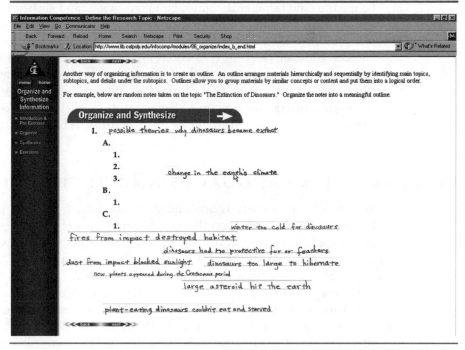

From California Polytechnic State University, San Luis Obispo. Available: http://www.lib.calpoly.edu/infocomp/modules/06_organize/index_b_end.html.

FIGURE 6.21
Rollovers Used in a URL Exercise

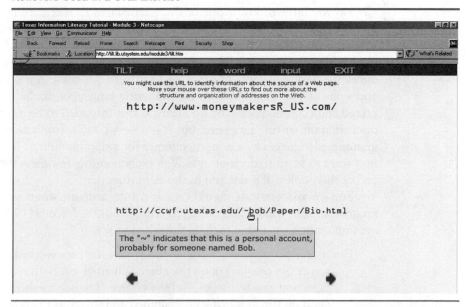

Screenshot copyright clearance received from the Digital Information Literacy Office on behalf of the University of Texas System Digital Library, Austin. Available: http://tilt.lib.utsystem.edu/module3/tilt.htm.

progress of students, a database will facilitate the collection of data and data analysis and can make that data available to the students online. A database can be used to establish user accounts, build quiz pools, and authenticate access. If you are going to consider implementing a database for these functions, there are many to choose from with a wide range of prices. As with other software choices, consider platform restrictions and complexity. If building a database from scratch and programming the interaction is beyond your team's technical capabilities, keep in mind that course-shell software programs use databases to accomplish interactive functions. For example, Blackboard's CourseInfo uses MySQL, a free database (http://www.mysql.com) as its back-end application.

INTERACTIVITY LANGUAGES AND TECHNOLOGIES

Web-based interactivity is accomplished most often via Web programming languages. The most common (but not the only) types of Web programming languages used to accomplish this are known as script languages. A simple definition of a script language from Whatis.com (http://whatis.com) is "a program or sequence of instructions that is *interpreted* or carried out by another program rather than by the computer processor." Traditional programming languages (like C++) are *compiled*, meaning that the instructions or commands are transformed into machine language that is read by the processor. This results in a program that is executed much faster than one composed in a script language, but it is much more complex to write. In contrast, a script language is designed to encourage rapid development because it is easier to learn and faster to code than is a traditional language. Script languages are often called "glue" languages because they excel at gluing separate application components together—often necessary when bringing interactivity to a Web page.

Do you have to know one of these languages to integrate interactive elements into your tutorial? Of course not. (We will look at tools for nonprogrammers shortly.) However, it is useful to have an understanding of the different methods used to program dynamic, interactive Web sites. This section introduces the basic concepts of scripting (writing a program in a script language) and some of the common Web programming languages, including both interpreted and compiled ones. By no means is this intended to be a comprehensive discussion on writing programs, but it is a very basic introduction to Web programming languages by a nonprogrammer to nonprogrammers. If you think you may want to learn to do your own Web programming, resources included at the end of this book will point you in the right direction.

Some considerations should be taken into account when selecting a Web programming language. According to Ford, Wells, and Wells (1996), issues that are important to examine include the following:

> *Power and performance* Scripted tasks have to be executed either on the server (server-side) or on the client (client-side). Both ways have advantages and disadvantages, and the choice of which method to use will depend on the task being programmed and the power necessary to execute

the program and how these requirements will affect its performance. Again, you must consider the specifications of the computers your users will be using, the network connectivity, and the server capabilities.

Platform independence As with HTML, you don't want to have to worry whether the application you create can function on a specific operating system. Your application should be platform independent. If that is not possible, then be sure to choose a language that will work with your existing system.

Preserving intellectual property Many of the script languages can easily be read by viewing the source of an HTML page. If this is a concern, you may want to consider using a language that will offer some protection of your intellectual property.

Safety Creating a safe environment for your users as well as your data and server is very important. Some languages are safer than others, so this is something you should research.

Web Programming Languages

A few prevalent languages like Perl and JavaScript have become familiar to Web designers. However, these are not the only Web programming languages out there. The following subsections, presented here in alphabetical order, briefly describe several languages that are used in Web programming. Refer to figure 6.22 for a comparison of the languages introduced.

ActiveX

ActiveX Microsoft's answer to Sun Microsystems' Java technology. It is used to create a component called an ActiveX Control (similar to a Java applet). A control is a self-sufficient program that can run on an ActiveX network (Windows and Macintosh only). An ActiveX control is a Dynamic Link Library module (.dll). Microsoft maintains an ActiveX Control Web site at http://www.microsoft.com/com/tech/ActiveX.asp.

Java

Java really isn't considered a scripting language, but it is included here because it is so closely associated with Web interactivity. Java is much closer to being a full-featured programming language than are the script languages. It was developed specifically as an Internet application by Sun Microsystems and is platform independent. It can be used to create complete applications or to build small application modules called applets. One use of an applet is shown in figure 6.23. When a user clicks in one of the check boxes (lower right screen), he or she is advanced to a module on that particular topic. An applet is sent along with a Web page to a user. Applets can perform different tasks, such as animations or calculations, without the user having to send data back to the server. In an

FIGURE 6.22
Web Programming Languages Comparison Chart

LANGUAGE	PLATFORM SUPPORT	LOCATION	TYPE	FILE EXTENSION	NOTES
ActiveX	Windows/ Macintosh	Downloads from server to client	Compiled	.dll	Developed by Microsoft ActiveX control is similar to Java applet
Java	Platform independent	Can be client-side or server-side	Compiled	.class (compiled) .jav, .java (source code)	Developed by Sun Microsystems Write small programs called applets (which run on clients) and servlets (which run on server)
JavaScript	Platform independent	Can be client-side or server-side	Interpreted	.js	Developed by Netscape
Jscript	Multiplatform	Can be client-side or server-side	Interpreted	.js	Developed by Microsoft Microsoft's equivalent to JavaScript
Lingo	Windows, Macintosh	Downloads from server to client	Compiled	.dcr, .swd	Developed by Macromedia Specific to Director
Perl	UNIX, Macintosh, Windows	Server-side	Interpreted, but can be compiled	.pl	Used often to write CGI scripts Open source, freely available
PHP	Cross-platform	Server-side	Interpreted	.php, .php3, .phtml	Chiefly used on Linux Web servers Developed strictly to serve Web pages Open source, freely available
Python	Multiplatform	Server-side	Interpreted but can be compiled	.py, .pyc (compiled)	Copyrighted but freely usable and distributable

LANGUAGE	PLATFORM SUPPORT	LOCATION	TYPE	FILE EXTENSION	NOTES
Tcl	Multiplatform	Server-side	Interpreted	.tcl	Often used for CGI scripting Open source, freely available
VBScript	Cross-platform	Can be client-side or server-side	Interpreted	.vbs	Developed by Microsoft Subset of Visual Basic Freely available Comparable to JavaScript Not supported by Netscape

FIGURE 6.23
Java Applets Used in a Library Information Access Tutorial

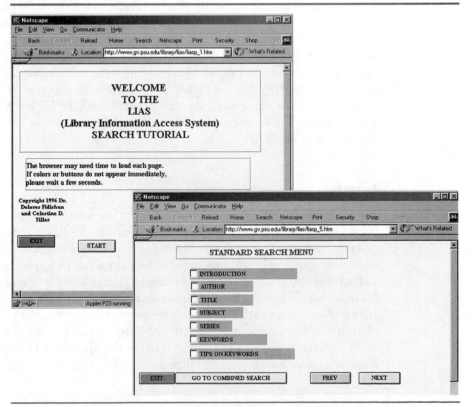

From Penn State Great Valley Library, Malvern. Available: http://www.gv.psu.edu/library/lias/liasp_1.htm.

HTML page, applets are handled much like an image. An <applet> tag tells the browser to transfer the compiled code to the browser and execute the code (as long as the browser is Java enabled). An applet is named with an extension of ".class" (e.g., Applet.class). Because a download to the browser is required, users' access speed capabilities should be a consideration when incorporating applets. Visit Sun's site for detailed information about Java: http://java.sun.com.

JavaScript

JavaScript is one of the best-known script languages for Web authors who want to create dynamic pages. It is commonly used to respond to user events such as mouse clicks, mouseovers, page navigation, and form input and is a flexible way to integrate animation, sound, and other multimedia elements. Developed by Netscape, JavaScript is not a subset of Java. It is an interpreted language rather than compiled. Also, it is an open language that can be used by anyone without purchasing a license. A JavaScript program can be embedded right into an HTML page, meaning that it can function totally on the client side. To embed JavaScript, the code is inserted in a <script> tag in the <head> of HTML documents. If preferred, the JavaScript code can also be in a separate file that is called from the HTML page. These files end with the extension ".js" (e.g., Script.js). JavaScript is a safe language, meaning that it isn't able to access any system controls or hardware on a user's computer. Although JavaScript is best known as a client-side script, it is also available as a server-side language to accomplish such tasks as communicating with a relational database or conducting file manipulations on a server. It is handled a bit differently on a server. The script resides in an HTML document on the server, but the page is compiled into an executable file. Instead of the <script> tag, a <server> tag encloses the script. One benefit of a server-side JavaScript is that it can be read by any browser, not just ones that are JavaScript enabled. To learn more about JavaScript, go to Netscape's JavaScript Development site at http://developer. netscape.com/javascript.

Jscript

Microsoft has developed Jscript specifically for use within Web pages. It is an interpreted, object-oriented language that is not a cut-down version of a more powerful language. It adheres to the ECMAScript standard (visit http:// www.ecma.ch), the Web's standard scripting language. Jscript is designed for use in browsers and other applications that use ActiveX controls and Java applets. It comes bundled with Microsoft Internet Explorer and with Microsoft Internet Information Server (MIIS), or it can be downloaded at no charge. It has multiplatform support. As is the case with JavaScript, to embed the script in a document the code is inserted in a <script> tag in the <head> of HTML documents. For more information, go to http://msdn.microsoft.com/scripting.

Lingo

Lingo is the scripting language that programs behind the scene in Macromedia's Shockwave Director. It is specific to Director.

Perl

Perl (Practical Extraction and Reporting Language), created by Larry Wall, is popular in the world of Web development for being the primary language used to create dynamic content through CGI (Common Gateway Interface—see the discussion later in this chapter) programming. However, Perl is not synonymous with CGI; Perl can be used for a wide variety of purposes. It derives from the C programming language and has its roots in the UNIX environment. Yet because it is an interpreted language, it is portable across platforms, but it isn't strictly an interpreted language. Perl has been described as a "compiled scripting language." This means a Perl program can be handled in different ways depending on its intended purpose. Without delving into complex details, the result is a language that is easier to learn and faster to code than traditional programming languages, but it has more sophisticated capabilities than a strictly interpreted language. A program written in Perl will have an extension of ".pl" (e.g., form.pl). For comprehensive information on Perl visit http://www.perl.com.

PHP

Originally written by Rasmus Lerdorf and known as Personal Home Page and now called PHP Hypertext Processor, this interpreted language is similar to JavaScript and VBScript and is used chiefly on Linux Web servers. Unlike JavaScript, however, PHP is a server-side HTML-embedded scripting language. This means that the PHP script is embedded in a Web page along with its HTML. Before the page is sent to the user who has requested it, the server interprets the code and executes the script. A Web page that contains a PHP script will typically be given a name with an extension ".php," ".php3," or ".phtml" (e.g., webpage.php). Unlike most of the other languages, PHP was developed strictly to serve Web pages rather than being based on an existing language. PHP can be used to do the same sort of tasks that can be done with a CGI script, but, according to its developers, its strength lies in the large number of database applications it supports. It is an open source and is freely available for download from http://www.php.net.

Python

Guido van Rossum, its creator, selected Python's name because he was a fan of *Monty Python's Flying Circus*. Python is similar to Perl because it, too, is an interpreted language that supports compilation. It is known for its readability and portability to multiple operating systems. Python is deemed to be easy to learn because it is object oriented (programming that is organized around objects rather than actions). As with some of the other languages, it is made available at no charge. The download and a site full of comprehensive information are accessible at http://www.python.org.

Tcl and Tk

Tcl stands for Tool Command Language (pronounced t-c-l or tickle). It is an interpreted language, and like Perl, it is used on the Web for CGI scripting (although not as extensively as Perl). It, too, is open source and is touted as being easy to learn and allowing rapid development. It is often compared with Perl, and both have their disciples. One advantage of Tcl comes with its Tk (Tool Kit), which is a tool for creating GUI (Graphical User Interface, pronounced gooey) front-ends. John Ousterhout created Tcl. A good place to find thorough information on Tcl is from the Tcl Developer Xchange at http://www.scriptics.com.

VBScript

Microsoft's VBScript (Visual Basic Script) is that company's answer to JavaScript. Like JavaScript, it is an interpreted script language. It is a subset of the Visual Basic programming language. As is the case with JavaScript and Jscript, to embed a VBScript in a document you insert the code in a <script> tag in the <head> of HTML documents. Not surprisingly, it is a free language and enjoys cross-platform support. It is included with both Microsoft Internet Explorer and Microsoft Internet Information Server or can be downloaded from http://www.microsoft.com/msdownload/vbscript/scripting.asp. Visit Microsoft's Scripting Technologies Web site for further information: http://msdn.microsoft.com/scripting.

Web Server Application Technologies

This section presents a few important technologies that are often included when a discussion on scripting occurs but that can't really be classified as Web programming languages. Instead, these are technologies that permit a Web server to serve dynamic data.

CGI

The Common Gateway Interface (CGI) is actually a protocol for transferring information between a Web server and a program. Its purpose is to provide a means to process interaction between users and the server. A CGI script is stored and executed on the Web server in response to a request from a user. A typical example for a use for a CGI program is to process forms from an HTML page. The user fills in the form and clicks on the submit button. At that point, the CGI program takes control to process the information that was submitted. It might e-mail that data to a person, or it might write the information to a spreadsheet. Although most people associate CGI with Perl, CGI is not language specific. CGI can be written in any language, including Perl, Python, and Tcl. The main shortcoming of CGI is that it tends to be slow because each request submitted by a user causes a new program to be launched. If there is high traffic, this can result in overtaxing the server. The big advantage of using CGI is that you are assured that all of your users will be able to use the program (unlike those technologies that are client-side and can be turned off in the browser by users or may not be supported by a particular browser version). If you are interested in learning CGI or finding CGI scripts, check out the CGI Resource Index at http://www.cgi-resources.com.

ASP

An Active Server Page (ASP) is a Web page that includes one or more embedded scripts that are executed on a Microsoft Web server before the page is sent to the user. The script responds to input from the user and then builds a Web page on the fly before sending it out. ASP works well to dynamically change, edit, or add content to a Web page; to respond to user queries; and to access databases and then return results. ASP can be written using VBScript, Jscript, or ActiveX controls. Pages that have been built via ASP end in the extension ".asp" (e.g., data.asp). Because ASP is designed to run on a Microsoft Web server, required server software includes Windows NT and Internet Information Server (IIS). However, technologies are being developed that will permit ASP to run on non-Windows operating systems. One example is Chili!Soft ASP, a product that provides platform-independent ASP (http://www.chilisoft.com).

To deliver ASP pages to your audience you will need a server, of course, but it is possible to run ASP on your own PC using Microsoft's Personal Web Server, which is included with Windows 98 (look in the Add-ons folder). This capability can be useful as you go through the process of learning ASP because you don't have to be connected to a remote server to test your scripts. Since it is a server-side technology and ASP is delivered to the end users as plain HTML, there are no browser limitations for reading the output. Microsoft is developing the next version of ASP, called ASP+. The purpose is to enhance the functionality of ASP, and one of the main outcomes is that ASP+ pages are compiled rather than interpreted. A good starting point to learn more about ASP is at the ASP Resource Index at http://www.aspin.com.

JSP

JavaServer Page is Sun Microsystems' technology similar to Microsoft's ASP. However, unlike ASP, JSP is designed to be platform and server independent. The language used to create JSP is Java. Small programs called servlets (the server-side version of an applet) are specified in a Web page and are run on the server, resulting in a modified page that is then sent to the requester. JSP technology is also known as the Servlet Application Program Interface (API). JSP pages will end with an extension ".jsp" (e.g., journalist.jsp). One benefit of servlet technology over CGI and ASP is that once a servlet is started, it stays in the server memory and can be executed multiple times to fulfill requests. A CGI program and an ASP page have to be reinterpreted every time they are requested, resulting in slower response times. Sun Microsystems' Java technology site is the place to find additional information: http://java.sun.com/products/jsp.

Markup Languages and Interactivity

By now, you understand that HTML pages, by themselves, are static documents. Interactivity is added to them through the integration of scripts and other technologies. However, there are "newer" and more advanced markup languages that are associated with Web interactivity: dHTML, VRML, XML, and XHTML. The following subsections discuss what they are and how they are considered interactive.

dHTML

Dynamic HTML (also discussed in chapter 5 in reference to animation) is not an actual specification. Rather, it is a collective term for a combination of new tags and options introduced in HTML 4.0 along with increased programming possibilities. A dynamic page is one that has the capability to change, even after it's been loaded into a browser. Some of the simple interactions that would be considered dHTML are rollovers and the ability to drag and drop objects from one place on a page to another. The three main technologies that are the primary components making up dHTML include client-side scripting, DOM, and CSS.

Client-Side Scripting   One of the best-known ways that Web authors create dynamic pages is through client-side scripting. It is the part of the equation that actually makes changes in a page.

DOM   Considered the core of dHTML, DOM stands for Document Object Model, a programming interface. The model encompasses the structure of a document as well as its behavior and the behavior of the objects that make up a page. It deals with objects, which include all the HTML page elements such as divisions, paragraphs, images, links, etc. All of the objects can be manipulated, and this is what makes interactivity possible. DOM is platform and language neutral; it allows programs and scripts to dynamically access and update page content, structure, and style of documents. This is accomplished by exposing DOM to scripting through browsers. While scripting makes the actual changes, DOM is the component that allows objects to be changeable. The best place to find in-depth information about DOM is at W3C's site: http://www.w3.org/DOM.

CSS   Cascading Style Sheets (which were discussed in chapter 4) are a part of DOM, meaning that they are accessible to the scripting languages. Because CSS allows specific location placement of objects on a page (through specification of coordinates in the *x*, *y*, and *z* planes), a script can be used to move the object (or element), hide or show it, and otherwise change its properties (such as color and style).

VRML

Now called Virtual Reality Modeling Language, VRML was originally called Virtual Reality Markup Language. As we learned in the section on animation in chapter 5, VRML is a screen-description language that describes the geometry and behavior of a 3-D world. This language is highly interactive as it allows users to determine how to move through a scene.

XML

XML (Extensible Markup Language) is similar to HTML in that they both use tags to describe the contents of a page. However, in HTML, tags and attributes have specific meanings and control how elements will appear on a page. For instance, <p> stands for paragraph, and when it is used, a space is inserted in the line above it. With XML, tags are used to delimit pieces of data, and the meanings of tags are completely up to the application that reads it. If <p> is used in an XML file, it can stand for whatever data is being described (price, person, etc.). An XML tag describes the data that is contained within it. The meanings of tags can be decided on an individual level or can be determined by a group who may want to share information in a consistent way. Because the markup symbols are unlimited and self-defining, the language is said to be extensible. XML is actually a subset of SGML (Standard Generalized Markup Language). Because XML is designed to deal with data, it isn't meant to be a replacement for HTML because it isn't meant to be read. Instead, HTML and XML serve two different purposes and, thus, can complement each other. HTML handles presentation; XML handles content.

Where does interactivity come into play? Like HTML, XML is static. It is a very effective means to structure data, but it must be paired up with a programming or script language to extract data and to interface with different applications. Once again, W3C is the site to visit to find out all about XML: http://www.w3.org/XML.

XHTML

XHTML—Extensible HyperText Markup Language—is the W3C's latest recommendation for HTML. It is a reformulation of HTML 4.01 in XML, bringing the strengths of XML to HTML. As of this writing, XHTML is the W3C's current recommendation for the latest version of HTML (http://www.w3.org/MarkUp).

INTERACTIVITY DEVELOPMENT TOOLS FOR NONPROGRAMMERS

The previous section showed that there are many choices for incorporating interactivity if you are a programmer or have one on your project team. However, what about all the rest of us who want to build an interactive tutorial but don't have the background, programming skills, or desire to do our own scripting? It is hoped that the previous section didn't scare you off because now we are going to talk about the variety of existing tools available to nonprogrammers to facilitate building an interactive site. Keep in mind that this is a rapidly evolving industry, and between the time this is written and the time you are reading this, many more tools will be available to help you. Thus, we will consider broad categories of interactivity development aids, but don't limit your consideration to the examples that are mentioned. Use your Internet searching skills to ferret out new and exciting utilities.

Web Editors

As Web editors evolve, many are including additional features that permit behind-the-scenes scripting functionality, cascading style sheets support, and sometimes, ready-to-use scripting actions. As was mentioned in chapter 3, Selecting Project Development Tools, choose a Web editor that supports advanced features including CSS, layers, animations, JavaScript, applets, forms, and image maps.

Script Libraries

One of the greatest things about the Web is how willing people are to share what they have created. There are plenty of script libraries (sometimes called script archives) in existence in which you can find prewritten scripts that will perform just about any interactive function you need. It's easy to locate one; try going to your favorite search engine or directory and input the kind of script library or interaction you would like to find: "JavaScript script library" or "rollover script." Depending on what type of script you are getting, the retrieval process may be a simple cut-and-paste or a file download for files like a CGI program that have to be copied to your server. For example, as shown in figure 6.24, the JavaScript Source provides instructions for cutting and pasting code that will give a description of a link when a user passes a mouse over the link. Note that the script includes a credit line for the author. This will not display on the page, but it will reside in the <head> section of the document. Often the script is ready to use as written, but you may find that you will want to modify it to customize it to your specific situation. Good script libraries include instructions for modification and installation procedures.

Be sure to read and follow the rules that have been established at each library. Because most of these libraries collect scripts from many authors, there

FIGURE 6.24
JavaScript Source Script Library

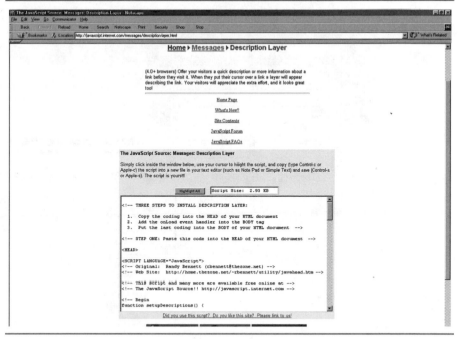

may be different use conditions depending on the authors' wishes. Typical conditions include leaving author credit information inside the script or providing a link to the script library. You will find a list of several script libraries in the resources section at the end of this book.

Applications and Online Services

A specialized application that can be used to develop interactive components is a very useful tool. Some are offered at no charge to educational institutions. Hot Potatoes, from the University of Victoria Humanities Computer and Media Centre, is one example of this type of application that offers its application at no charge to nonprofit educational organizations who make their materials freely available over the Web. It includes six different applications; each one creates a different kind of interactive exercise. The example shown in figure 6.25 uses JMatch (top screen) to build a quiz where students match correct associations by dragging items from the right column and then dropping them next to the appropriate answer on the left (bottom screen). Some applications are designed to give client-based interactivity and feedback only; others provide a feedback mechanism to the instructor or collect data to grade and track students' progress.

FIGURE 6.25
Hot Potatoes Quiz Creation Tool

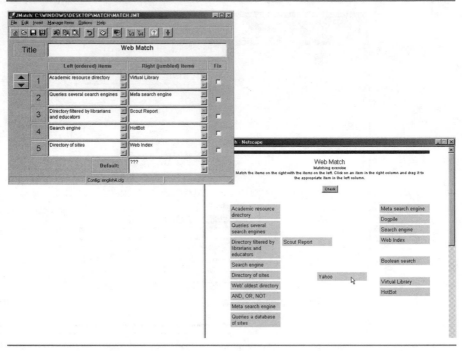

From University of Victoria Humanities Computing and Media Centre, Victoria, B.C. Available: http://web.uvic.ca/hrd/halfbaked.

Some tools don't require you to download and install software to use them. There are sites that offer services that permit you to build interactive quizzes, tests, and exercises and store them on their servers. Quia is an example of this type of service (http://www.quia.com). It allows instructors to create games and quizzes, administer them, and track scores. Another interesting service, FormSite. com (http://www.formsite.com), is one that permits you to create forms and store the data in a database on its server. It offers two levels of service: one free and one fee-based.

The Centre for Curriculum, Transfer and Technology, in British Columbia, Canada, has put together a useful site that can help you discover different tools and compare their advantages and disadvantages. It contains information on more than one hundred educational-delivery applications including testing systems and course shells. The URL is http://www.ctt.bc.ca/landonline.

Course Shells

We examined course shells in chapter 3 and learned that they are designed to be a complete package to deliver all aspects of online education. Of course, this includes interaction for communication, information transfer, file exchange, and online surveys and quizzes. If you have access to a course shell, it can provide you with an environment that permits you to concentrate on instructional design and content building without having to be a technology guru.

Web-Development Sites

An abundance of sites are devoted to Web-development issues. Often, they include tools to help Web authors build dynamic sites. CNET Builder.com (http://home.cnet.com/webbuilding/0-3880.html?tag=st.cn.1.dir.3880) is just one example of this type of site. In previous chapters a few contributions from that site were introduced: The Mighty Mouseover Machine (http://builder.com/Program ming/Kahn/012898/index.html) and Window Builder (http://builder.com/Pro gramming/Kahn/092497/toolwb.html). Those are just two of the tools that are freely available. Two other sites that are similar to CNET are WebDeveloper.com (http://www.webdeveloper.com) and About.com (http://about.com), which has subsites that focus on HTML/XML, Perl, JavaScript, and Java.

NOTES

Ford, S., D. Wells, and N. Wells. 1996. Web Programming Languages. Baltimore, Md.: Object Services and Consulting. Retrieved 4 March 2001 from http://www.objs.com/survey/lang.htm.

Rutkowski, K. 2001. Categories of Interaction. Washington, D.C.: George Washington University. Retrieved 4 March 2001 from http://www.gwu.edu/~220i2i/lectures/unit3/lectset1.htm.

7 Evaluation and Testing

In chapter 2, evaluation was identified as a crucial part of the design and development cycle. Establishing effective methods to evaluate the different stages of a Web-based project is the best way to make sure the project stays on track and accomplishes its established goals. However, the evaluation process is often the part of the design and development cycle that falls by the wayside. Whether it's due to time or budget constraints or to lack of knowledge on how to proceed, it's not unusual to hear of projects that are not evaluated in any fashion or that have chosen the wrong measurements altogether. In this chapter, you will be introduced to an overview of evaluation and testing methods that have been determined to be useful for measuring the effectiveness of the interface design process as well as the effectiveness of the completed project. The purpose of this chapter is to provide you with some ideas about which method will best suit your project. It is beyond the scope of this book to cover research methodology and analysis, as there are many sources that address this in great depth.

WHY, WHAT, AND HOW MUCH EVALUATION?

You've assembled a knowledgeable team for your project who have a good technical and design experience. You've done the analyses of your audience and have a good sense of how the project should be developed. Why, then, should you take on the extra time and expense of conducting tests and evaluations?

It's important to recognize that those most deeply involved in the creation of your Web-based tutorial have become so immersed that it is impossible to maintain complete objectivity. The only way to find out if the design your team has developed functions as intended is to have it evaluated by people outside the project. What seems obvious to those closest to the project may not be understandable at all to outsiders. The purpose for conducting testing is to discover and correct usability flaws during the iterative design of the interface. External users can give you a fresh perspective.

Choices of evaluation methods can range from a costly multiphase test to a one-hour test with a few key users. Which method(s) you select will depend on several factors. Ben Shneiderman (1998) identified these determinants for the selection of an evaluation plan:

Stage of design Are you at the project's beginning, middle, or end?

Novelty of project Is the project well defined, or is the project more exploratory in nature?

Number of expected users Is the tutorial for a class of 20 or for more than 1,000 students?

Criticality of the interface How critical is the function of the interface you are designing? For example, an interface for a medical system will warrant a more comprehensive evaluation effort than an interface for a library tutorial.

Costs of product and finances allocated for testing How much money has been invested in producing the tutorial, and what amount has been delegated for testing?

Time available How much time is there to conduct an evaluation? If time is limited, a lengthy evaluation may not be the answer.

Experience of the design and evaluation team Do your team members have any experience executing similar projects, or is this their first?

What should you try to discover through evaluation? Focusing on the wrong evaluation objective will result in a waste of time and money. Once again, Shneiderman has compiled a list of measurable human factors central to the evaluation of an interface:

Time to learn How long does it take a regular user to learn to use the interface?

Speed of performance How fast can a regular user work through a set of tasks?

Rate of errors by users How many and what kind of errors do users make?

Retention over time How much of the knowledge obtained in the instruction do users retain after a length of time?

Subjective satisfaction What do users think about the learning experience that took place?

CATEGORIES OF EVALUATION

Two main types of evaluation are formative and summative. Both methods are important components of the evaluation story.

Formative Evaluation

A formative evaluation is one that takes place during the development or implementation of a project. The goal of formative evaluation is to help the development team recognize problems in the design of the tutorial so that those problems can be corrected and improved prior to the completion of the project. When the results of a formative evaluation are incorporated into the design, it becomes an iterative process because each modified interface is then a candidate for a new evaluation. A variety of methods can be used for a formative evaluation, some qualitative and some quantitative. Examples are surveys, focus groups, and observations. However, time is an important factor in conducting a formative evaluation because results must be analyzed and then be included in the modified interface quickly enough to stay on schedule.

Summative Evaluation

A summative evaluation is one that occurs at the end of a project and is used to determine the impact of the project. It is used to measure whether the goals of the project have been met, including whether the final design and implementation were successful, as well as whether mastery of content took place. A summative evaluation is often the tool that is used by decision makers and other stakeholders to judge the project's worth. In a multimedia project, this evaluation often serves as the basis for later revisions to the program. Some common summative evaluations are observation, student achievement, and interviews.

EVALUATION METHODS

This section presents some of the established software evaluation methods. Some may be more appropriate for either formative or summative evaluations, but there are methods that can be used for both processes. In addition, some evaluation methods involve users, and others rely on experts.

User Evaluation Methods

The intended audience for your project should be involved in the evaluation process. This section examines two common methods of evaluation that involve the user: prototyping and usability testing.

Prototyping

Prototypes are primitive interface designs that are quickly assembled and cheap to produce. A prototype allows user feedback at the very beginning of the design process. Design issues can be discovered early before time and money have been invested in any actual production of the tutorial.

Prototyping may be at a low-, medium-, or high-fidelity level. Low-fidelity prototypes are those that are very quickly constructed, such as paper sketches and storyboards that have no functionality but that demonstrate design concepts and layout. A low-fidelity prototype presentation for user feedback requires a facilitator who knows the intended functionality to demonstrate it. The users who will be part of the test should be representative of your targeted audience. In addition to having a facilitator present it, development team members should act as observers and take notes on the participants' comments and reactions. If your budget allows, it may be useful to videotape the session for later reference.

Medium-fidelity prototypes simulate or animate some but not all of the features of the intended system. Some approaches to medium-fidelity prototypes are computer-based and slide/video simulation. High-fidelity prototypes are those that are fully functional. Both of these prototyping methods are more expensive than low-fidelity. Although most prototyping takes place in the early stages of the design process, medium- and high-fidelity prototypes make their appearances during the later stages because of the time required to produce them. Medium and high-fidelity prototyping do not require a facilitator, but they do require an observer to record user actions. If you are interested in more detail about prototyping, visit http://www.cpsc.ucalgary.ca/~saul/681/1998/prototyping/survey.html and read "Prototyping for Design and Development."

Usability Testing

The purpose of usability testing is to assess your design and tutorial structure by having actual users work through the program. This type of testing should be part of the formative evaluation so that any usability issues can be addressed and resolved.

Is it necessary to recruit a large number of users to get conclusive answers to your questions? According to Jakob Nielsen (2000), good results can be obtained from testing no more than five users. In research he conducted, he found that a single user provides almost ⅓ of all the data there is to know about a design's usability. With a second user, there is some overlap with what the first person found, so the second user doesn't contribute as much new information as did the first. This trend continues as you add more users. By the time the fifth user is tested, there is nothing much new to discover. Because of the iterative nature of the design process, you may choose to run a test at each stage of the redesign and involve five users for each test. The only time you really need to think about using more than five testers is when your audience straddles disparate user groups. Then you will want to include testers who are representative of each different group. Be sure that the people you select to participate are "ordinary" users. Students who work in your library have a higher knowledge of how a library functions, so it is preferable to find students who are just regular library users.

Testing should be held in a computer lab or wired classroom where there won't be interruptions. However, it doesn't have to be a sterile, noiseless location because the more normal a setting you can come up with, the closer to reality the test will be.

If the testing method you are using requires interaction between the user and a facilitator, prepare a list of questions and key points that you are interested in exploring so that the facilitator has a guide that will be the same for all participants. The guideline is just that, however, because issues that you never considered may crop up during a session, and these will need to be addressed with other participants.

The facilitator should have an assistant who acts as an observer and records the feedback. As with prototyping sessions, a video recording can be a valuable tool if it doesn't make participants self-conscious.

The final step in a usability test is to compile the findings and assimilate the results into potential solutions. Share these with your team, form a consensus about what actions are best, and proceed with the interface modifications.

Different measurement methods can be used during a usability test. Some will provide you with quantitative data; others will give you qualitative insight into users' thinking.

Success Rate   This is a very straightforward way to test usability. You simply record the percentage of users who are able to accomplish the task they were assigned.

Thinking Aloud   This method is one in which users are asked to verbalize their thoughts as they work their way through the tutorial.

Task Performance   This measurement is accomplished by timing how long it takes users to perform assigned tasks.

Checklist-Based Testing   For budgetary reasons, you may decide that you prefer to do user testing without a facilitator or observer. A checklist-based test is very cost-effective and easily executed. Prepare a checklist of criteria that you want your testers to evaluate, and give them the list. Then leave the room, and let the testers work through the checklist as they interact with your program.

Subjective Satisfaction   A big measurement of a design's success is how satisfied users are when they interact with it. A questionnaire can be useful in soliciting user satisfaction.

Usability Inspections

Users can provide important evaluation information. On the other hand, bringing in experts to review your interface design can be instrumental to design improvement during an iterative process. The term *expert* can refer to interface design authorities or to staff members who know the content and the tasks that are going to be included in the tutorial. As in the case of user testing, usability inspections (also often called "expert reviews") should involve more than one person because no single inspection will uncover every design flaw. Arrange for three to five experts to participate in the review process. Expert reviews can occur at any point in the design phase and are useful because they usually can be done quickly and cheaply. The reviews can be scheduled to take place at various stages of the design process when the development team is ready for feedback. Depending on the scope of the project, feedback from the experts can be a formal report or an informal discussion with the team. The different methods of expert review that you can choose include those in the following subsections.

Heuristic Evaluation

Developed by Jakob Nielsen, heuristic evaluation is one of the most popular types of usability inspection. To conduct this type of evaluation, evaluators are given a short list of design-usability principles (heuristics), such as Shneiderman's eight golden rules (see chapter 4), or Instone's usability heuristics for the Web (1997). Each expert inspects the interface alone and determines its conformance with the list. Each inspector usually will go through the interface at least twice; the first time to become acquainted with the system and the second to focus on the specific principles. After all of the evaluators have completed their solitary inspections, they meet and aggregate their findings. Additional in-depth information about conducting heuristic evaluations can be found at Nielsen's site: http://www.useit.com/papers/heuristic.

Guidelines Review

If your organization has established specific guidelines to which your Web documents must conform, then you may want to perform a guidelines review. In this type of evaluation, the interface is checked for adherence to any organizational interface design requirements.

Pluralistic Walkthrough

In a pluralistic walkthrough the users, developers, and usability experts meet in a group setting and work through task scenarios, evaluating the usability of a system. A benefit of this type of evaluation is that the participants will be a diverse group that brings in different levels of skills and points of view. Normally, this type of session would include a facilitator who coordinates the discussion and participant input.

Consistency Inspection

The purpose of a consistency inspection is to ensure consistency across multiple products from the same development effort. In the case of library instruction tutorials, if you are developing two or more separate tutorials on various topics, having the same look and functionality among all of them will benefit the students using them. Consistency can be checked in regard to such factors as color, screen layout, terminology, and navigation format.

Cognitive Walkthrough

A cognitive walkthrough involves experts playing the role of users walking through the program interface to carry out tasks. Often, users prefer to learn by exploring a new interface rather than by reading formal instructions. By putting themselves in the users' shoes, the inspectors can break down different tasks into specific steps and identify sequences that are likely to cause difficulty. To prepare for a cognitive walkthrough, team members decide which tasks should be tested and then compile a list that breaks down each task into a sequence. Experts should have some knowledge of the targeted audience profile so they understand the goals and purposes. These goals should be defined and listed. During the evaluation phase, the information that was gathered in the preparatory stage is analyzed, and predictions are made about the degree of difficulty users are likely to encounter as they try to reach their goals.

Formal Usability Inspection

A formal usability inspection is the most structured type of inspection. Adapted from software inspection methodology, it formalizes the discovery and recording of usability problems. It is done with a team of several people who, in addition to inspecting the design, each have a specific role assigned: moderator, designer, recorder, and inspector. These roles are played during a formal meeting that is held following the inspection of the design. During the meeting, the moderator walks the team through each scenario or task, and the inspectors report each defect found at that particular stage. The recorder logs each reported defect. The final step is to assign the identified defects to be fixed to the appropriate development person. Although this method is very detailed, it takes longer to prepare and requires more people to carry out than do some of the other inspection methods.

Inquiry Methods

In addition to user evaluations and usability inspections, much valuable information can come by asking users questions and soliciting their feedback. You can discover what they like or dislike, what their needs and expectations are, and how well they comprehend the program. Following are several avenues for collecting information from users.

Questionnaires

A questionnaire is a written list of questions that you distribute to one or more users. They then complete it and return it to you. Although the term *questionnaire* is often used interchangeably with the word *survey*, a questionnaire is an instrument that can be used to conduct a survey, but a survey can also be conducted in person or over the phone. Keep in mind when using a questionnaire that you are putting the burden on your users to return it to you; you are asking them to expend more effort on their part than with some other feedback methods. A possible compromise is to use an online questionnaire to survey users so that you reduce the cost of printing, mailing, and collecting paper forms.

Interviews

Interviews are direct person-to-person interaction with users. Their opinions can be solicited, and follow-up questions can be posed to clarify any issues that arise. Types of interview methods include structured interviews, with specific predetermined agendas, and unstructured, more informal interviews. It is always a good idea to tape the interview so that the subject isn't distracted by the interviewer's note taking.

Focus Groups and Group Discussions

Focus groups and group discussions can be used to gather users' impressions both before design and after implementation. To run a focus group, you gather together six to eight people with a moderator who keeps the group on task. The moderator may demonstrate a prototype and then solicit response from the group. The main problem with focus groups as an information-gathering mechanism is that what is being collected are opinions about how participants *think* the program will or should work rather than actual data about how they would really interact if they were to sit in front of the screen and work through the program. Focus groups can be beneficial for exploring what users want from a program. However, what users want may not be what they need.

Field Observation

Unlike observation in a usability test, field observation takes place in the users' environment. The purpose of this type of observation is to see users in action at their normal place of work or study. Part of a field observation is to interview users about their work or study habits and how they would normally use the tutorial.

Online Feedback

As a part of the summative evaluation process, consider providing a vehicle for users to give you feedback from within the tutorial. This method can be beneficial because you will receive impressions and opinions during or soon after they have worked through the tutorial.

CONTENT MASTERY

Measuring the usability of the interface is an important part of ensuring the success of your tutorial. However, the most vital goal of an online instruction project is for learning to occur. Remember that Shneiderman identified "retention over time" as one of the factors central to the evaluation of an interface. As you are planning evaluation procedures, build in methods to measure if students have mastered the content and to what extent. Even if your institution or the class instructor doesn't require a grade, a testing system will help you assess how effective your online instruction has been. This can be a crucial factor in decision making for future online instruction projects.

NOTES

Instone, K. 10 Oct. 1997. "Site Usability Heuristics for the Web." *Web Review*. San Francisco, Calif.: CMP Media. Retrieved 4 March 2001, from http://www.webreview.com/1997/10_10/strategists/10_10_97_2.shtml.

Nielsen, J. 19 Mar. 2000. Why You Only Need to Test with 5 Users. Alertbox. Retrieved 23 Sept. 2000, from http://www.useit.com/alertbox/20000319.html.

Shneiderman, B. 1998. *Designing the User Interface: Strategies for Effective Human-Computer Interaction*. 3d ed. Reading, Mass.: Addison-Wesley.

Resources

Accessibility

Bobby. Available: http://www.cast.org/bobby.

> Use this site to test your tutorial's accessibility.

Color Challenged Applet. Available: http://www.InternetTG.org/newsletter/mar99/color_challenged_applet.html.

> Use this applet to test the color accessibility of your text and background.

W3C Web Accessibility Initiative. Available: http://www.w3.org/WAI.

> W3C's site is a storehouse of information on making the Web accessible to the disabled.

Animation

About Animation Software Reviews. Available: http://animation.about.com/arts/animation.

> About.com's animation subsite contains links to animation software reviews, animation tools, and GIF animators.

Farrell, C. 1999. Make Your GIFs Dance. Available: http://builder.cnet.com/Graphics/Webanim/index.html.

> Learn about the benefits and uses for animated GIFs, as well as how to create them.

Flash. Available: http://www.macromedia.com/software/flash.

> Macromedia's product site includes Flash frequently answered questions, white papers, and a features tour.

King, A. 2000. Optimizing Animated GIFs. Webref.com. Available: http://www.webreference.com/dev/gifanim.

> Learn the steps involved to optimize animated GIFs.

Kirsanov, D. 1999. The Art of Animation. Available: http://www.webreference.com/dlab/9904.

> This is a thoughtful discussion on the basics of animation.

McMillian, A., and E. Hobson. Animation Tutorial. Webmonkey. Waltham, Mass.: Lycos. Available: http://hotwired.lycos.com/webmonkey/multimedia/animation/tutorials/tutorial1.html.

> This tutorial can teach you about GIF 89, DHTML, and Flash as well as about design and integration issues.

Macromedia Director Shockwave Studio. Available: http://www.macromedia.com/software/director.

> Information about Director and Shockwave is plentiful at Macromedia's site.

Multiple-Image Network Graphics. Available: http://www.freesoftware.com/pub/mng.

> The home site for MNG is the best source of information about this format.

3-D Animation Workshop. Webreference.com. Available: http://www.webreference.com/3d/indexa.html.

> This workshop comprises more than sixty lessons that will instruct you about how to do 3-D animation.

VRML Works. Available: http://home.HiWAAY.net/~crispen/vrmlworks.

> There are links to many of the available VRML tools at this site.

Wagstaff, S. 1998. "Animation Basics." In *Animation on the Web*. Berkeley, Calif.: Peachpit Press. Available: http://beta.peachpit.com/ontheweb/animation/chap2.html.

> This sample chapter from Wagstaff's book is a good introductory overview to animation.

Applications for Building Interactivity

Castle: Computer Assisted Teaching and Learning. Available: http://www.le.ac.uk/cc/ltg/castle.

> The site contains download tools that can be used to create interactive quizzes. It is written in Java to ensure cross-platform compatibility; the latest version of the Castle tool kit also includes the capability to log grades and time stamp student activity.

FormSite.com. Available: http://www.formsite.com.

> Create HTML forms and store the data collected from them for free on their server.

Hot Potatoes. Available: http://web.uvic.ca/hrd/halfbaked.

> The Hot Potatoes program available on this site consists of six applications that can be used to create interactive multiple-choice, short-answer, jumbled-sentence, crossword, matching/ordering, and gap-fill exercises.

Online Educational Delivery Applications: A Web Tool for Comparative Analysis. Available: http://www.ctt.bc.ca/landonline.

> Compare the features and functionality of more than forty educational delivery applications and examine information on another sixty.

Quia. Available: http://www.quia.com.

> Quia is a free service that permits the creation of quizzes and provides virtual classroom space as well.

QuizCenter. Available: http://school.discovery.com/quizcenter/quizcenter.html.

> Here is another free service that allows creation of quizzes and server space to store them. Quizzes are automatically graded, and there is password protection to provide privacy to students.

Audio

Classical Music Archives. Available: http://www.prs.net/midi.html.

> This site contains more than 11,000 MIDI files from more than 850 composers.

Findsounds.com. Available: http://www.findsounds.com.

> This search engine finds sound effects and sample sound files on the Web.

Hitsquad.com. Available: http://www. hitsquad.com.

> The site contains comprehensive information about audio editing and batch encoders.

Multimedia Sound. Available: http:// mmsound.about.com/compute/mmsound.

> About.com's topic site covers just about everything you need to know about producing and using sound on the Web.

Browser Compatibility

Webmonkey Browser Chart. Available: http://hotwired.lycos.com/webmonkey/ reference/browser_chart.

> This chart lists which features are supported by specific browser versions.

Web Site Garage. Available: http:// websitegarage.netscape.com.

> This utility will check your site for browser compatibility.

Cascading Style Sheets

Bos, B. 2000. Web Style Sheets. Available: http://www.w3.org/Style.

> The home page for cascading style sheets is located at W3C.

Clip Art

About.com's Web Clip Art. Available: http:// webclipart.about.com/internet/webclipart.

> This site attempts to provide clip art links that help you locate all types and topics of clip art for your Web pages.

Clipart.com. Available: http://www.clipart. com.

> This site is a clip-art directory with links to clip art, font, photo, and Web graphic sites.

Colors

Color in Web Design. Available: http:// webdesign.about.com/compute/Webdesign/ msubcolor.htm.

> About.com provides links to sites that talk about color issues.

Green, M. 1998. Basic Color & Design SBCFAQ. Available: http://www.ergogero. com/FAQ/cfaqhome.html.

> Green feels that many people don't know the right questions to ask about color, so he has put together "Should Be Frequently Asked Questions."

Kennedy, J. R. 1999. Introduction to Color: Color Theory 101. *Web Design Clinic* 1, no. 1 (March). Available: http://www.webdesign clinic.com/ezine/v1i1/color/index.html.

> Kennedy discusses the basics of colors: the color wheel; hue, tint, shade, tone, value, and intensity; and no-fail color schemes.

Communication Tools

Discus: Free Discussion Board. Available: http://www.discusware.com/discus/home.

> This free software package can be run on UNIX or Windows. It is easy to install and use.

Microsoft NetMeeting. Available: http:// www.microsoft.com/windows/netmeeting.

> NetMeeting is full-featured conferencing and collaboration software that is included with Windows 2000 or can be downloaded from Microsoft's Web site. It runs only on a Windows platform.

Course Shells

Jensen's Survey of High-End Web Authoring Courseware Shells. Available: http:// www.trinity.edu/rjensen/245soft1.htm.

Jensen combines reviews of courseware shells with easy-to-understand information about the technology involved.

Online Educational Delivery Applications: A Web Tool for Comparative Analysis. Available: http://www.ctt.bc.ca/landonline/evalapps.html.

Compares the features and functionality of more than forty educational delivery applications including many course shells.

Design and Development Cycle

Lee, W. W., and D. L. Owens. 2000. Multimedia-Based Instructional Design: Computer-Based Training, Web-Based Training, Distance Broadcast Training. San Francisco, Calif.: Jossey-Bass/Pfeiffer.

This book contains a step-by-step process for completing multimedia projects. It focuses on the development process and includes customizable job aids for readers' use.

WBT Information Center. The Development Process. Available: http://www.filename.com/wbt/pages/process.htm.

This is a concise list of components in the development cycle.

Evaluation and Testing

Dickstein, R., and V. Mills. 2000. "Usability Testing at the University of Arizona Library: How to Let the Users in on the Design." *Information Technology and Libraries* 19 no. 3 (Sept.): 144–50.

This article tells about the processes the University of Arizona Library used to make its Web information gateway a user-focused site.

Gordon, S. 2000. User Testing: How to Plan, Execute, and Report on a Usability Evaluation. CNET Builder.com. Available: http://www.builder.com/Graphics/Evaluation/index.html.

This site has information on defining goals, setting up testing, and reporting findings.

Laberge, J. 1998. The Cognitive Walkthrough Inspection Method: An Overview. Available: http://www.cpsc.ucalgary.ca/~saul/681/1998/cogwalk/Introduction.html.

Laberge's article provides a detailed description of the cognitive walkthrough inspection method and a discussion of the theory behind it and its strengths and weaknesses.

Lu, G. 1998. Prototyping for Design and Evaluation. Available: http://www.cpsc.ucalgary.ca/~saul/681/1998/prototyping/survey.html.

This site, prepared as part of Lu's course requirements, contains a detailed overview about prototyping.

Nielsen, J. n.d. Heuristic Evaluation. Available: http://www.useit.com/papers/heuristic.

The creator of heuristic evaluation has prepared a Web site that details the method.

———. 1997. The Use and Misuse of Focus Groups. Available: http://www.useit.com/papers/focusgroups.html.

In this article, Nielsen talks about the benefits and drawbacks of using focus groups to assess interface decisions.

Nielsen, J., and R. L. Mack, eds. 1994. Usability Inspection Methods. New York: John Wiley.

This is a guide to usability inspections that discusses techniques and compares them to other testing methods.

Glossaries

Webopedia. Available: http://www.webopedia.com.

> This is an online computer technology dictionary/encyclopedia.

Whatis.com. Available: http://whatis.com.

> Here is a very helpful site for finding information technology definitions. It contains more than 2,000 topics and links to more than 12,000 hyperlinked cross-references.

Graphics

All About Graphics Software. Available: http://graphicssoft.about.com/compute/graphicssoft.

> About.com's site contains information on selecting and buying graphics software (including buying on a budget), reviews that rate different applications, and a graphics-software help center. In addition, there is a plethora of links to information about most aspects concerning digital imaging.

Designer-Info.com. Available: http://www.designer-info.com/index.htm.

> The purpose of Designer-Info.com is to provide the information you need to choose the right graphics tools. Use this site to read reviews on different graphics applications and to find tutorials on using specific software.

PNG (Portable Network Graphics) Home Site. Available: http://www.freesoftware.com/pub/png.

> The official site for the emerging Web graphics format contains comprehensive information.

W3C. Graphics on the Web. Available: http://www.w3.org/Graphics.

> Read about what the W3C is doing and has already done about graphics on the Web.

Image Optimization

GIF Lube. Available: http://giflube.netscape.com.

> This utility optimizes GIF, JPEG, and PNG files.

JPEG Wizard. Available: http://www.jpg.com/products/wizard.html.

> Here is a free JPEG optimization utility from Pegasus Imaging.

Library Instruction on the Web

ACRL Internet Education Project. Available: http://cooley.colgate.edu/dbs/acrliep.

> The intention of this project is to provide an effective method for librarians to display and share instructional materials that they have designed for teaching about seeking and evaluating information in a networked environment.

ACRL Instruction Section Teaching Methods Committee. Tips for Developing Effective Web-based Library Instruction. Available: http://www.lib.vt.edu/istm/WebTutorialsTips.html.

> Here are seven instruction objectives that contribute to good pedagogy in Web education.

Caspers, J. S. 1998. "Hands-on Instruction across the Miles: Using a Web Tutorial to Teach the Literature Review Research Process." *Research Strategies* 16, no. 3, 187–97.

> This article talks about using a flowchart diagram as a navigational tool for a Web tutorial. (See figure 4.7 for a screen shot of the diagram.)

Library Instruction Round Table. Library Instruction Tutorials. Available: http://Diogenes.Baylor.edu/Library/LIRT/lirtproj.html.

> This listing of library tutorials is organized into categories including general guides to research, subject-specific guides, interactive tutorials, and guides to the Internet.

Library Orientation Exchange. LOEX Clearinghouse for Library Instruction: Instruction Links. Available: http://www.emich.edu/public/loex/ISLINKS/ISLINKS.HTM.

> LOEX's instruction links include sections on virtual tours, tutorials, evaluating resources, and assignment suggestions.

Markup Languages

Dynamic HTML Developer Central. Available: http://developer.netscape.com/tech/dynhtml/index.html.

> Netscape's dHTML site contains a good assortment of resources about developing dynamic HTML.

XML. Available: http://www.w3.org/XML. W3C has the official word on XML.

XML.com. Available: http://www.xml.com.

> The mission of this site is to help users learn about XML and how it can be used to solve real-world problems.

Multimedia

Adam's Multimedia Tutorial. Available: http://hotwired.lycos.com/webmonkey/multimedia/tutorials/tutorial3.html.

> Eight lessons will teach you about audio, video, streaming media, and animation with Flash.

Navigation

Muehlbaurer, J. May 1998. The Navigation and Usability Guide. Webreview.com. San Francisco, Calif.: CMP Media. Available: http://www.webreview.com/1998/05_15/designers/ 05_15_98_2.shtml.

> This article lists twelve rules for navigation and usability.

Page Optimization

HTML Optimization. Available: http://www. webreference.com/programming/optimize.

> Webreference.com provides links to optimization tools and tutorials.

King, A. 2000. Extreme HTML Optimization. Available: http://www.webreference. com/authoring/languages/html/optimize/index.html.

> This article explains the importance of optimizing HTML documents and provides tips for doing so. Some suggestions are "extreme" and violate W3C standards.

Research Literature

Axeen, M. E. 1967. *Teaching the Use of the Library to Undergraduates: An Experimental Comparison of Computer-Based Instruction and the Conventional Lecture Method.* Urbana: University of Illinois.

Cherry, J. M., and M. Clinton. 1991. "An Experimental Investigation of Two Types of Instruction for OPAC Users." *The Canadian Journal of Information Science* 16, no. 4: 2–22.

Dewald, N. H. 1999. "Transporting Good Library Instruction Practices into the Web Environment: An Analysis on Online Tutorials." *Journal of Academic Librarianship* 25, no. 1: 26–32.

Drueke, J. 1992. "Active Learning in the University Library Instruction Classroom." *Research Strategies* 10: 77–83.

Emerson, J. D., and F. Mosteller. 1998. "Interactive Multimedia in College Teaching. Part II: Lessons from Research in the Sciences." *Educational Media and Technology Yearbook* 23: 59–75.

Ester, D. P. 1994. "CAI, Lecture, and Student Learning Style: The Differential Effects of Instructional Method." *Journal of Research on Computing in Education* 27, no. 2: 129–40.

Garrett, R. L. 1995. "Computer-Assisted Instruction in Two-Year Colleges: Technology for Innovative Teaching." *Community College Journal of Research and Practice* 19: 529–36.

Germain, C. A., T. E. Jacobson, and S. A. Kaczor. Jan. 2000. "A Comparison of the Effectiveness of Presentation Formats for Instruction: Teaching First-Year Students." *College & Research Libraries* 61, no. 1: 65–72.

Kaplowitz, J., and J. Contini. 1998. "Computer-Assisted Instruction: Is It an Option for Bibliographic Instruction in Large Undergraduate Survey Classes?" *College & Research Libraries* 59, no. 1: 19–27.

Thompson, A. D., M. R. Simonson, and C. P. Hargrave. 1996. *Educational Technology: A Review of the Research*. Washington, D.C.: Association for Educational Communications and Technology.

Rollovers

Kahn, C. Mouseover Machine. Available: http://www.builder.com/Programming/Kahn/012898.
> Try this free utility to create simple or advanced image rollovers.

Script Languages and Web Interaction Technologies

ActiveX Controls. Available: http://www.microsoft.com/com/tech/ActiveX.asp.
> Microsoft's site containing articles, white papers, and links to ActiveX Web sites.

ASP Resource Index. Available: http://www.aspin.com.
> This site is an index of ASP components, applications, scripts, tutorials, and references.

CGI Resource Index. Available: http://www.cgi-resources.com.
> More than 2,200 resources about CGI are available from this site.

CGI Scripts: Writing and Using CGI. Available: http://html.about.com/compute/html/cs/cgiscripts/index.htm
> About.com's HTML site contains a variety of information on CGI.

Hotscripts.com: Web Development Portal. Available: http://www.hotscripts.com.
> Hotscripts.com is a directory that compiles and distributes Web-programming-related resources. You'll find sections that cover the prevailing languages and Web interaction technologies.

Java.sun.com. Available: http://java.sun.com.
> Here is the official Java technology site from its creator, Sun Microsystems.

JavaScript Source. Available: http://javascript.internet.com.
> This site includes JavaScript tutorials as well as cut-and-paste scripts that you can use.

JavaScript Development Central. Available: http://developer.netscape.com/javascript.
> Access complete documentation (guides and reference manuals) to both client-side and server-side JavaScript at this site.

JavaServer Pages. Available: http://java.sun.com/products/jsp.
> Sun's site for JSP technology is worth a visit.

Perl. Available: http://www.perl.com.
> Here you'll find the central Web site for the Perl community.

PHP: Hypertext Processor. Available: http://www.php.net.
> PHP's home site contains detailed documentation on how to program by using PHP.

Python Language Website. Available: http://www.python.org.
> This is the official Python site.

Tcl/Tk Developer Xchange. Available: http://dev.scriptics.com.
> This site contains comprehensive information on all aspects of Tcl.

Web Developer's Virtual Library. Available: http://wdvl.internet.com.
> Here are resources on all aspects of Web development, including programming. You will find tutorials, discussion lists, software, etc.

Windows Script Technologies. Available: http://msdn.microsoft.com/scripting.
> Microsoft's site includes coverage of VB-Script and Jscript.

Script Libraries

CGI Resource Index: Programs and Scripts. Available: http://cgi.resourceindex.com/Programs_and_Scripts.
> This section of the Resource Index contains more than 2,000 scripts.

JavaScript Source. Available: http://javascript.internet.com.
> The library at this site has hundreds of ready-made scripts.

Matt's Script Archives. Available: http://www.worldwidemart.com/scripts.
> This archive is a good place to find CGI scripts.

100% Free Scripts at Surfzilla. Available: http://scripts.surfzilla.com.
> A nice assortment of scripts from various places has been indexed on this site.

Scriptsearch. Available: http://www.scriptsearch.com.
> Here you will find scripts written in a variety of script languages.

Selecting Development Tools

Focus on Mac Hardware. Available: http://machardware.about.com/compute/machardware.
> From About.com, here is a site that links to information about Macintosh hardware.

MacWorld. Available: http://macworld.zdnet.com.
> If you are a Mac user, this online magazine is a good resource for hardware and software reviews.

PC Guide. Available: http://www.pcguide.com.
> You'll find general reference information about IBM-compatible computers at this site. "Systems and Components Reference Guide" is particularly useful.

PC Magazine. Available: http://www.zdnet.com/pcmag.
> Here you can find hardware and software reviews on a wide realm of PC products.

PC Technology Guide. Available: http://www.pctechguide.com.

This Web site contains a great deal of information that explains PC components and peripherals. It includes a glossary and is available for download or in CD format (for a small fee).

SMIL

Just SMIL. Available: http://streamingmediaworld.com/smil/smilhome.html.

Streaming Media World's site contains tutorials, reviews of authoring software, and links to other SMIL resources.

W3C. Synchronized Multimedia. Available: http://www.w3.org/AudioVideo.

W3C's site includes the official specifications for SMIL and links to tutorials, players, authoring tools, and updates to SMIL information.

Streaming Media

Streaming Media World. Available: http://streamingmediaworld.com.

This site is dedicated to information about streaming media of all types, including audio, video, and SMIL.

Typography

Web Page Design for Designers: Typography. Available: http://www.wpdfd.com/wpdtypo.htm.

This site has good information, illustrates various concepts, and provides practical tips, too.

User Interface Design

Jakob Nielsen's Top Ten Mistakes Revisited. Available: http://www.useit.com/alertbox/990502.html.

Here is the update to his original list of the top ten mistakes in Web design.

Jakob Nielsen's Website. Available: http://www.useit.com.

This Web site on usability is presented by one of the foremost experts on Web design.

Morkes, J., and J. Nielsen. 1997. Concise, SCANNABLE, and Objective: How to Write for the Web. Available: http://www.useit.com/papers/webwriting/writing.html.

This article tells the results of three studies conducted to discover how people read on the Web.

Nielsen, J. 2000. *Designing Web Usability: The Practice of Simplicity.* Indianapolis, Ind.: New Riders.

Jakob Nielsen's book contains many of the articles that can be found on his Useit.com site, but it's handy to have them on hand, nicely organized, and with color examples of the points he makes.

Ten Guidelines for User Centered Design. Available: http://stc.org/pics/usability/newsletter/9807-webguide.html.

This concise set of guidelines can be a useful tool for ensuring that you approach user-centered design in the most effective manner.

Usable Web. Available: http://usableweb.com.

Here is a collection of links about human factors, user-interface issues, and usable design specific to the World Wide Web.

Video

Desktop Video. Available: http://desktopvideo.about.com/compute/desktopvideo.

This is About.com's topic site for digitizing video. It includes information concerning both hardware and software issues.

Digital Video. 15 Sept. 2000. PC Magazine Online. Available: http://www.zdnet.com/pcmag/stories/reviews/0,6755,2628008,00.html.

> This in-depth article compares DV hardware and software, including streaming video.

Miastkowski, Stan. 2000. "Move over Spielberg" *PC World* 18, no. 5 (May). Available: http://www.pcworld.com/heres_how/article/0,1400,15824,00.html.

> This provides a step-by-step, easy-to understand guide to digitizing video.

MPEG Home Page. Available: http://www.cselt.it/mpeg.

> This is the home site of the Moving Pictures Experts Group, which is in charge of developing MPEG standards.

Pinnacle Systems. Available: http://www.pinnaclesys.com.

> This company manufactures integrated video-production packages.

Virtual Experiences

Virtual Reality in Education: Education and MOO, MUD, MUSH. Available: http://www.skally.net/eduvr.

> Links to an abundance of sources on educational uses for virtual reality can be found at this site.

Web-Development Sites

About.com. Available: http://about.com.

> Subsites devoted to HTML/XML, Perl, JavaScript, and Java include scripts and utilities.

CNET Builder.com. Available: http://home.cnet.com/webbuilding/0-3880.html.

> This site has information on all aspects of building a Web site, including utilities for incorporating interaction on Web pages.

WebDeveloper.com. Available: http://www.webdeveloper.com.

> Here is another good resource for all facets of Web development.

Web Editors

Editors. Available: http://webdesign.about.com/compute/webdesign/cs/editors/index.htm.

> About.com's Web-design subsite has information about and reviews on both code-based and WYSIWYG editors.

HTML Editors. Available: http://webdeveloper.com/html/html_editors.html.

> A long list of editors is available at Webdeveloper.com.

Index

Notes: References to figures are in italics.
See the list of acronyms for all acronyms that are not spelled out in full.
Corporate names are given in parentheses.

About.com, 46, 169
Academic Search Elite, 152
accessibility, 31–2, 92–4
    resources, 179
accessories, camera, 37
active learning, 5, 13, 55. *See also*
    interactivity
ActiveX, 157, 160, 163
ad hoc navigation systems, 64
Advanced Streaming Format
    (ASF), 134
AIFF (.aiff, .aif), 118
alignment, text, 87
ALT attributes, 93, 117
American Society of Composers,
    Authors and Publishers
    (ASCAP), 120
analog camcorders, 38
analog/digital conversion, 34, 38,
    39, 118
animated GIF (.gif), 122
animation, 120–8
    applications, 46–7
    basic concepts of, 121–2
    interactive, 153–4
    prerendered, 121
    resources about, 179–80
    types of, 122–8
applets, 157, 160
application servers, 51–2, 162–4
applications, 167–8
Arizona, University of, Tucson, 98,
    99
arrows, 68
ASF (Active Streaming Format),
    130

ASP, 163
assignment-related instruction, 5,
    10
ATAPI (AT Attachment Packet
    Interface) connectivity, 40
AU (.au), 118
audience, 23, 28, 54. *See also* user
    accessibility; user interfaces
    evaluation of instruction,
        172–3
    needs analysis, 17, 54
audio, 29–30, 34, 118–20
    controls, *120*
    resources about, 180–1
    software, 47
authoring software, 32, 40–52
Authorware (Macromedia), 50,
    152, *153*
automated indexing programs,
    23
AVI (.avi), 129–30, 132

backgrounds, 85
bandwidth, 104
batch encoders, 47
batteries, camera, 37
BBEdit (Bare Bones Software), 42
bitmapped images. *See* raster
    images
Blackboard, 50, *51*, 156
BMP, 44
Bobby, 94, *94*
bookmarks, 69, 70, 72
Boolean logic, 103, 122
Bowling Green State University
    Libraries, 20, *21*, 141–2

brainstorming, design, 18
breadcrumb trails, 67–8
Broadcast Music, Inc. (BMI), 120
browsers, 22, 29
    and color, 81–3
    and fonts, 88–9
    issues with, 30–1
    and plug-ins, 104
    resources about, 181
    and second windows, 56
    style support for, 75
budget, 24
Builder.com (CNET), 56, 114,
    126, 169
Butler University, Irwin Library,
    101, *102*, 113, 142, *143*

Café Moolano, 140
California Polytechnic State
    University, San Luis Obispo,
    125, *126*, *155*
California, University of
    Berkeley, *141*
    Los Angeles, College Library,
        59
    San Diego Libraries, *81*, *154*
    Santa Cruz, *149*
camcorders, 37–9
Camden County Library System,
    71
cameras, 35–7
Camtasia, 132
cascading style sheets (CSS),
    74–5, 88, 125, 164–5
    resources about, 181
case, text, 88

CD-Rewritable (CD-RW) drives, 40
central processing units (CPUs), 29
Centre for Curriculum, Transfer and Technology, 168
Centre Pompidou, *129*
CGI, 161, 162–3
Chapman University, Thurmond Clarke Memorial Library, 8, *8*
charge coupled devices (CCDs), 35, 36
chats, 137, 144–5, *146*
Chili!Soft ASP, 163
Cincinnati, University of, 7, *7*
Claremont Colleges Libraries, *62*
clarity, 75
client needs analysis, 16–17
client relations, 27
client-side maps, 112–13
client-side scripting, 164
clip art, 111–12
    resources about, 181
closure, 60
Club 2000, Inc., *83*
CMOS (complementary metal-oxide semiconductor) sensors, 35
code-based editors, 41–2, 43
codec, 38
Codec Central, 38
cognitive walkthroughs, 175–6
ColdFusion (Allaire), 52
collaborative learning, 5, 13, 139
colors, 29, 33–4, 76–84, 93
    of backgrounds, 85
    browser-safe, 81–3
    and capability of monitors, 33–4
    coding of, 81
    combining, 78–80
    linking, 83–4
    meanings and perceptions of, 77
    number of, 83, 115
    resources about, 181
    symbolism of, 77–8
communication
    with clients, 27
    online, 142–5
    resources about, 181
    as social interaction, 137
CompactFlash, 36
compression. *See individual formats*
CompuServe, 107
computer competence, 17
computer selection, 32–3
conferencing, 139, 145

connectivity
    of cameras, 36
    of databases, 154, 156
    of removable storage devices, 40
    of scanners, 35
consistency, 60, 175
content
    and design, 18, 55–9
    and information needs, 17
    mastery of, 177–8
    and navigation, 61
    project team responsibilities for, 25
    sequence of, 20
    writing, 57–9
contrast, 80
Cool Edit (Syntrillium), 47
copyright, 120
CorelDRAW (Corel), 44, *45*
course evaluation, 150–1
course-related instruction, 5, 9
course shells, 50, 168–9
    resources about, 181–2
CourseInfo (Blackboard), 156
Curtin University of Technology, *138*
cycling (looping), 121

database, 51–2
    connectivity, 154, 156
    search skills, 8–9
Dazzle Video Creator, 39
decorative typefaces, 87
Delphion, 153
demonstration/simulation, 101, 103
design
    instructional, 54–5
    user-centered, 54
    of user interfaces, 59–61
design and development cycle, 15–27, *16*
    resources about, 182
development hardware, 32–40
    resources about, 186–7
Dewald, Nancy, 5–6
dHTML Layer-based animation (.htm, .html), 125–7, 164
digital camcorders, 38–9, 47
digital cameras, 35–7, 106
digital zoom lenses, 37
Director (Macromedia), 49, *49*, 124–5
Director Shockwave (.swd, .dcr, Macromedia), 124–5
discipline-specific research skills, 9

discussion forums, 137, *137*, 143–4, *145*
display capabilities, 29
distance education, 1, 7, 145, 151
dithering, 82
DOM, 164
dpi, 35
Dreamweaver (Macromedia), 42, *42*, 46, *113*, 126, *127*
drop-down menus, 67
Duke University Libraries, 12, *13*
DV, 38
dynamic fonts, 92, 125

e-mail, 137, 143, 144
EBSCOhost, 152
ECMAScript standard, 160
Emmanuel College, Cardinal Cushing Library, *153*
enrichment, 55
errors, 60
evaluation, *19*, 24, 26, 55, 170–8
    categories of, 171–2
    course, 150–1
    forms, 146, *149*, *150*, *151*
    methods, 171, 172–7
    objectives, 171
    resources about, 182
expert reviews, 174–6
extrusion, 127

feedback
    for evaluation of tutorial, 146, 172–3, 174, 176–7
    instructional, 55, 60, 138, 146, 149, 151
field observation, 177
file formats, 37
FireWire (Apple), 39
Fireworks (Macromedia), 45
First Page, *43*
flash capability, 37
Flash (Macromedia), 46, 123–4, *124*, 125, *125*, 153
flexibility, 49, 56, 61, 68
Florida Distance Learning Reference and Referral Center, 145, *146*
flowcharts, 18, 20, *21*, 26
focus groups, 54, 172, 177
follow-up assistance, 6
fonts, 85–6, 88–9
    dynamic, 92, 125
    and HTML font sizes, 88
formal usability inspection, 176
formative evaluation, 171–2
formats, graphic, 44

forming, and small-group development, 26
forms, online, 145–51, *147, 149, 150, 151*
FormSite, 168
Fort Lewis College, John F. Reed Library, 14, *14*
frames, 56, 69–72, 153
Freehand (Macromedia), 44
functionality, 18, 23

Gantt charts, 24, *25*
GIF Construction Site (Alchemy Mindworks), 46
GIF (.gif), 44, 107–8
    advantages, disadvantages, and uses, *109*
GIF Lube (Netscape), 115, *116*
GIFDancer (Paceworks), 46
global navigation systems, 63
glossaries, resources about, 183
goals, 1, 5, 16–17, 26
GoLive (Adobe), 42
graphics, 25, 105–17
    applications, 44–6
    cards, 34
    editing software, 35
    formats, 107–11
    for navigation, 64–5
    resources about, 183
    as text, 89
group discussions, 177
GUI (Graphical User Interface), 162
guidelines review, 175

hardware, 17
    development, 32–40
    issues, 28–30
    requirements, 105
Harry Fox Agency, Inc. (HFA), 120
Harvard University, Wiedener Library, 131–2, *131*
headphones, 34
heuristic evaluation, 175
hexadecimal values, 82–3
hierarchical navigation systems, 62–3
highlighting, 61, 64, 84
    advantages and disadvantages, *84*
Hoffman, B., 55
Holzschlag, M. E., 77
HomeSite (Allaire), *41*, 42
Hot Potatoes, 167, *168*
hot spots, 112, 113

Houston, University of, Libraries, 100, *100*
HTML, 28
    and animation, 46
    editors, 40–3
    font sizes versus point size, 88
    and image slicing, 116–17
    limitations of, 72
    publication of tutorial, 22, 25
    and style, 74–5
HTML (Un)Compress, 96
hues, 34, 78, 82
hyperlinks, 59, 60, 141–2, *142*

icons, 65, 111, *112*
identification of location, 100
IEEE (Institute of Electrical and Electronic Engineers), 39
i.LINK (Sony), 39
Illinois State University, Milner Library, 101, *101*
illustration, 101
    software, 44
Illustrator (Adobe), 44, 107
image editors, 44. See also raster images
image maps, 64–5, 112–13, *113, 143*
images, 98, 100–1, 105–17
    background, 85
    labeling, 117
    optimizing, 114–15
    quality of, 36
    resources about, 183, 185
    rollover, 113–14, 154
    slicing of, 116–17
    as text, 89
imaging software, 35
Info Trekk, 138
information
    literacy, 1, 13–14
    needs analysis, 17
    transfer interaction, 137–8, *138*
inquiry methods, 176–7
Instone, K., 175
instructional design, 54–5
Intellectual Property Network, 153
interactive animations, 153–4
interactivity, 18, 43, 136–69. See *also* active learning
    and application technologies, 162–4
    categories of, 136–40
    development tools, 166–9
    and markup languages, 164–5
    methods, 140–56

resources about, 180
    and Web programming languages, 157–62
interlacing, 110
Internet Explorer (Microsoft), 30, 160, 162
Internet Information Server (Microsoft), 160, 162, 163
Internet skills, 10–11
interviews, 172, 177
IRCAM (Institut de Recherche et Coordination Acoustique/ Musique) Multimedia Library, 128
ISA (Industry Standard Architecture), 34

Java, 118, 157, 160, 163
JavaScript, 113, 119, 160, *167*
JavaScript Source, 166
Jaz Drive, 40
JMatch, 167
JPEG (.jpeg, .jpg), 37, 44, 108–9, 115
    advantages, disadvantages, and uses, *109*
Jscript, 160, 163
JSP, 163–4

keyframes, 121, 126
King, Andrew, 95
knowledge building interaction, 139, *140*

labeling images, 117
layers, 126
LCD panels, 36, 37
learning experiences, 147
Learning Space (Lotus), 50
lectures, 1, 5
    online, 138
legibility, 80
lenses, 36–7
Lerdorf, Rasmus, 161
library instruction on the Web, resources about, 183–4
Library Online Basic Orientation (LOBO), 69
library orientation, 12
Linfield College, 66
Lingo (Macromedia), 161
links
    color of, 83–4
    to sound files, 119
LIRT (Library Instruction Round Table), 18
live access, 153, *154*

LiveMotion (Adobe), 45, 46
load times, 31
  and bandwidth, 104
  and image slicing, 116–17
  and page optimization, 95–6,
    114–15, 116–17
  and streaming, 133
  and video, 129
local navigation systems, 63–4
LZW compression, 107

M-JPEG, 38
marketing strategy, 23
markup, 93
markup languages, 164–5
  resources about, 184
Matrox, 47
mechanics, 6
mediums, 5, 6, 13
MEDLINE, 152
memory, short-term, 61
Memory Stick (Sony), 36
memory storage, 36
menu trees, 65
menus, drop-down, 67
microphones, 34
MIDI (.midi, .mid), 34, 118
MNG (.mng), 122–3
mock-ups, 22, 49
modeling, 127
Monash University Library, 9, 10
monitors, 29, 33
monospace typefaces, 87
Montgomery College Libraries, 76
MOOs, 140
Morkes, J., 57
motivation, 55
Mouseover Machine, 114, 114,
  169
MPEG (.mpeg, .mpg, .mp3, .mp4),
  119, 132
MPEG-1, 37, 38
MPEG-2, 38
MPEG-4, 38, 131, 132, 134
MP3 (.mp3), 119
multimedia, 25, 97–135
  appropriateness of, 98–103
  benefits and limitations, 97–8
  considerations, 103–5
  resources about, 184
  types, 105–35
MySQL, 156

navigation, 56, 60, 61–72, 94, 98
  hierarchical, 62–3
  linear versus nonlinear, 69

methods, 64–7
  and placement of tools, 68–9
  resources about, 184
  systems, 61–4
needs analyses, 16–17
Netcenter's Web Site Garage
  (Netscape), 31, 31, 32, 115,
  116
NetMeeting (Microsoft), 145
Netscape, 30
Netscape's Composer, 41
NetTrail, 149
net.TUTOR, 150
networks, 26
Nevada, University of, Libraries,
  65, 152
Newby, T. J., 97
Nielsen, Jakob, 53, 57, 69, 88,
  120–1, 173, 175
nodes, 131
nonprogrammers, 166–9
norming, and small-group
  development, 26
North Carolina State University
  Charlotte, J. Murrey Atkins
    Library, 57
  Raleigh, 69, 70
Northern Colorado, University of,
  85, 86
Notepad, 40
Notes, 155

object-based editors, 44, 45–6
object movies, 132
objectives, 6, 55
observation, 172
OCR software, 35
Ohio State University Libraries,
  151
Old Dominion University, Perry
  Library, 90
online
  catalog skills, 7–8
  chats, 137, 144–5, 146
  discussion forums, 137, 137
  feedback, 177
  forms, 145–51, 147
  lectures, 138
  services, 167–8
  survey, 147
Open Type (Adobe & Microsoft),
  92
operating systems, 28, 29
  and application servers, 52
  sound recording software in, 47
optical zoom lens, 37

optimization, 95–6, 114–15
Ousterhout, John, 162
outlines, 18–19, 20

page layout, 72–5
page optimization, 95–6
  resources about, 184
PC Technology Guide, 35
PCI, 34
Penn State Lehigh Valley Library,
  91
Penn State Libraries, 122
Pennsylvania State University
  Libraries, University Park,
  104, 123
performing, and small-group
  development, 26
peripheral selection, 33–4
Perl, 161, 163
Personal Web Server (Microsoft),
  163
PFR files, 92
Photoshop (Adobe), 44
PHP, 161
Pinnacle Systems, 47
pixels
  of digital cameras, 36, 37
  and peripheral selection, 33
  of raster images, 105–6, 106
  and site design considerations,
    29, 68, 72, 85
  in Windows versus Macintosh,
    89, 90
platforms, 28, 32, 35
plug-ins, 49–50, 104
pluralistic walkthroughs, 175
PNG (.png), 109–10, 122
point sizes, 86–7
  and HTML, 88
pop-up windows, 56, 153
postproduction, 23
Powell, Adam, 104
PowerPoint (Microsoft), 48
Premiere (Adobe), 47–8
preproduction, 15–22
prerendered animation, 121
presentation tools, 48
primitives, 127
processor speed, 29
production, 22
programming, 50–1
progress reports, 27
Project (Microsoft), 25
project management, 24–7
project teams, 18, 25–6
ProQuest (Bell & Howell), 138

prototyping, 17–18, 22, 49, 54, 172–3
publication, 22
Python, 161–2, 163

QTVR (QuickTime Virtual Reality), 131–2
quality control, 27
questionnaires, 146–7, 174, 176
Quia, 168
QuickTime (.mov, .qt, Apple), 46, 130–1, *131*, 133, 134, 135
QuickTime 4 (Apple), 134
QuickTime Pro (Apple), 46, 134
QuickTime VR Authoring Studio (Apple), 47

RAM, 29, 34, 37
raster images, 44, 105–10
    and animation, 46, 121
    and object-based editors, 45
    versus vector images, *108*
readability, 80, 87
real-time, 153
    animation, 121
RealAudio, 133
RealMedia (.ram, .rpm), 133–4
RealNetworks, 46, 48, 134
RealPlayer, 134, 135
RealProducer, 46, 47, 134
RealSystem G2, 133–4
RealVideo, 133
Recording Industry Association of America (RIAA), 120
remediation, 55, 60
remote access interaction, 138, *139*
removable file storage, 39–40
reports, 27
research literature, resources about, 184–5
research skills, 6–7
resizing, 106
resolution
    of camcorders, 38–9
    of digital cameras, 36
    and peripheral selection, 33
    of raster images, 105–6
    of scanners, 35
    and site design considerations, 57, 68, 72–3
    in Windows versus Macintosh, 89, *90*
resource allocation, 26–7
resource needs analysis, 17, 24
responsibilities of team members, 25–6

reversal of actions, 60
revision, 23
Ritchie, D. C., 55
robots, 23
roles, 26
rollover images, 113–14, 154, *155*
    resources about, 185
Rutkowski, Kathy, 136

sans serif typefaces, 87
Saskatchewan, University of, Libraries, 129, *130*
scaling, 106
scannability of text, 58–9
scanners, 35, 106
screen-capture movies, 132
screen
    captures, 101, 103
    layout, 72–5
    size, 29, 33
ScreenCam (Lotus), 101
scripts, 18–19, *20*, 25, 67
    languages, 50–1, 156–62
    libraries, 67, 166–7, *167*
    resources about, 185–6
    rollover, 114
SCSI connectivity, 40
search engines, 23, 68
self-assessment, 149, *149*
serial connections, 36
serif typefaces, 87
server-side maps, 112
servers, 26, 50, 51–2, 133, 134
Servlet Application Program Interface (API), 163
servlets, 163–4
SGML, 165
Shippensburg University, Ezra Lehman Library, 8, *8*
Shneiderman, Ben, 53, 59–61, 83, 171, 175, 177
Shockwave (Macromedia), 153
Shockwave Director (Macromedia), 161
shortcuts, 60
Simpletext, 40
simplicity, 75
simulations, 151–2, *152*, *153*
site
    architecture, 18–19, 22
    construction, 22
    design, 22, 29
    indexing, 23
    maintenance, 23
skills practice, 138, 151–3, *152*, *153*, *154*

SmartMedia, 36
SMIL (.smi), 46, 134–5
    resources about, 187
social interaction, 137
software
    animation, 46–7
    audio, 47
    authoring, 32, 40–52
    course shells, 50
    graphics, 35, 44–6
    imaging, 35
    OCR, 35
    and platforms, 28
    presentation, 48
    for project management, 24
    requirements, 17, 105
    resources about, 186–7
    specialty, 50
    and specific search skills, 8–9
    video editing, 47–8
    Web editor, 40–3, 56, 95, 166, 188
sound. *See* audio
Sound Blaster (Creative Technology), 34
sound cards, 34
sound files, 47, 119–20
Sound Forge (Sonic Foundry), 47
SoundEdit 16 (Macromedia), 47
space, white, 75–6
Spazz3D (Virtock Technologies), 47
speakers, 34
specialty tools, 50
speed, 29
    scan, 35
sprites, 121
staffing, 25–6
storage, removable, 36, 39–40
storming, and small-group development, 26
storyboards, 18, *20*, 22, 26, 48
streaming media, 46, 131, 132, 133–4
    resources about, 187
structure, open versus closed, 55–6
student achievement, 172
style sheets, cascading, 74–5, 88, 125, 164–5
    resources about, 181
summative evaluation, 172
surveys, 138, 146–7, 172, 176
SVG (.svg), 110–11
SVGA, 33–4

SWF (Shockwave Flash) format, 46
system requirements, 32–3

tables, 72–3, 93, 95
tabs, 65
tags, 23, 41, 119, 165
taskbars, 56
Tcl, 162, 163
teams, 18, 25–6
TeleEducation, 66
testing. *See* evaluation
tests, 138, 149–50
Texas, University of, System Digital Library, 124, *125, 140, 155*
Texas Information Literacy Tutorial (TILT), 124, 154
text, 89
    alignment, 87
    case, 88
    for navigation, 64
    on the Web, 88–9
theme, 98, 100
3-D, 127–8, *128*
TIFF, 44
time lines, 24, 48, 49, 121, 126
Tk (Tool kit), 162
tone, 98, 100
tool bars, 64–5
Top Class (WBT Systems), 50
traditional bibliographic instruction, 1–2
training, 139
transparency, 110
tripods, 37
TrueDoc (Bitstream), 92
Tuckman, B., 26
tweening, 121
typefaces, 85–7
typography, 85–92
    resources about, 187

URLs, *22*, 56
usability inspections, users', 174–6
usability testing, experts', 173–4
USB connections, 36, 39, 40
user accessibility, 92–4
user interfaces, *22*, 25, 53–96
    guidelines and principles, 59–61
    resources about, 187
users. *See* audience

Utah, University of, Spencer S. Eccles Health Sciences Library, 11, *12*

VBScript (Visual Basic Script), 162, 163
vector images, 44, 106–7, *107*
    and animation, 46, 121, 124
    and GIF, 108
    and object-based editors, 45
    and SVG, 110–11
    versus raster images, *108*
VGA, 34
Victoria, University of, Humanities Computing and Media Centre, 167, *168*
video, 37, 37–9, 129–32
    adapters, 34
    capture cards, 37, 38, 47
    editing applications, 47–8
    file formats, 48
    resources about, 187–8
virtual experiences interaction, 139–40
    resources about, 188
visual-based editors, 41, 42–3
visual design, 75–92
visualization, 103
von Rossum, Guido, 161
VRML Works, 47
VRML (.wrl), 47, 128, *129*, 165
VSE Web Site Turbo (Voget Selbach Enterprises GmbH), 96

Wake Forest University, Z. Smith Reynolds Library, 10, *11, 20, 63, 98, 99, 102 ,117, 127, 137, 139, 144, 145, 147*
Wall, Larry, 161
WAV (.wav), 118
Web Accessibility Initiative Standard, 92
Web-based library instruction
    best practices, 5–6
    types of, 6–14
Web Content Accessibility Guidelines 1.0, 92
Web Developer's Virtual Library, The, 51
Web-development sites, 169
    resources about, 188
Web editors, 40–3, 56, 166
    resources about, 188

visual-based, 95
Web interaction technologies
    resources about, 185–6
Web Player (Macromedia), 50
Web programming languages, 156–62
    comparison chart, 158–9
Web server application technologies, 162–4
Web Site Garage. *See* Netcenter's Web Site Garage
Web-team responsibilities, 25–6
WebCT (WebCT), 50, 150
WebDeveloper.com, 169
Weinman, Lynda, 82, *82*
white space, 75–6
Window Builder (CNET), 56, *58*, 169
windows, 56, 153
Windows Media (.asf, .asx, Microsoft), 133, 134
Windows Media Player (Microsoft), 134
Windows Media Services (Microsoft), 134
Windows Media Tools (Microsoft), 134
Windows 98 (Microsoft), 163
Windows NT (Microsoft), 163
wire-frame prototypes, 54
Wisconsin, University of, Parkside, *73*, 150, *150*
WMF (Windows Metafile), 44
World Wide Web Consortium (W3C)
    accessibility guidelines, 92, 94
    and DOM, 164
    format recommendations, 110, 111
    language recommendations, 134, 165
    style sheet recommendations, 74
    and XML, XHTML, 165
writing, 57–9
WYSIWYG Web editors, 41, 42–3, 95, 126

XHTML, 165
XML, 134, 165

Zip drives (Iomega), 40
zoom lenses, 37